DATE DUE

~~MR 1 2 '97~~			
~~DE 8'99~~			
~~OC 24 '05~~			

DAMNED

WOMEN

ELIZABETH REIS

DAMNED WOMEN

Sinners

and Witches

in Puritan

New England

CORNELL UNIVERSITY PRESS

ITHACA AND LONDON

First published 1997 by Cornell University Press

Library of Congress Cataloging-in-Publication Data
Reis, Elizabeth (Elizabeth Sarah)
   Damned women : sinners and witches in Puritan New England /
Elizabeth Reis.
      p. cm.
   Includes index.
   ISBN 0-8014-2834-3 (cloth : alk. paper)
      1. Women—New England—History—17th century. 2. Women—New
England—Social conditions. 3. Women—New England—Religious life.
4. Puritans—New England—History. 5. Witchcraft—New England—
History—17th century. I. Title.
HQ1438.N35R45   1997
305.4'0974'09032—dc21   96-53411

Printed in the United States of America

Cornell University Press strives to use environmentally responsible suppliers
and materials to the fullest extent possible in the publishing of its books. Such
materials include vegetable-based, low-VOC inks and acid-free papers that are
recycled, totally chlorine-free, or partly composed of nonwood fibers.

Cloth printing   10 9 8 7 6 5 4 3 2

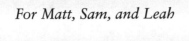

For Matt, Sam, and Leah

CONTENTS

ILLUSTRATIONS

PREFACE

THIS book examines the relationship among women, evil, and Puritanism in seventeenth-century New England. Far more women than men were accused and convicted of witchcraft. What was it about New England Puritanism that linked women more closely with the devil? And why did some women themselves come to believe that they had in fact forged a pact with Satan and become witches?

In focusing attention on the darker side of Puritan thought and experience, I do not want to suggest that women's existence was unremittingly desolate. My discussion of women, sin, and the devil is intended to revise our understanding of gender in early New England. Nonetheless, it should be read within the context of new scholarship on women and religion in Puritan New England, a body of work which shows that women could live full and meaningful lives offering considerable satisfaction. They were not simple victims of a misogynist plot to keep them dependent or, worse, to destroy them bodily.

Indeed, Puritan women may have been less subordinate than many European women of their day. Laurel Thatcher Ulrich, for example, has amply demonstrated that in the new societies of colonial New England women's roles could be as expansive as the family economy required. As a "deputy husband," a rural Puritan farm woman could be expected to perform a wide range of tasks that middle-class Victorians would later define as "unladylike," from routine gardening, butchering, and dairying to the more unusual commercial trading in the marketplace or, indeed, running an entire farm when her husband was unavailable. Town women, too, frequently performed duties and labors beyond conventional expectations; as Ulrich has explained, the practice of their lives proved less rigid than prescriptions might suggest.[1]

New England in the seventeenth century, like other colonial settlements in North America, was a new society, and as such it offered women as well as men new opportunities and demanded of them new responsibilities. The story of the Great Migration of 1630–1642 is well known. Thousands of English people traveled to New England in family groups to construct a Bible Commonwealth, new congregations of saints, and prosperous communities in the wilderness. A balanced ratio between the sexes, the persistence of patriarchal control and the commitment to family and community, the comparative health and longevity of the population, and the relatively short duration of the migration (which meant that New England's subsequent population growth would occur through natural increase) all contributed to making New England more stable and more like old England than any other early North American colonial settlement.[2] New England women, as a result, may have lacked the "advantages" of contemporary Chesapeake women, whose rarity in a world characterized by high mortality rates and a heavily imbalanced sex ratio gave them greater independence and power through marriage and widowhood.[3] On the other hand, most New England women would hardly have understood the world in such terms or have sought out the dangers of disease, the toil of indentured servitude, or the instability and perils of widowhood. And given the nature of the New England economy, in which the household constituted the primary unit of production, women played critical—and, most likely, satisfying—economic roles within the family, even as that family defined and confined them.[4] Finally, despite its

1. Laurel Thatcher Ulrich, *Good Wives: Image and Reality in the Lives of Women in Northern New England, 1650–1750* (New York, 1980), esp. 35–50.

2. See especially Virginia DeJohn Anderson, "Migrants and Motives: Religion and the Settlement of New England," *William and Mary Quarterly,* 3rd ser., 58 (1985), 339–83.

3. Lois Green Carr and Lorena S. Walsh, "The Planter's Wife: The Experience of White Women in Seventeenth-Century Maryland," *William and Mary Quarterly,* 3rd ser., 34 (October 1977), 542–71.

4. Mary Beth Norton, "The Evolution of White Women's Experience in Early America," *American Historical Review* 89 (June 1984), 593–619.

patriarchal quality, Puritanism seems to have offered women unique opportunities for involvement, even leadership, as Anne Hutchinson's challenge to the new Puritan orthodoxy in New England both demonstrated
and sorely tested.[5]

Leaving behind the English church they considered corrupt, New England Puritans cultivated a more vital, primitive faith, abolished certain
Anglican religious rituals, and rejected the hierarchical ecclesiastical
structures of the establishment. Community and family dominated social, cultural, and religious life; a family, wrote William Gouge, was "a
little Church, and a little commonwealth, at least a lively representation
thereof."[6] Men—husbands and fathers—dominated this domestic world,
as Milton's famous lines from *Paradise Lost* (4.297) express: "he for God
only, she for God in him." Early in the eighteenth century, Benjamin
Wadsworth's *Well-Ordered Family* would explain that "the Husband is
call'd the Head of the Woman. . . . It belongs to the Head to rule and
govern. . . . Wives are part of the House and Family, and ought to be under the Husband's Government."[7]

Yet Wadsworth's caution that a husband's rule "should not be with
rigour, haughtiness, harshness, severity; but with the greatest love, gen-
tleness, kindness, tenderness that may be," and his admonition that a
husband must not treat his wife "as a Servant, but as his own flesh; he
must love her as himself," perhaps suggest that such a hierarchical relationship could nonetheless operate through mutuality and reciprocity.[8]
As John Cotton elaborated, the family itself represented a covenant, with
parents and householders bound to "wives, and children, and servants,
and kindred, and acquaintances, and all that are under our reach, either

5. On the threat Hutchinson posed as a woman, see Jane Kamensky, *Governing the
Tongue: The Politics of Speaking in Early New England* (New York, forthcoming 1998);
and Marilyn J. Westerkamp, "Puritan Patriarchy and the Problem of Revelation," *Journal
of Interdisciplinary History* 23 (Winter 1993), 571–95. See also Westerkamp, "Anne
Hutchinson, Sectarian Mysticism, and the Puritan Order," *Church History* 59 (1990),
482–98; on Hutchinson's relationship to the clergy, see James F. Cooper Jr., "Anne
Hutchinson and the 'Lay Rebellion' against the Clergy," *New England Quarterly* 61 (September 1988), 381–97.

6. William Gouge, *Of Domesticall Duties* (1622), quoted, appropriately, in an epigraph
in John Demos, *A Little Commonwealth: Family Life in Plymouth Colony* (New York,
1970), xix.

7. Benjamin Wadsworth, *A Well-Ordered Family,* 2nd ed. (Boston, 1719), 35–37.

8. Ibid.

by way of subordination, or coordination." [9] While the Pilgrims' pastor John Robinson could characterize a wife's proper attitude toward her husband as "a reverend subjection," Samuel Willard could say that "tho the Husband be the head of the wife, yet she is an head of the family." Recognizing the partnership between the husband and wife, Willard reasoned, "of all the orders which are unequals, these [between husbands and wives] do come the nearest to an Equality, and in several respects they stand upon an even ground. These two do make a pair, which infers so far a parity." [10] Within these ambiguities and amid the day-to-day negotiations of family life, women could craft lives of meaning and worth.

Women's roles within the confines of the church were similarly more elastic than is generally imagined. In the reformed tradition of Protestant theology, women and men were equal in the sight of God. Although women could not participate in the congregational governance of churches, they experienced conversion, they signed the covenant and joined the church (more frequently than their husbands), they studied the Scriptures, they baptized and instructed their children, and they used their considerable influence to promote religiosity in their households and communities. New England Puritanism could offer women spiritual fulfillment and even particular opportunities for organizing and controlling their family relationships, as Amanda Porterfield has detailed. [11]

Yet in acknowledging the meaning and purpose that shaped the economic, religious, and social lives of New England Puritan women and al-

9. John Cotton, *The Covenant of God's Free Grace* (London, 1645), 19. Quoted in David Hackett Fischer, *Albion's Seed: Four British Folkways in America* (New York, 1989), 70.

10. John Robinson, quoted in Demos, *Little Commonwealth*, 83; Samuel Willard, *A Compleat Body of Divinity* (Boston, 1726), 610. For a discussion of the relationship between husbands and wives, see Edmund S. Morgan, *The Puritan Family: Religion and Domestic Relations in Seventeenth-Century New England* (New York, 1944), esp. 29–64; and Helena M. Wall, *Fierce Communion: Family and Community in Early America* (Cambridge, Mass., 1990), esp. 49–85.

11. Amanda Porterfield, *Female Piety in Puritan New England: The Emergence of Religious Humanism* (New York, 1992), 80–115. On the numbers of women and men joining churches, see Mary Maples Dunn, "Saints and Sisters: Congregational and Quaker Women in the Early Colonial Period," *American Quarterly* 30 (1978), 582–601; Gerald F. Moran, "Sisters in Christ: Women and the Church in Seventeenth-Century New England," *Women in American Religion,* ed. Janet Wilson James (Philadelphia, 1980), 45–65; Richard D. Shiels, "The Feminization of American Congregationalism, 1730–1835," *American Quarterly* 33 (1981), 46–62.

lowed them to live in ways they found satisfying, we need not deny the particular trials they faced as women. The sunnier moments in a woman's life—a well-arranged marriage, a successful delivery and joyful baptism, an overwhelming conversion experience and admission to the church— could be balanced or challenged in her spiritual and ecclesiastical life by darker realities, such as the perceived presence of Satan and his special ability to entrap women. In this book I examine these realities, which, like women's work, worship, and social presence, also shaped the complex Puritan conception of women as well as women's own understanding of themselves.

If witchcraft episodes were extraordinary, they did not emerge out of thin air. Derogatory cultural images of women fueled witchcraft accusations and proceedings, and women's guilt over their perceived spiritual inadequacies could even lead them to confess to specific transgressions they apparently had not committed. Puritans—men as well as women— lived a roller-coaster life, alternately assured of their salvation and convinced of their depravity. Here I focus appropriate attention on the "down" side, particularly as it affected the spiritual lives of women. My explication of the pessimism inherent in Puritan women's religious experience I hope will contribute to the fuller, more nuanced understanding of early American women which is taking shape.

The witchcraft episodes that erupted intermittently in the seventeenth century and culminated in 1692 were ordeals intimately related to the religious culture of New England Puritanism. This is not to say that Puritanism caused the "witch craze" or that persecution of "witches" would not have happened if the settlers had not been Puritans. Persecution of women for witchcraft had a long European history stretching back to the eleventh century. Estimates of the number of people executed throughout the centuries of witch hunting in Europe vary widely (from tens of thousands to millions). It is generally recognized that most of those killed were women (about four-fifths by conservative estimate), though the actual numbers and percentages are a matter of conjecture in the absence of accurate records.[12]

12. For a perceptive discussion of the numbers debate and how these figures are used within the contemporary feminist spirituality movement, see Cynthia Eller, *Living in the Lap of the Goddess: The Feminist Spirituality Movement in America* (New York, 1993), 162–76.

Some 95 percent of all known witchcraft accusations and more than 90 percent of executions for witchcraft in the British North American colonies occurred in New England. Carol Karlsen has identified 334 accusations and 35 executions in New England between 1620 and 1725. If Puritans like Michael Wigglesworth feared that the New World was "A Waste and howling wilderness, / Where none inhabited / But hellish fiends, and brutish men / That devils worshipped," it must have been even more distressing, indeed terrifying, that Satan continued to stalk New England even after the establishment of the New Jerusalem and the first, pioneer generation had given way to a well-established second and a third. The wrath of the devil alarmed New Englanders, especially when it afflicted them through the action of witches, defined as those who made compacts with the devil and agreed to enter his service. Such a definition and the fact that so many accused "witches" were women (approximately 78 percent) emphasized both Satan's relentless pursuit and women's eventual submission.[13] But it has only been since the early 1970s that scholars have heeded the words of the nineteenth-century feminist Matilda Joslyn Gage, that in order to comprehend the European witch persecutions (and, by extension, those of the American colonies), we need to substitute the word "woman" for "witch."[14]

It would be easy, but inaccurate, to characterize the Puritans simply as misogynists. In fact, Puritan New Englanders considered themselves rather more enlightened than others when it came to woman's place in society and in their cosmology. They did not subscribe to the prevailing European view that women were inherently more evil than men. Yet the

13. Carol F. Karlsen, *The Devil in the Shape of a Woman: Witchcraft in Colonial New England* (New York, 1987), 47; Michael Wigglesworth, "God's Controversy with New England," in *Proceedings of the Massachusetts Historical Society, 1871–1873,* vol. 12 (Boston, 1873), 83. See also Richard Godbeer, *The Devil's Dominion: Magic and Religion in Early New England* (Cambridge, 1992), 235–42, for useful appendixes of names and outcomes of cases before and during the Salem crisis. For other cases that never came to trial, see John Demos, *Entertaining Satan: Witchcraft and the Culture of Early New England* (New York, 1982), 402–9.

14. Matilda Joslyn Gage, *Woman, Church, and State* (1893; New York, 1972), 243. For a recent examination of the European witch hunts which places women's experiences and gender issues at the center of the analysis, see Anne Llewellyn Barstow, *Witchcraze: A New History of the European Witch Hunts* (San Francisco, 1994).

"witches" in Puritan New England were also primarily women. Karlsen's study of witchcraft in New England makes significant strides in explaining why. She argues that some women were singled out because of their potentially powerful status as inheritors of money or property.[15] My interest centers on the religious reasons for the persecution of women as witches in early America. Puritan theology demanded an unrelenting self-scrutiny from which a true beliver—man or woman—could never derive too much optimism about salvation. Indeed, saints and sinners alike—and, we shall see, women in particular—believed themselves more likely to be bound to Satan than to God. Convinced of their abiding sinfulness and guilt, some women needed little provocation to imagine that they had succumbed to the devil more literally and become witches.

Although I refer to "Puritans" and "Puritan belief" throughout the book, I do not mean to imply that Puritanism, even New England Puritanism, was a coherent body of thought. Puritan scholars, most notably David D. Hall, have reminded us not only of the diversity among New England Puritan communities but also that people in those communities subscribed to Puritanism in varying degrees. There were those who attended church services regularly, who delivered their conversion narratives and became full members of the church, and who had their children baptized; there were others who merely attended meetings and never underwent conversion; and there were others whom Hall has called "horse-shed Christians," men and women who restricted their religious involvement, preferring the talk of their neighbors behind the church to their minister's sermons.[16] Despite the difficulty of ascertaining the precise nature, texture, or depth of any one person's belief, it is nevertheless possible to speak of Puritan belief and Puritan culture. Ministers taught its doctrines in their sermons, and conversion narratives and more mundane acts indicate that lay members grasped, internalized, and even helped shape and reshape those messages. It is no surprise that Puritan religiosity pervaded the discourse of New Englanders, particularly the documents of the witch trials. Puritanism was not discrete, something to listen

15. Karlsen, *Devil in the Shape of a Woman.*
16. David D. Hall, *Worlds of Wonder, Days of Judgment: Popular Religious Belief in Early New England* (New York, 1989), 15.

to in weekday sermons or at Sunday meetings and then to put away as one went about one's daily business; it saturated the culture. I hope that in these pages I have discovered something of its essence.

I HAVE RECEIVED enthusiastic support for this project from friends, colleagues, and family. Most recently, I became indebted to the Center for the Study of American Religion at Princeton University, where I spent a fruitful year revising the manuscript in the most collegial and encouraging atmosphere possible. Surrounded by lively intellectual exchange and wonderful library resources, and free of teaching duties, I was able to devote myself completely to the book revisions. The center's weekly seminar, attended by faculty and graduate students from several different departments, helped me to sharpen my thinking, forcing me to make my work accessible to an audience with diverse interests and backgrounds. I thank John Wilson and Robert Wuthnow for making each Friday seminar such a delightful and thought-provoking afternoon, and Jody Shapiro Davie and Lynn Davidman, my fellow fellows at the center, for sharing countless coffees and conversations.

I thank Robert Middlekauff, James Kettner, and William Simmons at Berkeley for their help and guidance. Several others read various chapters or the entire manuscript and made beneficial suggestions: David D. Hall, Karen O. Kupperman, John Murrin, Michael McGiffert, Bernard Rosenthal, Robert St. George, Jane Kamensky, Richard Godbeer, Stephen Aron, Anita Tien, John Giggie, Brad Verter, Cynthia Eller, Nina Silber, James F. Cooper Jr., John Theibault, Daniel Pope, Carla Pestana, Margaret Masson, Ruth Bloch, Karen Halttunen, Bonnie Bassler, Patty Barber, and Nina Dayton. Among these, John Murrin must receive special recognition. I am deeply grateful for his thorough, perceptive reading of the manuscript, first as an anonymous referee for Cornell University Press and later when he revealed his identity so we could discuss the substantive issues. My editor at Cornell, Peter Agree, has been supportive throughout.

My work has been supported by the National Endowment for the Humanities as well as by the Center for the Study of Women in Society at the University of Oregon. I thank the staff of the Princeton University Library, the American Antiquarian Society, the Huntington Library, the Beinecke Rare Book and Manuscript Library at Yale University, the Connecticut State Library, the Connecticut Historical Society, the Essex Institute, and the Massachusetts Historical Society. I am also grateful to the readers at the *Journal of American History* and David Thelen for their comments on "The Devil, the Body, and the Feminine Soul in Puritan New England," which appears in a slightly different version here as Chapter 3.

My family deserves special mention. My parents, Pamela Tamarkin Reis and Ronald Reis, have provided unfailing support, both emotional and financial. They, together with my brother, David Reis, form what I have dubbed the Reis Foundation—the only granting institution, I have often joked, for which no application or letters of recommendation are required. My children, Samuel and Leah Reis-Dennis, are too young to read the book now, but both in their own way understand what it is about. Neither helped at all, in fact they continue to be a constant though delightful distraction. Such distractions are the very essence of life.

I have often wondered what the technical limit is on the amount of help, editing, and advice I may receive from a single person before I should confess that the true authorship of this book is Elizabeth Reis as told to Matthew Dennis. We shared an office during our year at Princeton, and I interrupted Matt's own writing regularly with "How does this sound?" Not only did he read and critique each chapter several times, but he patiently discussed every detail, from the conceptually difficult matter of organizing chapters to the mundane particulars of formatting the footnotes. I cannot imagine writing a book without Matt's critical intellectual insights and his round-the-clock support of my work. There are several advantages to living with an early American historian, other than being able to share libraries, and Matt has shown me that collegial support can blend quite nicely with the demands of researching, writing, teaching, and raising a family.

ELIZABETH REIS

Eugene, Oregon

DAMNED
WOMEN

INTRODUCTION

PURITAN WOMEN AND
THE DISCOURSE OF DEPRAVITY

WERE seventeenth-century Puritan women damned? I contend that many women believed they were and, in fact, that New England culture as a whole regarded women as more likely to be damned than men. These beliefs are curious for two reasons. First, Puritans believed in predestination; salvation and damnation were foreordained by God, not chosen by individuals—female or male—and only God knew who would end up in heaven or in hell. Theology and lived religion, however, often collided. Women and men did not simply wait for God to reveal their fates to them on Judgment Day. As many scholars have noted, laity and clergy alike searched constantly for clues about their destiny, alternating between strongly felt hope and fear. Central to this cycle of anxiety and assurance was the very real dread of the devil. The imminent possibility of damnation—made certain by complicity with Satan—terrified the Puritans. The idea of the covenant, the cornerstone of Puritan belief, seemed to make God more accessible and directed attention to the glorious possibility of salvation, but New England Puritans more often focused on what seemed all too probable: their possession by Satan followed by their deserved tumble into an agonizing hell.

Women, in particular, internalized their ministers' messages. They were more likely to think of themselves as utterly depraved, as "rebellious wretches against God," bonded to Satan and bound for hell; lay men, by contrast, were more likely to repent for particular sins than to dwell on the worthlessness of their essential natures. This gendered difference brings us to the second curious feature of the idea of "damned women": Puritans never explicitly confronted their belief that women were more sinful than men. In fact, they maintained that women as well as men could share in the glory of conversion, oneness with Christ, and ultimately salvation. Nevertheless, the understanding women expressed about themselves betrays feelings about the soul and its relation to God and the devil which differed from those of men.

The witchcraft episodes of the seventeenth century, when women were accused and convicted far more than men and when women actually confessed to being in the devil's snare, display the sense of women's inherent wickedness which the community—women and men—endorsed. Puritans may have professed publicly that the sexes were equal before God, but they were not equal before the devil.[1] It was women, by and large, whom the devil tortured, hoping to recruit them into his service as witches. The women who confessed to witchcraft were so assured of their essential sinfulness that they became convinced they had actually covenanted with Satan rather than with God. Believing themselves to be sinners in any case, women easily blurred the line between ordinary sinning, which necessitated repentance, and the more egregious act of signing the devil's book and becoming a witch.

The community's response to the very different ways women and men confessed to such illicit covenanting—as well as the differences in the confessions themselves—suggests that women, rather than men, were expected to be witches. Exoneration from this loathsome crime required more of women than of men. Women had to prove not only that they had not compacted with the devil but that they were blameless in every respect. Demonstrating freedom from all sin was, of course, an exceedingly difficult task for any Puritan; for a Puritan woman, so thoroughly permeated by her religion's ideology that she considered herself by nature a vile

---

1. This is not to suggest that New England Puritanism did not provide women with spiritual fulfillment and even opportunities for organizing and controlling their family relationships, as Amanda Porterfield, *Female Piety in Puritan New England: The Emergence of Religious Humanism* (New York, 1992), 80–115, has discussed. Nonetheless, the possibilities for more nearly equal status and social power which theology seemed to offer women were diminished by the covenant's underside, which subverted women's spiritual and social efficacy and left them more vulnerable to Satan.

and evil creature hopelessly unworthy of Christ's love, the task was virtually impossible. To comprehend the complexity of both the witchcraft crisis and women's subjectivity in seventeenth-century New England, we must truly understand Puritan religious belief, which conceived a world in which Satan and God vied for souls in a literal as well as metaphorical sense. During the witchcraft crisis, the battle became a vicious confrontation between Satan's accused handmaid and her alleged victim.

I hope to shed light on two related issues confronting students of early America and women's history: how Puritanism functioned as lived religion and how gender was constructed socially. As Judith Butler and others have shown us, gender is partially invented through performative acts that are shaped and constrained by the very culture in which they are produced.[2] Analysis of seventeenth-century confessions (in the meetinghouse and in the courtroom) suggests that some Puritans enjoyed greater flexibility in performing their identities than others, as men seemed more able than women to refashion themselves through their deeds while divorcing themselves from their "true"—that is, according to orthodoxy, their depraved—natures. In several chapters I look specifically at three questions that illuminate this theory: why were women accused of witchcraft more often than men, why did more women than men confess to witchcraft, and why did women accuse other women of witchcraft? In the answers we can see how female identity and place were constructed, by the larger community and by women themselves.

In addition, I examine the nature of New England Puritanism—not merely the formal, theological dimension of the religion, which many scholars have already explored, but also the way lay women and men actually lived their theology. Building on important earlier social and intellectual histories that considered common people and the more prominent ministry discretely, I explore the dynamic relationship between lay and clerical thought and action. The laity shared with the clergy a common theological understanding of the devil's powers and of how to defeat his suggestions and tortures. During the witchcraft trials, when so many saw the devil insistently breaking into the thoughts and lives of the people of Massachusetts and Connecticut, both the lay public and the ministry ex-

2. On the notion of gender performativity, see Judith Butler, *Gender Trouble: Feminism and the Subversion of Identity* (New York, 1990).

pected his intrusion and had prepared strategies to defeat it. I agree with
David D. Hall that no rigid line divided clerical thought from popular religion. In fact, as Hall argues, the term "popular religion" should not be
read as the ways in which laity broke with clergy on various issues. Rather,
ministers and the lay public shared certain assumptions about their religious and folk traditions. Sometimes clerical interpretations held sway;
sometimes the two strains of thought merged imperceptibly; and often, as
we shall see, the laity, implicitly encouraged by the clergy, voiced the
meaning of commonly held beliefs in unpredictable and gendered ways.[3]

The language ministers used in sermons, which audiences could not escape, articulated the notion that the devil's presence was ubiquitous.
Ministers made it perfectly clear that intimacy with Satan annihilated
any chance of attaining saving grace and damned a person to an eternity
in hell. They preached that unreformed sinners who served the devil
rather than God were doomed, and they peppered their sermons with images of hell's dark abyss. Puritan anxiety owed less to the unattainability
of heavenly glory than to the likelihood of hellish horror. Calvinism made
salvation an uncertain reward for even the most righteous, but it surely
damned those who followed the devil's path. Predestination notwithstanding, sinners could indeed work their way to hell.

Because complicity with Satan implied such dire consequences, ministers felt it was their obligation to warn their congregations of the devil's
objectives. In weekly sermons and written tracts, they repeatedly admonished their flock not to fall prey to Satan's methods. Although the devil
could not force a person to lead a life of sin and degradation, he possessed a frightening array of persuasive tools and temptations and would
go to any length to lead people into sin, thereby possessing their souls.

Perhaps unwittingly, with their evocative language and constant warnings about the devil's intrusions, the clergy reinforced folk beliefs about
Satan—in their own minds as well as in those of the laity. True, in their
sermons ministers did not specifically describe the devil's actual, physical
appearance in all its horror; his existence remained ethereal rather than
corporeal. Yet during the witchcraft episodes, when both the accusers
and the accused detailed their encounters with the devil, neither the

3. David D. Hall, *Worlds of Wonder, Days of Judgment: Popular Religious Belief in
Early New England* (New York, 1989).

clergy nor the court challenged lay images of Satan. Whether he was said
to appear in the shape of a dog, a yellow bird, or a hideous creature, part
monkey and part man, the testimony was eagerly accepted. In the zeal to
rout the devil from the godly commonwealth, belief in Satan's direct
physical presence prevailed.

Clergy and laity shared assumptions about their world, about God and
the devil, about sin and salvation, and about how the devil afflicted the
body in order to possess the soul (and seemed to possess women more
readily than men). During the witch trials, lay visions of the devil's powers pushed ministers' teachings into compliance. The consequences for
women, who predominated among the accused, could be grim, placing
them in a deadly double bind. Whereas the clergy had taught that Satan
tortured the body to capture the soul (a soul construed in gendered terms
as a feminine entity), witnesses described the devil's torments more literally, in ways consonant with their earthly understanding of women's and
men's bodies and souls. Women's feminine souls were seen as unprotected
in their weaker female bodies, vulnerable to the devil's molestations.

Secular concerns similarly impinged on religious understanding during
examinations of suspected witches. Accused women were damned if they
did and damned if they didn't: if they confessed to witchcraft charges, their
admissions would prove the cases against them; if they denied the charges,
then their very intractability, construed as the refusal to admit to sin more
generally, could mark them as sinners and hence allies of the devil. Thus,
although Puritan theology held that women and men would be equal before God and the devil, the mundane world mediated those tenets, making it easier for Puritans to imagine that women were more likely than
men to submit to Satan and become witches.

After the Salem crisis the theology of the devil shifted subtly, as did
women's and men's relationship to Satan and sin. In the eighteenth century, sinners feared God's wrath, and they dreaded the thought of eternal
hellfire, but they rarely linked the devil's possession of their souls with this
horrific end. Ministers cautioned against imagining that the devil lurked
around every corner and urged their congregations to differentiate between mere temptation and possession. Likewise, sinners assumed that
the devil belonged in hell, roaming this earth only metaphorically as a
tempter or symbolically as the embodiment of a human villain. Women
continued to think of themselves as vile sinners, but they dissociated their

souls from the devil, took more responsibility for the commission of particular sins, and by midcentury seemed far more confident that they could
successfully overcome Satan's inveiglements.

By the eighteenth century New Englanders had come to attribute
bizarre behavior to unneighborliness, unwomanly conduct, or even in-
sanity, rather than to the devil's machinations, but such was emphatically
not the case in the seventeenth. For this reason, I interpret the witchcraft
episodes through the lens of religious belief. To be sure, other accounts of
what took place at Salem (and elsewhere earlier in the 1600s) remain
credible. In *Salem Possessed* Paul Boyer and Stephen Nissenbaum analyze
long-standing community frictions in the context of increasing commercialization, concluding that tensions exploded in the form of witchcraft
accusations. Carol Karlsen's feminist social and economic interpretation
also retains its explanatory power. She finds that many of the accused
were potentially powerful women on the verge of inheriting substantial
amounts of property. This interruption of the customary transfer of
property from one generation of males to the next rendered them con-
spicuous and suspect.[4]

By focusing on sociological or economic reasons for witchcraft outbreaks, or on psychological ones as John Demos did in his pathbreaking
Entertaining Satan, these historians and others may underestimate the religious context. Seeking to rationalize the seemingly aberrant witchcraft
phenomena, scholars have largely discounted what the colonists actually
said about the devil's power. They have interpreted claims of spectral evidence in individualized terms, for example, as one neighbor's means of
retaliation against another, and they have explained witch hunts generally as the manifestation of economic, social, and psychological conflicts
within Puritan communities. I am not denying that such conflicts existed
or that they precipitated and influenced the course of events. These other
perspectives provide important clues about the peculiar nature, magni-
tude, and timing of the Salem crisis, as well as about the reasons for the
predominance of women among the accused. Yet by ignoring the relationship between New Englanders, particularly women, and the devil,
these interpretations obscure what Puritans saw as the primary focus of

4. Paul Boyer and Stephen Nissenbaum, *Salem Possessed: The Social Origins of Witchcraft* (Cambridge, Mass., 1974); Carol F. Karlsen, *The Devil in the Shape of a Woman:
Witchcraft in Colonial New England* (New York, 1987).

the witchcraft crises that ruptured their lives. The forces that could damn women in early New England were not simply social, economic, and political; though we might not expect it, given the trajectory of Puritanism's departures from Catholicism and from other Protestant movements, religion damned women too.[5]

Beliefs about the devil remained relatively consistent throughout the seventeenth century, and therefore I include material from earlier witchcraft cases in Connecticut and Massachusetts, but I focus on the 1692 crisis at Salem. Because the Salem episode occupies such a central place in the book, a brief summary of events might be helpful to set the context.[6]

In the winter months of early 1692, Betty Parris, age nine, and Abigail Williams, age eleven—cousins in the Reverend Samuel Parris's household—began to have bizarre fits and seizures. Observers first suspected illness but then concluded that the devil's intrusions were to blame. But who was behind the devil's entry into this godly family? In the Puritan world Satan's appearance signaled God's severe displeasure. And once Satan had successfully gained access to an individual or the community at large, Puritans believed he was very difficult to exorcise. Abigail Williams, Betty Parris, and others (not all of whom were young girls) continued to experience their afflictions and to accuse people of witchcraft. We will never know exactly why, but whether accusers and witnesses sincerely believed that the accused had signed a devil's pact and afflicted others, whether they contemplated political or familial revenge, whether they simply continued to play a game that had gotten out of hand, whether they pursued a strategy to deflect suspicion from themselves, or whether they calculated fraud, they knew that their stories would be

5. John Demos, *Entertaining Satan: Witchcraft and the Culture of Early New England* (New York, 1982). Other recent works, none of which focuses specifically on Satan and women, are Bernard Rosenthal, *Salem Story: Reading the Witch Trials of 1692* (Cambridge, 1993); Richard Godbeer, *The Devil's Dominion: Magic and Religion in Early New England* (Cambridge, 1992); Richard Weisman, *Witchcraft, Magic, and Religion in Seventeenth-Century Massachusetts* (Amherst, Mass., 1984). Weisman analyzes the relationship between religion and magic, emphasizing a division between elite and popular expressions of witchcraft belief. For an analysis of the witchcraft episodes which does take both religion and gender seriously, see Ann Kibbey, "Mutations of the Supernatural: Witchcraft, Remarkable Providences, and the Power of Puritan Men," *American Quarterly* 34 (1982), 125–48.

6. Readers interested in a more complete narrative might consult Rosenthal, *Salem Story*. Rosenthal's narrative reorders the primary material chronologically, thus contextualizing events and personalities.

believed.[7] In their religious world, witchcraft accusations (particularly against women, as we shall see) were credible and demanded action because they were so threatening.

Although several scholars have offered explanations for why the witchcraft accusations broke out when and where they did, simple definitive answers about Salem remain elusive. Perhaps, as Bernard Rosenthal suggests, to impose an overarching construction would be to trivialize an irreducibly complex affair.[8] In addition to chronic factionalism and disputation over property, Massachusetts was beset by social and political dislocation in the late 1680s and early 1690s, when it experienced renewed threats from neighboring Indians and the loss of its charter from England. But these problems, while serious, did not mechanically produce the witchcraft outbreak and witch hunting of 1692. Setting aside the question of cause, we might consider what Rosenthal terms a developing logic that allowed the crisis to take the course it did, including the accusations of approximately 156 people, the convictions of 30, and the hanging deaths of 14 women and 5 men.[9]

As other scholars have noted, the Salem episode was distinguished from earlier witchcraft accusations not by the intensity of belief but rather by the official response to the accusations.[10] Previous governors had been more cautious about jailing and trying witchcraft suspects, and their reticence had perhaps allowed potentially inflammatory outbreaks to die out. The trouble at Salem, however, began at a time of transition and instability as a new governor, Sir William Phips, took over from the inter-charter governor, Simon Bradstreet, who was about ninety years old.

7. For a persuasive argument emphasizing fraud, see Rosenthal, *Salem Story,* esp. 50. The episode, he says, "represents a desperate logic, rational and correct, that the safest way out of the web of accusation was through confession, accusation, or claims of affliction." I would not discount personal safety as a motive, although I emphasize that without the fundamental belief in the devil's powers, all of what Rosenthal sees as deception would have been impossible.

8. Ibid., 4–8.

9. Another man, Giles Corey, was pressed to death, and three women and one man died in prison. For complete lists of those accused and the outcome of their cases, see Godbeer, *Devil's Dominion,* 235–42. Boyer and Nissenbaum provide a good summary of the entire episode in their introduction to the collection of primary documents. See Paul Boyer and Stephen Nissenbaum, eds., *The Salem Witchcraft Papers: Verbatim Transcripts of the Legal Documents of the Salem Witchcraft Outbreak of 1692,* 3 vols. (New York, 1977), 1:3–30.

10. See especially Weisman, *Witchcraft, Magic, and Religion,* xi–xiii, 96–114.

Phips, in contrast to other, moderating governors, set up a special court
to deal with the situation and placed at its head the colony's staunchest
believer in the devil's ability to recruit witches: William Stoughton, the
lieutenant governor. Under Stoughton's guidance, the seven men named
to the court examined, tried, sent to prison, and hanged "proven" witches.
The court ignored the clergy's advice to proceed with caution, albeit offered irresolutely, and instead encouraged testimony that sent many to
their deaths.

Were there really witches? Did those who confessed to witchcraft really sign a devil's pact in blood and afflict others? The primary source for
an affirmative answer would have to be the fifty or so confessions. Admissions concerning the devil's book, the devil's sacrament, baptisms by
the devil, and witch meetings complete with weapons could, conceivably,
be taken at face value, even though our modern worldview discourages
such an explanation. My own reading takes us in a different direction.
I maintain that the confessions had multiple meanings, then and now.
Some women probably did believe that they had actually signed the
devil's pact; others may have confessed to save their own lives; and yet
others confessed to ordinary sin, indicating at least a temporary commitment to the devil. No doubt some of the accused practiced various forms
of magic, but magical practice was not uncommon; it was not what the
confessors admitted to; and it certainly was not what these trials were
about.[11]

The seventeenth-century New England witch trials were about religious loyalty, good and evil, God and the devil. Puritans knew that no
one could be faithful to both God and Satan, and yet during the episode
troubling, apparently contradictory evidence was presented. Here were
people, many of them church members, that is, saints and pillars of the
community, suspected of choosing Satan rather than God. The confusion, the anxiety, the terror of losing one's life, of imagining the "truth"
about one's neighbors, not to mention the agony of scrutinizing one's
own life, searching for past sinfulness must have been overwhelming and
frightening. The trials themselves have a scripted quality about them, but
it is important to remember that the participants, although they may

11. For a discussion of the ambiguous relation between magical practice and witchcraft,
see Godbeer, *Devil's Dominion*.

have come to know their parts, were not explicitly coerced; most had an intellectual, theological, and emotional commitment to the proceedings. For me, why the witch hunt happened becomes a less urgent issue than how it happened. This book is my exploration, then, of the belief system that made the drama possible and gave women center stage.

Because it is difficult to imagine the sensibilities of seventeenth-century Puritans, to understand the intensity and reality of their fears, I find the admittedly imperfect analogy of the sexual abuse of children useful. In today's world we live with the knowledge that many children are victims of such abuse. As parents, we warn our children about the dangers and teach them how to respond to such situations. The charge that some-one—a teacher, daycare worker, relative—has made sexual advances cannot be taken lightly. The Puritans' fear of Satan's threat was just as real to them, the charge that someone was a witch just as serious. Al-though the demons are different, the sense of threat is the same, and it ig-nites similar fear and action.

Surely "Salem" has become an icon in American culture. The trials have become a metaphor for hysterical persecution, unfounded accusa-tions, and confessions that have no reasonable explanation. From the controversy surrounding the McCarthy hearings in the 1950s to the more recent contentions of the False Memory Syndrome Society (whose members insist that they have been unfairly accused of abusing their chil-dren), the Salem trials have been invoked again and again. Obviously, the trials have had a much broader effect than their actual scope and dura-tion would lead us to expect.

I hope that this book about the Puritans' conceptions of sin and Satan will expand our cultural and historical understanding of how people act on their religious belief—especially belief in a specter of evil—and how those religiously informed actions both reflect and prescribe their own particular gender arrangements, often to the detriment of women. Satan has reappeared in our nation's discourse with surprising frequency. Reli-gious fundamentalists, for example, decry daycare centers as abodes of Satan, and in sensational cases children have testified about incidents of ritual Satanic abuse. Early in 1993 in Waco, Texas, David Koresh repre-sented the outside world as the demonic site of a grand war between God and the devil.

The rhetorical use of Satan—and perhaps belief in such a figure—

seems to be gaining strength in some quarters, suggesting that there are limits to secularization or "modernization" in America. Even religious leaders who downplay the direct intervention of the devil remain concerned about a more generalized evil and betray their own sense of America's proper social agenda. For example, Cardinal John O'Connor, archbishop of New York, exercised caution in his comments about growing Satanic cult activity and the increasing requests to the Catholic church for exorcisms, yet he affirmed that the devil's power could be seen in many worldly evils, notably divorce and abortion.

Evil, by whatever name we call it, continues to bedevil us, and like our colonial ancestors, many people use their particular (though sometimes vaguely articulated) theological beliefs to explain it, to identify sin, and to formulate their response to it. As in colonial New England, too, women are judged and at times condemned on the basis of religiously founded notions of their nature and proper sphere. Religion is a vital social and cultural force; I hope that books such as this one, while focused on the seventeenth century, will nonetheless help illuminate its effect on American life—in the mainstream and on the fringes—by giving a broader historical context to contemporary issues.

I

WOMEN'S SINFUL NATURES
AND MEN'S NATURAL SINS

F EAR of the devil permeated New England culture. Puritan ministers cautioned their flocks about Satan's omnipresence, and the laity worried in spiritual diaries and conversion narratives that the devil would likely win the battle for their souls. Despite Puritan ministers' insistence that women and men were equal in the sight of God, both sexes equally capable of cleaving to Christ or to the devil, women and men interpreted the message differently. In this chapter I explore the underside of covenant theology, both what it offered in common to women and men and how it became differentiated between the sexes.

What did Elizabeth Oakes mean when she said in her conversion relation, "I thought I was troubled in conscience yet under power of Satan, and I a curse"? Or Goodwife Jackson when she declared, "I thought I was a rebellious wretch against God, and so I continued long"?[1] Clergy and laity alike worried about going to hell, but in the midst of common obsessions a gendered division emerges which perhaps anticipates the feminization of American Protestantism: women more than men seemed to heed their ministers' words. Both men and women feared damnation, but women fashioned their identities and subjectivities in accordance with the most pessimistic clerical perspective. Insofar as there were any divisions between clerical and lay thought on the issue of damnation and

1. Mary Rhinelander McCarl, ed., "Thomas Shepard's Record of Relations of Religious Experience, 1648–1649," *William and Mary Quarterly,* 3rd ser., 48 (July 1991), 441, 446.

the devil's possession of souls, women sided with the clergy. Even in their most intimate spiritual confessions, lay men tended to distance themselves from the notion of complete depravity which Puritan ministers preached and Puritan women internalized.

Although Puritan men and women often experienced sin and sanctification, damnation and salvation differently, as we shall see, they nonetheless lived with each other in the same world, occupying common households and meetinghouses. If Puritanism tasted different to men and women, it was not necessarily because they imbibed it from separate cups. Thus we must first look to the ministerial messages offered indiscriminately to both women and men concerning sin, salvation, and damnation and then turn to the distinctive ways in which audiences interpreted and shaped their religious sensibilities. Before embarking on an analysis of difference, that is, we must examine the common ground. And nothing was more common than the forces that drew women and men alike toward the gaping mouth of hell.

Intellectual historians have examined the spiritual troubles of lay Puritans, such as Oakes and Jackson, as well as the religious musings of Puritan clerics. They have concluded that Puritan anxiety centered on the issue of assurance: how could believers be assured that they were of God's elect and would ultimately be saved? Intellectually, Puritans subscribed to the covenant of grace, holding that God's grace could neither be earned nor denied. Yet they spent much of their lives wondering if their deeds would prove worthy or their sins too great and souls too wicked for God to choose them for everlasting life. Many spent their spiritual lives speculating whether they would sit at God's right or left hand when Judgment Day arrived. By focusing on the central question of assurance of salvation, religious scholars emphasize the aspect of Puritan covenant theology that concerned justification and sanctification. This emphasis can distract us from the less sanguine implications of the covenant. It was the imminent possibility of damnation—made certain by complicity with Satan through sin—which generated overwhelming fear in the hearts of the Puritans.

The relationship between justification and sanctification troubled contemporaries as it does present-day scholars because of its intimate connection with salvation. Puritan ministers taught that justification—the righteousness or grace given to the elect as a result of Christ's sacrificial death for the sins of mankind—was one of the steps a regenerate soul must experience on the way toward salvation. Justified people lived saintly lives not to "earn" God's love but as a manifestation of the grace they had received.

Sanctification meant the repudiation of all sin in order to demonstrate that one was worthy of God's free gift. Sanctification, or the leading of a good life, did not necessarily indicate one's election, but Puritans interpreted it as a likely sign of sainthood. Ideally, some believed, justification and sanctification should take place almost simultaneously; when God granted grace, then behavior would change. Ministers argued about the degree of preparation required in order to receive grace. Could one live a saintly life in preparation for receiving grace? The constant examination of one's life and continued search for the true repudiation of sin as evidence of grace left many in despair. And that anxiety and desperation were hardly assuaged when churchgoers heard from their spiritual leaders that uncertainty of one's election was one of the signs of salvation, whereas complete assurance was a sure sign of damnation.[2]

Scholars have lately focused on the pietistic, rather than the intellectual, aspects of Puritan theology. Eager to prove that the Puritans' religious lives consisted of more than simple anxiety over salvation, these historians have argued convincingly that joy and enthusiasm pervaded believers' religious ardor.[3] Charles Hambrick-Stowe's study of private

2. On the cycle of anxiety and assurance, see Michael McGiffert, *God's Plot: Puritan Spirituality in Thomas Shepard's Cambridge* (Amherst, Mass., 1994), 3–29, 135–48. On the relation between justification and sanctification, see Norman Pettit, *The Heart Prepared: Grace and Conversion in Puritan Spiritual Life* (New Haven, 1966); William K. B. Stoever, *"A Faire and Easie Way to Heaven": Covenant Theology and Antinomianism in Early Massachusetts* (Middletown, Conn., 1978); Charles E. Hambrick-Stowe, *The Practice of Piety: Puritan Devotional Disciplines in Seventeenth-Century New England* (Chapel Hill, N.C., 1982); Charles Lloyd Cohen, *God's Caress: The Psychology of Puritan Religious Experience* (New York, 1986); and Edmund S. Morgan, *Visible Saints: The History of a Puritan Idea* (New York, 1963). See R. T. Kendall, *Calvinism and English Calvinism to 1649* (New York, 1979), for a discussion of the progression of ideas concerning faith and repentance from Calvin to John Cotton. Andrew Delbanco, *The Puritan Ordeal* (Cambridge, Mass., 1989), argues persuasively that the preparation doctrine increased rather than decreased anxiety because it tended to transfer responsibility for salvation from God to the self.

3. Charles Cohen has pointed out that, contrary to Max Weber's thesis connecting Puritan theology to the development of capitalism, love of God rather than the desire for assurance motivated godly works. Cohen remarks, "It is love that makes the Saints go round." See *God's Caress*, 119.

Puritan devotional practices clearly establishes a full range of intense personal religious experiences filled with hope and the love of God.[4] Certainly Puritans experienced joy and solace through their beliefs; authors of spiritual musings and conversion relations, for example, wrote or spoke of the comfort received from God's love. And yet this sense of blessedness was always tempered, perhaps fueled, by constant apprehension, not uncertainty of salvation but dread of damnation.

Ministers often delivered their sermons as if they had three distinct audiences in mind: those who considered themselves among the elect, those who remained anxious and unsure of their election, and those who were absolutely convinced of their place among the sinning reprobates.[5] The very premise of the covenant of grace, stipulating that those too sure of themselves would be damned, virtually demanded that Puritan listeners consider themselves members of the latter two categories, and so it is likely that most of the congregation "heard" and internalized the messages directed at those people still unwilling or unable to turn to God.

If there were indeed any listeners in the audience who felt confident of their estates, there were portions of the weekly sermons intended to reinforce such beliefs. Ministers assured these hearers that if their hearts were truly humbled they would not succumb to temptations, and the Lord would ultimately fulfill his promise of everlasting peace to them. Thomas Hooker told his congregation, "Howsoever the heart that is truly humbled may sometimes be tossed and troubled, yet he is not distracted,

4. Hambrick-Stowe, *Practice of Piety*, esp. 23–53. On the ritual aspects of assurance, confession, and repentance, see David D. Hall, *Worlds of Wonder, Days of Judgment: Popular Religious Belief in Early New England* (New York, 1989), 117–65.

5. Teresa Toulouse has maintained that the structure of the sermons, particularly those of John Cotton and Benjamin Colman, implied two kinds of listeners—those who were sure of their election and those who remained unsure. I arrived at my understanding of the material independently, and although I believe that three audiences were frequently addressed in the sermon literature, I agree with Toulouse that this multiplicity occurs because of the tensions between the desire to preach the mysteries of assurance and the necessity of preaching moral behavior. See Toulouse, *The Art of Prophesying: New England Sermons and the Shaping of Belief* (Athens, Ga., 1987). Edmund S. Morgan has argued that Puritan ministers preached primarily to the children of church members, so that they would convert, thereby retaining their church membership. Thomas Hooker was an exception; he addressed his sermons to all sinners, regardless of conversion status. See Morgan, *The Puritan Family: Religion and Domestic Relations in Seventeenth-Century New England* (New York, 1944), 174–75, and idem, *Visible Saints: The History of a Puritan Idea* (New York, 1963).

because he is contented, as it is with a ship upon the sea, when the bil-
lowes begin to roare and waves are violent, if the Anchor be fastened
deep, it stayes the ship." The tiny ship, Hooker explained, was the soul;
the raging ocean waters were the world; and the anchor was humiliation.
The deeper the humiliation/anchor, "the more quiet is the heart, and the
more it is calmed." [6]

The covenant of grace would be fulfilled, according to Hooker, if the
soul remained humbled throughout the storm. God protected the souls
he had chosen from temptations, and even the devil proved no match for
God's will. Hooker believed that it was "*impossible* that the exaltation
& glory of an humble Soule should be *hindered by men or devils*. Let the
devill and all his instruments labour to cast shame and disgrace upon
thee. . . . it cannot be hindered, but that the *Lord will exalt thee; the Lord
hath promised it*." No matter what evil threatened, if God had accepted a
soul into his divine grace, then, Hooker assured his congregation, "the
Lord [would] prevaile with you, the Lord emptie you, that Christ may fill
you, the Lord humble you, that you may enjoy happinesse, and peace for
ever." [7]

Thomas Shepard used the metaphor of a marriage with Christ to describe the irrevocable bonding that occurred between a saint and God
upon entering into the covenant of grace. "No sin shall part thee and
him," Shepard declared, "for Christ when he enters into marriage-
covenant, does not suspend his love on our Grace or Holiness, then he
might leave quickly, but on his Grace to wash away our filthiness." [8] In
Boston, Urian Oakes preached the fundamental premise of the covenant:
"If nothing can separate a Christian from the love of GOD in Christ, then
nothing can conquer him, but he is invincible." [9]

Belief in predestination may have given the saints some measure of security and confidence concerning their salvation.[10] The covenant of grace

6. Thomas Hooker, *The Soules Humiliation* (London, 1637), 138.

7. Ibid., 218, 224.

8. Thomas Shepard, *The Parable of the Ten Virgins* (Cambridge, Mass., 1695), 25. See
Morgan, *Puritan Family*, 161–69.

9. Urian Oakes, *The Unconquerable, All Conquering and More than Conquering
Souldier: or the successful warre which a believer wageth with the enemies of his soul*
(Boston, 1674).

10. Cohen, *God's Caress*, 116. Satan's assaults did not end, however, with one's conversion. In fact, Puritans believed that Satan would pursue this individual ever more steadfastly in order to win back the soul and keep it from salvation.

offered solace to those who had converted and entered into God's compact. Even if they backslid temporarily from their part of the bargain, God would not abandon those whom he had elected. John Cotton counseled those who lapsed, "If therefore thou seest any uncleannesse in thy heart, abandon it, and resolve with full purpose of heart against it, hold on your way, and you will increase your strength, Prov. 10:29. The Lord will show himself strong to all that are upright before him." Repentance and renewed faith, Cotton assured them, ensured God's promise.[11]

But just as the covenant made God slightly more accessible and knowable, it simultaneously rendered God's angry and vengeful side all too perceptible. For those who remained unsure of their election and uncomfortable counting themselves among the saints, the ministers presented two alternatives. Repentant sinners could reform their evil ways and hope that God would then offer his grace, or God would have no qualms about casting into hell those who refused his free gift of grace and chose sin and degradation instead.

Puritans unsure of their election and those utterly convinced of their reprobation were often one and the same. Historians have identified the cycle of anxiety and assurance as a characteristic feature of Puritanism, and so it is not surprising to find tormented souls alternately relieved at the prospect of salvation and terrified at the possibility of damnation.[12] Depending on their particular state of mind on any given day, people could be expected to lend more credence to their ministers' encouragement or admonitions.

Samuel Willard's classic collection of sermons, published posthumously, offered hope for both saints and sinners.[13] The saints were told that, once converted, they would remain forever in God's hands, and the

11. John Cotton, *The Way of Life* (London, 1641), 107. As Robert Middlekauff has pointed out, the language of the covenant was just one of several ways in which the clergy appealed to their audiences. See Middlekauff, *The Mathers: Three Generations of Puritan Intellectuals, 1596–1728* (New York, 1971), 60–61. I believe, however, that the idea of a heavenly contract could be of vital importance to Puritan New Englanders, not for its assurances of salvation but rather for its realization of hell's imminence.

12. See Michael McGiffert, ed., *God's Plot: The Paradoxes of Puritan Piety, Being the Autobiography and Journal of Thomas Shepard* (1640; Amherst, Mass., 1972). McGiffert has described this cycle in the introduction to Shepard's autobiography. See also the revised edition as cited in note 2.

13. On the importance of Willard's body of sermons, see Gerald Goodwin, "The Myth of 'Arminian-Calvinism' in Eighteenth-Century New England," *New England Quarterly* 41 (1968), 227.

sinners were reminded that there was hope for their salvation, however doubtful it might seem to them. To those whom "Satan seeks to drive . . . to despair," Willard extended reassuring declarations of God's generosity in choosing his elect: "Consider that you are Men and not Devils. You are not of that company whom God hath for ever forsaken . . . but you are of that sort whom God hath pleased to restore from death to life; of that race whom God hath his Elect among." In September of 1694 he pledged to his insecure listeners that God "will gather a *great number* to make them partakers in eternal salvation. Hope then, and do not despair and dye." [14]

Willard's distinction between "men" and devils was not meant to exclude women but to distinguish between devils, who would never be among the elect, and people—female and male—who could hope for election. Willard's point in this sermon was to encourage all sinners to repent and choose God. His promise that God would select a great number for eternal salvation may have given some sinners cause for hope, but if they listened further, those hopes may yet have been dashed.

Whether the road to heaven was narrow or wide was a matter of some debate. Even sermons delivered by the same minister often betrayed two conflicting convictions. On the one hand, preachers felt obligated to offer hope to unrepentant sinners, with the expectation that they would abandon their reprobate practices and let God into their hearts. "There is hope for the oldest sinner, if yet he will hear the voice of Christ," Willard promised. "The arms of a Saviour are now open to receive you if you will come to him." [15] On the other hand, Calvinist theology taught that Christ had died for only a small and discriminating number of elect. The preacher Henry Smith exhorted, "Heaven is large, but the way to heaven must be narrow." [16] Thomas Hooker concurred: "There is a most narrow way of Gods Commandements, and there is but one way or gate into this happinesse, it is narrow, and a little gate; . . . and if you misse this gate, you lose all your labour, and shall never come to Salvation." [17] Indeed, even Willard advised sinners that conversion was not simple. Quoting from

14. Samuel Willard, *The Compleat Body of Christian Divinity* (Boston, 1726), 275.
15. Ibid., 241.
16. Thomas Fuller, ed., *The Works of Henry Smith; including Sermons, Treatises, Prayers, and Poems,* 2 vols. (Edinburgh, 1867), 2:18.
17. Hooker, *Soules Humiliation,* 212.

Acts 14:22, he warned "that we must through much tribulation enter into the Kingdom of God. . . . [You] are not to ly upon a bed of ease, but to engage in a field of war . . . and endure to the end." [18]

On the issue of salvation, the sermons reflected a belief in an unknowable God who selected for eternal glory only those who had faith and had received the free gift of grace. Slightly altered within the context of covenant theology, however, the Puritan version of predestination was not quite as harsh as a more orthodox Calvinism. [19] Covenant theology could offer believers a more accepting God, allowing them to dwell on the joyful prospect of salvation; nevertheless New England Puritans more typically focused on what seemed all too likely: their merited descent into the terrors of hell.

Sermons delivered by the clergy often emphasized the horrors that would befall a sinner. Ministers made it perfectly clear that intimacy with Satan through sin ended one's chance of attaining saving grace and damned one to an eternity in hell. They insisted that unreformed sinners were doomed and filled their sermons with images of hell's dark abyss. Samuel Willard, for example, threatened his listeners: "If you are resolved in your way . . . know and be assured that you are going to a bottomless pit. . . . [Y]ou are going to dwell with the devils and damned spirits, and to be tormented with the flames of the botomless pit, where you shall be filled brim full in soul and body with the wrath of God." [20]

Calvinism viewed salvation as uncertain for even the most righteous but damnation as sure for those who followed the devil's path. "It is true," warned Thomas Hooker, "though thy good workes are not perfectly good and cannot save thee, yet thy bad workes are perfectly naught and will condemne thee." [21] In practice, the theology of predestination was Calvinist when it came to getting into heaven, but Arminian in terms of getting into hell. In short, the glories of heaven were entirely the result of God's good grace and mercy, but the miseries of hell awaited deserving reprobates who had only themselves to blame.

18. Samuel Willard, *The Christians Exercise by Satans Temptations* (Boston, 1701), 148.

19. On the relationship between Calvinism and covenant theology, see Perry Miller, "The Marrow of Puritan Divinity," Publications of the Colonial Society of Massachusetts, no. 32 (1937), 247–300. For a fuller discussion, see idem, *The New England Mind: The Seventeenth Century* (Cambridge, Mass., 1939), 365–97.

20. Willard, *Compleat Body,* 241.

21. Hooker, *Soules Humiliation,* 55.

Although seventeenth-century English and American Puritans seldom illustrated their texts, their word portraits represented hell as a place of perpetual torture and horror, as in this fifteenth-century French illuminated manuscript of Saint Augustine's *City of God* (courtesy Bibliothèque Sainte Geneviève, MS. 246, folio 389).

The minister Michael Wigglesworth's popular poem *Day of Doom,* published in 1662, explained the theology well:

> High God's Decree, as it is free,
>   so doth it none compel
> Against their will to good or ill;
>   it forceth none to Hell.
> *They have their wish* whose Souls perish
>   with Torments in Hell-fire,
> *Who rather choose their souls to lose,*
>   than leave a loose desire.
>
> God did ordain sinners to pain
>   *yet he to Hell sends none*
> *But such as swerv'd and have deserv'd*
>   destruction as their own.
> His pleasure is, that none from Bliss
>   and endless happiness
> Be barr'd, *but such as wrong'd him much,*
>   *by willful wickedness.*[22]

God would gather in the select few, but the sinful merited their eternal torment among "piercing groans of creatures lying upon a terrible rack, and scorched with the flames of a seven times heated furnace."[23]

Preachers envisioned the everlasting fiery lakes of hell and tried to make their flocks tremble at the likelihood that this would be their destination. Willard exhorted the unregenerate in his audience: "The Devil is your master, you have no command of your selves, but do and will obey his commands; and Oh! remember, he is driving you to the chambers of death, and hurrying you down the steep precipice of overlasting destruction."[24] Audiences—women and men sharing the same pews—heard a powerful, emphatic message; no one could serve God and the devil. One was either a saint who might possibly end up in heaven or a sinner who would definitely end up in hell.

---

22. Michael Wigglesworth, *Day of Doom: or, a Poetical Description of the Great and Last Judgment* (Cambridge, 1662; Boston, 1828), v. 149, 150, p. 47, emphasis added.
23. Willard, *Compleat Body,* 241.
24. Ibid., 230.

Church disciplinary actions reinforced the pessimistic message of the sermons. Although sinners were given the chance, and sometimes several chances, to reform their ways, to apologize, and to commit themselves anew to Christ, they were warned repeatedly of the implications of failing to repent adequately. In 1664 the Salem congregation censured Samuel Archer Sr. for drunkenness. Several witnesses had seen him staggering and falling as he walked along with an Indian woman. Archer's written confession, read aloud, stated "that he had sinned against God, dishonoured his profession and grieved the Spirit of his brethren by his often drinking more than was meet etc." The pastor spoke to him of 1 Corinthians 6:10—"that drunkards are excluded from the kingdom of heaven"—and reminded him that this was not the first time he had been warned. Archer was left to contemplate his repentance, until he was called again before the church three weeks later. This time he was not contrite. In fact, the record states, "he was farre from manifesting any repentance in his expressions." He maintained that God had already pardoned him. Others spoke against him, testifying that since the last incident he had been drinking excessively again. As there was "no signe of repentence appearing in him, but rather signes of one besotted and hardened in his way," the pastor and brethren voted to excommunicate him. The following Sabbath the pastor used Archer's excommunication as a warning to others, underscoring that "*inpenitent* drunkards are excluded from the Kingdome of Heaven." [25]

The Beverly, Massachusetts, congregation dealt similarly with inpenitent sinners. In 1669 Benjamin Morgin, the son of a church member, showed "presumptuous contempt of the worship of God." He had stolen some horses and oxen and then he added to his misdeeds "ye haynous sin of lying to cover his sinne." When the church sent for Morgin so that he could repent, he failed to show up. Not only did he refuse to appear the second time he was summoned, but he "also spake very reproachfully of ye Church & publick worship of God." Morgin received one more chance, accompanied by an ultimatum demanding that he repent not only for the theft and lying but also for his behavior toward the church or he would

25. Richard D. Pierce, ed., *The Records of the First Church in Salem Massachusetts, 1629–1736* (Salem, 1974), 100–102, emphasis added.

be "proceeded with as A Scandalous & Inpenitent sinner." Morgin defied the ultimatum and showed no signs of remorse; instead, he proved himself to be "a lamentable spectacle of A stupifyed sinner." As the church records state unequivocally, "Hee was by Censure of Excommunication *delivered to Satan.*" [26]

Ministers presented the world to their audience as if it were divided into two camps—those who succumbed to temptation, sinned, and thereby followed Satan, and those who had repented and followed God. According to the Reverend William Adams, "If thou art none of Christ's, thou art the Devil's. The possession of men in the world is divided between Christ and Satan." [27] People had to choose their master. One was either a regenerate saint who would "cleave together [with Christ] as moulded into one loafe," or a reprobate sinner committed to giving one's body and soul to the devil.[28] Of the wicked, Thomas Hooker said, "The divell rules in them; he speakes by their tongues, and workes by their hands, and thinks, and desires by their minds, and walkes by their feet." [29]

God would divide and separate the two camps, the saints and the sinners, on Judgment Day. Ministers affirmed God's blueprint for the day of reckoning as a way of persuading the unregenerate to turn to God before

26. "Beverly First Church Records," *Essex Institute Historical Collections* 35 (July 1899), 189. See Chapter 4 for a fuller discussion of the gendered nature of confession and apology. It was not unusual for church disciplinary action to take years to resolve. In Beverly, for example, sinners—women as well as men—would often come before the church two or three times before their confessions were deemed convincing enough to warrant restoration to the church, including authorization to partake in the Lord's Supper. See the cases of Bethia Stanly, Ephraim Hirreck, and John Dodge, for example (188, 193, 197, 201). On lay and clerical attitudes toward the decision to participate in the Lord's Supper, see Hall, *Worlds of Wonder,* esp. 156–62. See also David D. Hall, ed., *Works of Jonathan Edwards,* vol. 12: *Ecclesiastical Writings* (New Haven, 1994), esp. 26–38.

27. William Adams, *The Necessity of the Pouring Out of the Spirit from on High upon a Sinning Apostatizing People* (Boston, 1679), 38. Such examples abound in sermon literature; during the Salem crisis, the Reverend Samuel Parris declared, "Here are but 2 parties in the World, the Lamb & his Followers, & the Dragon & his Followers: & these are contrary one to the other. . . . Here are no Newters. Every one is on one side or the other." See James F. Cooper Jr. and Kenneth P. Minkema, eds., *The Sermon Notebook of Samuel Parris, 1689–1694,* Publications of the Massachusetts Historical Society, no. 66 (Boston, 1993), 203.

28. John Cotton, *The Way of Life* (London, 1641), 375.

29. Thomas Hooker, *Soules Humiliation,* 35.

it was too late. Samuel Whiting told his flock that his "hearts desire, knowing the Terrour of the Lord," was to persuade them to become godly before Judgment Day so that they could "look upon Jesus Christ with Comfort at that Day and . . . be set at his Right Hand, and hear that blessed Sentence of Absolution pronounced." [30]

If Whiting's sermon was meant to prevail upon sinners to reform their evil ways, however, its tone nevertheless conveyed a fearful and ominous vision of what would befall the sinners who failed to repent. He assured the evildoers that Christ would be able to differentiate the saints from the sinners, so that not one elect would remain among the reprobate nor one reprobate among the elect. Whiting acknowledged that in this world there was no such thing as a visible church peopled solely by the elect. Inevitably, "some Hypocrites will get in and trouble and defile and leaven them." But on Judgment Day, he warned, "Christ will be exact in separating the one from the other, no wicked persons shall thrust in among the elect saints." [31]

Christ's motive for the rigid delineation on Judgment Day was twofold. He did it for the godly, who would bask in the fellowship of other pious people as well as in the light of God. And more important, according to Whiting, Christ separated the wicked "for the augmentation of the misery of the Reprobate who when they all come together shall be torture and torment one to another." Whiting emphasized the horrors the sinners would endure when death deprived them of the ability to repent and reform. "O what a wofull condition will they then be in," Whiting proclaimed; "its unspeakable what their misery will be, inconceiveable what the torment of their Soules will be, when . . . this separation is all be made between the Elect and them." [32] The wicked would be severed from the just and cast into a "furnace of fire."

Speculation about Judgment Day plagued some Puritans both day and night. John Bunyan, a particularly imaginative writer of the Puritan experience, exemplified the dread of hell and God's wrath. Bunyan's seventeenth-century autobiography, *Grace Abounding to the Chief of Sinners,* widely read in New England, portrays a man convinced of his

30. Samuel Whiting, *A Discourse on the Last Judgment* (Cambridge, Mass., 1664), A5.
31. Ibid., 17.
32. Ibid., 18.

own damnation and tortured by thoughts of what awaits him upon his demise.[33] "[I] should tremble at the thoughts of the fearful Torments of Hell fire," wrote Bunyan, "still fearing that it would be my Lot to be found at last among those Devils and hellish Fiends, who are there bound down with the Chains and Bonds of Darkness, unto the judgment of the great day." Fearful that he could not receive God's grace because his sins were too heinous, Bunyan imagined Jesus looking upon him, "as if he did severely threaten me with some grievous Punishment for these and other my ungodly Practices."[34]

Despite Bunyan's fears of God's wrath, he found himself still wanting to sin. And yet he somehow managed to abstain from serious offenses without receiving God's grace and undergoing conversion. For twelve months Bunyan sought freedom from temptations. One day he overheard a conversation between two pious women and realized that their faith far surpassed his own. He wrote of how "God had visited their souls with his love in the *Lord Jesus,* and with what words and promises they had been refreshed, comforted, and supported against the temptations of the Devil."[35] Bunyan himself felt none of God's encouragement, no freedom from Satan's fiery darts; he constantly struggled against sin and Satan's hold.

Bunyan's autobiography suggests that his efforts at godliness stemmed primarily from fear of God's wrath rather than faith and trust in God's mercy. He described an encounter with an old friend whom he had forsaken because the man's habits were a bad influence. Bunyan asked him, "But Harry, said I, Why do you swear and curse thus? What will become of you, if you die in this condition?"[36] Bunyan knew that those who died

33. See Leopold Damrosch Jr., *God's Plot and Man's Stories: Studies in the Fictional Imagination from Milton to Fielding* (Chicago, 1985), for an insightful discussion of allegory and experience in all of Bunyan's writings; and Vincent Newey, ed., *The Pilgrim's Progress: Critical and Historical Views* (Liverpool, 1982). See Hall, *Worlds of Wonder,* 43–61, for a more general discussion of New England readers. Stories of sensational spiritual experience, such as Bunyan's, sold quite well, especially if the protagonist ultimately overcame the devil and attained grace.

34. John Bunyan, *Grace Abounding to the Chief of Sinners,* ed. Edmund Venables (1666; Oxford, 1879), 298, 302.

35. Ibid., 307.

36. Ibid., 308.

in a state of sin have "neither rest nor quiet in their Souls," and he declared his unwillingness to live with that terrifying thought.

Like Bunyan, other Puritans understood that they could indeed affect at least one possible outcome of their futures. Messages in sermons and in other writings mapped a wide passage leading to hell. Wigglesworth's *Day of Doom,* which sold 1,800 copies in its first year of publication, thoroughly detailed the procedure that awaited one after death, including facing Christ on Judgment Day and arriving at one's final destination. *Day of Doom* so effectively depicted the popular interpretation of Puritan theology that it merits closer textual analysis. Wigglesworth admitted from the outset that his purpose was to prepare his readers for death so that they might reform their ways before that fateful day. On the Day of Judgment it would be too late to change one's attitude and behavior. The sheep, or those for whom Christ had died, would sit on one side of Christ, and the goats, the unregenerate, on the other.

> Apostates base and run-aways,
>   such as have Christ forsaken,
> Of whom the Devil, with seven more evil,
>   hath fresh possession taken;
> Sinners ingrain, reserv'd to pain,
>   and torments most severe,
> Because 'gainst light they sinn'd with spite,
>   are also placed there.
>   · · · · ·
> With dismal chains, and strongest reins
>   like Prisoners of Hell,
> They're held in place before Christ's face,
>   till He their Doom shall tell.
> These void of tears, but fill'd with fears,
>   And dreadful expectation
> Of endless pains and scalding flames,
>   stand waiting for Damnation.[37]

Wigglesworth's intention may have been to prepare his audience for Judgment Day, but his words conveyed a frightening message. If sinners could not realize their own spiritual weaknesses, turning to God out of

37. Wigglesworth, *Day of Doom,* v. 28, 37, pp. 17, 19–20.

faith and love, then perhaps reading this familiar poem would scare them into piety. *Day of Doom* reproved those readers who deluded themselves that they might appeal to Christ's mercy for salvation and castigated those who qualified their sins as minor violations. Wigglesworth offered no hope for these poor sinners. His strikingly pessimistic message portrayed Christ as unrelenting in his wrath toward those who refused his grace.

> Without true Faith, the Scripture saith
>   God cannot take delight
> In any deed that doth proceed
>   from any sinful wight
> And without love all actions prove
>   But barren empty things;
> Dead works they be and vanity,
>   the which vexations brings.
>   . . . . .
> Your blinded spirit hoping to merit
>   by your own Righteousness,
> Needed no Savior but your behavior,
>   and blameless carriages. . . .
> *Your haughty pride laid me aside,*
> *And trampled on my Blood.*[38]

Christ's words in the poem emphasize that the unregenerates' sins were their own fault; they knew of the consequences of sin, and they should have reformed their evil ways.

> *Eternal smart is the desert*
>   *ev'n of the least offense;*
> Then wonder not if I allot
>   to you this Recompense;
> But wonder more that since so sore
>   and lasting plagues are due
> *To every sin, you liv'd therein,*
>   *who well the danger knew.*[39]

Wigglesworth depicted Christ chastising the wayward sinners for rejecting God's grace when it was offered. Christ's words in *Day of Doom*

---

38. Ibid., v. 100, 102, p. 35, emphasis added.
39. Ibid., v. 142, p. 61, emphasis added.

coupled with other Puritan sermons imply that going to hell involved a
conscious decision on the part of the unrepentant sinner. Sinners experienced a moment when they might have chosen the way of the Lord, but,
deserting Christ, they apparently preferred their lives of iniquity, in bondage to Satan.

Innately corrupt and depraved, sinners had to defeat Satan's possession
of their souls before they could fully embrace Christ. "The Mind of Man
is corrupted and blinded by the Fall," preached Benjamin Colman, "and
so are the Will and Affections, and by the Corruption of these Conscience is defiled and debauched; All these give Satan an easy *access* unto
the soul and a mighty *Power* over it by his Temptations." [40] The presence
of original sin, inherited from Adam's fall, ingrained in each person a
natural inclination to sin, thus paving the way for Satan's entry into his
or her soul.[41] John Davenport declared in his profession of faith to a New
England church that all men were created in Adam's image, conceived in
iniquity, and thus were "children of wrath, dead in trespasses and sins, altogether filthie and polluted throughout in soul and body; utterly averse
from any spirituall good, strongly bent to all evill." [42]

Ministers made a sharp distinction between persons in their natural
states and their converted souls. All the prayers and godly works that one
might do in the natural state were abhorred by God. One could not serve
both the devil and the Lord simultaneously, and the Puritans believed
that a person in the natural state, so easily lured by temptation, was Satan's servant. Thomas Hooker professed, "Every naturall man is an un-
believer, and therefore stands under the sentence of condemnation." If
the Lord did not grant grace to "draw him from that estate, he is like to
perish, and goe to hell for ever." [43] Samuel Willard was no more optimistic. "If the enquiry be, what is man?" Willard told his audience, "he
is a creature utterly void of all goodness, and a seminary of all manner of

40. Benjamin Colman, *Sermons Preached at the Lecture in Boston, from Luke
XI.21, 22*, American Antiquarian Society, Dated Books (Boston, 1717), 104. On the relationship between sexual imagery and the soul, see Chapter 3.

41. Because of original sin, Puritans believed that people could sin without Satan's instigation. See Willard, *Christians Exercise*.

42. *Letters of John Davenport, Puritan Divine*, ed. Isabel MacBeath Calder (New
Haven, 1937), 69. Despite the gendered language and imagery, it seems clear that such admonitions and prescriptions were intended for women and men equally.

43. Hooker, *Soules Humiliation*, 34.

abomination." Man was so not because of any particular sin committed but because he was a descendant of Adam, and therefore "he is enslaved to sin." [44]

Willard's and Hooker's descriptions of natural "man" was not meant to exclude women from the consequences of the Fall. Quite the contrary, women and men were considered equally reprehensible in the natural state. Regardless of what we might see today as biased language, Puritan women themselves knew all too well that these words were spoken to them as much as to their husbands, brothers, and sons. The important dissimilarity was between the natural state and the converted state, not between women and men.

Both Willard's and Hooker's language representing the natural state vividly described the soul gripped by Satan's clutches. "A company of divels like so many carrion crowes prey upon the heart of a poore creature, and all base lusts crall, and feed, and are maintained in such a wretched heart," wrote Hooker. "We can pitty poore drunkards, and sorrow for them; but we are as able to make worlds, and to pull hell in pieces; as to pull a poore Soule from the paw of the divell." Hooker's words demonstrate two points. Surely they were intended to persuade unrepentant sinners to turn from Satan to the Lord. "Either goe to Christ," he warned, "or there is no succour for thee." [45] More important, Hooker described the soul, held captive by Satan, as utterly irredeemable by mere mortals. Only Christ could save natural "man."

At the same time, God did not bestow the gift of grace lightly. Willard explained that while God does offer saving grace to some, *all* who remain in the natural state, even God's elect, are equally children of wrath and God's enemies.[46] And Hooker berated his audience, "Doest thou thinke that a few faint cold prayers, and lazy wishes, and a little horror of heart can plucke a dead man from the grave of his sinnes, and a damned soule from the pit of hell, and change the nature of a divell to be a Saint?" [47] Conversion from the natural state and Satan's power assumed, according to Willard, "the *turning* [of] the Soul *from* Sin and *Satan unto God.* . . . It is the subverting of the dominion of other lords, and bringing the sinner

44. Willard, *Compleat Body*, 211.
45. Hooker, *Soules Humiliation*, 37.
46. Willard, *Compleat Body*, 347.
47. Hooker, *Soules Humiliation*, 36; Willard, *Compleat Body*, 221.

into obedience to God; . . . for as long as we are the servants of sin, we cannot be the servants of God. *There is no communion between light and darkness, no fellowship with God and Belial.*"[48] Jonathan Mitchel described the conversion from the natural state to the state of salvation similarly. Before conversion, he explained, people are in a "state of darkness & bondage to Satan & consequently of perdition."[49]

The religious experiences and teachings of the Reverend Joseph Green typify the Puritan understanding of the depraved natural soul, the possession by Satan, and the significance of conversion. A teacher at Roxbury Latin School in the 1690s and later minister at Salem Village, Green filled his commonplace book with religious meditations and pious advice to his students and his family. He penned these words not only for the edification of others but also that he might maintain his own piety throughout each week.[50]

Green tried to impress upon his readers the Puritan belief that their souls would live for eternity. He hoped that consideration of their souls' immortality would convince some sinners to resist temptation before it was too late. "Remember that by nature those souls of yours are heirs of hell & eternal destruction," he chided, "and if you dye in that natural estate in which we all come into the world, you will surely have your portion with Devils & damned spirits forever." He encouraged his audience to think seriously about the possibility of eternal damnation. He said that if they had the opportunity to speak with only one of the souls damned to hell, "to hear what torments it endures for refusing Christ," they would long to have their souls saved.[51] He predicted that when all the souls from hell were reunited at Christ's second appearance, the wretched creatures would be filled with sorrow and shame, but it would be too late for them to escape their fate.

48. Willard, *Compleat Body,* 347. Willard makes biblical reference to Acts 26:18 and Matt. 6:24.
49. Jonathan Mitchel, *Continuation of Sermons concerning Man's Misery,* unpublished sermons, November 9, 1653–November 7, 1655, Massachusetts Historical Society. Mitchel preached this sermon on August 15, 1655, based on Acts 26:18, "From the power of Satan unto God."
50. *Commonplace Book of Joseph Green,* Publications of the Colonial Society of Massachusetts, no. 34 (Boston, 1943), 191–253.
51. Ibid., 199.

The threat of impending death and judgment dominated Green's religious musings and instructional advice. If you were to stand naked before Christ, Green speculated, could you "claim an interest in Christ, or would your hearts sink within you for sorrow[?]" The living had a chance to repent, believe, and love God, and Jesus "is abundantly willing to save [them]." But should they refuse and "neglect to get an interest in him; then he will look with an angry countenance on them that have despised him." Emphasizing the imminence of judgment, Green warned, "You may be in hell before to morrow if you defer your repentance." He offered his readers a reasonable option: they could either accept Christ's offer or ignore it, die in their natural states, face Christ on Judgment Day, and endure eternal wrath. "Let not the Devil perswade you to tarry any longer. [B]e not put off 'til to-morrow for you are not sure of to-morrow." [52]

Ministers counseled that the opportunity for accepting God's grace and abandoning the devil came during one's youth. Increase Mather feared that it would be too difficult for an incurable sinner ever to turn to the Lord. "When Satan hath held possession on a long time, it is not an easy work to out him, and disposses him." In fact, he warned the children in the congregation, "Truly, they that spend their childhood in the Service of Satan, if ever they be converted, are wont to have dreadfull Conversions at last. Therefore Young men should turn to God betimes, that so they may escape those bitter pangs, which otherwise they must expect to undergoe if ever good come of them." Mather told his listeners that "men are either converted in their youth or not at all." [53]

Advice to the young regarding conversion consisted primarily of such ominous admonitions. John Cotton's widely circulated *New England Primer* taught young readers the alphabet and the catechism, but chiefly it told in verse the fate of children who served God and those who unfortunately did not. "G" stood for "Godliness": "Godliness is profitable unto all things, having the promise of the life that now is, and that which is to come." And "I": "It is good for me to draw near unto God." But at "L," the children learned: "Liars shall have their part in the lake which burns with fire and brimstone." And at "U": "Upon the wicked, God shall rain an horrible tempest." Urged to trust in God and stand strong in their faith, the young readers of this alphabet verse encountered the practical

52. Ibid., 209, 212, 215.
53. Increase Mather, *A Call from Heaven* (Boston, 1679), 100–101, 106.

interpretation of the covenant. "Wo to the wicked," the message for "W" read, "it shall be ill with him, for the reward of his hands shall be given him." Children learned at an early age that they were to blame for their own sins and that their punishment would be both cruel and everlasting.[54]

David Stannard maintains that Puritan children learned about death when they were very young so that they might pray for their own salvation. The knowledge that they were sinners would help prepare them for death's imminence and inevitability.[55] The section "Verses for Children" in Cotton's primer contained a poem that warned: "Tho I am young yet I may die, / and hasten to eternity: / There is a dreadful fiery hell, / Where wicked ones must always dwell: / There is a heaven full of joy, / Where godly ones must always stay: / To one of these my soul must fly, / As in a moment when I die." [56] The *Primer's* catechism posed the youngsters a series of questions and answers concerning sin:

Q. What is your birth sin?

A. Adam's sin imputed to me, and a corrupt nature dwelling in me.

Q. What is your corrupt nature?

A. My corrupt nature is empty of grace, bent unto sin, only unto sin, and that continually.

The primer reviewed the Ten Commandments and then asked:

Q. Whether have you kept all these commandments?

A. No, I and all men are sinners.

Q. What are the wages of sin?

A. Death and Damnation.

Q. How then look you to be saved?

A. Only by Jesus Christ.[57]

54. John Cotton, *The New-England Primer . . . to which is added The Assembly of Divines and Mr. Cotton's Catechism* (1st ed. probably 1691; Boston, 1777). The pages are not numbered.

55. David E. Stannard, *The Puritan Way of Death: A Study in Religion, Culture, and Social Change* (New York, 1977). On child-rearing and the threat of eternal damnation, see Emory Elliot, *Power and the Pulpit in Puritan New England* (Princeton, 1974), 63–87.

56. Cotton, *New England Primer.*

57. Cotton, *The Shorter Catechism and Spiritual Milk for Babes,* in *New England Primer.*

Puritan children early absorbed a conviction of their sinfulness. Mindful of their mortality and assured of their blameworthiness, they must have perceived the specter of hell's dark furnace as threateningly close. Of course, these verses also taught of the grace of Jesus Christ, but the very sentence that gives some hope for salvation also drops a note of despair: "Q. How doth the ministry of the Gospel humble you yet more? A. By revealing the grace of the Lord Jesus in dying to save sinners, and yet convincing me of my sin in not believing on him, and of my utter insufficiency to come to him, and so I feel myself utterly lost." [58]

Guidance for the young did not always take the form of conventional religious study. Poems that personified good and evil, truth and conscience, conveyed the same messages in a lighter but no less didactic manner.[59] Cotton's *Primer* contains "A Dialogue between Christ, Youth, and the Devil," a lively conversation meant to persuade youngsters to turn to God. At first the youth tells Christ that he is committed to seeking pleasure at every opportunity while he is still in his prime. He is going to defy his parents' counsel to behave righteously and choose instead to spend his time in less godly pursuits. The devil, naturally, is thrilled by the youth's determination to join his ranks. He rejoices, "If thou my counsel wilt embrace, / And shun the ways of truth and grace, / And learn to lie, and curse and swear, / And be as proud as any are; / And with thy brothers wilt fall out, / And sisters with vile language flout; / Yea, fight and scratch, and also bite, / Then in thee I will take delight." The youth agrees to follow Satan's path, much to the amazement and disappointment of Christ. Incredulous that the youth would choose the devil over the Lord, Christ reminds the youth of the devil's dishonesty and of his allurements of folly which will turn out to be only bittersweet. Instead, Christ offers the youth everlasting joy if he would break away from the devil's snare.

The youth, content in his ways and not especially concerned about his future, refuses Christ's offer of sweet eternity because, he says, "Thy ways, O Christ! are not for me, / They with my age do not agree. / If I unto thy

58. Ibid.
59. "A Dialogue between Christ, Youth, and the Devil," in Cotton, *New England Primer*. For a much longer and more complex verse, see Benjamin Keach, *War with the Devil: or the Young Man's Conflict with the Powers of Darkness* (London, 1676). This was also printed in the colonies; in 1714 William Bradford published the twelfth edition in New York.

laws should cleave, / No more good days then should I have." Ignoring Christ's admonitions, the youth admits that at his young age he would rather have fun; he consciously rejects Christ and chooses the devil. "Don't trouble me," he dismisses Christ, "I must fulfil, / My fleshly mind, and have my will."

Justified in his anger, Christ turns the youth over to Satan. Christ reproaches the young sinner for his iniquities and pledges, "For all such things I'll make thee know / To judgment thou shall come also / *In hell at last thy soul shall burn, / When thou thy sinful race hast run* / Consider this, think on thy end / Lest God do thee in pieces rend." The youth, scared by Christ's fury, trembles in fear, promises to be more religious, and begs for Christ's help. All the while the devil pursues him, tries to convince him that there is no hell such as Christ describes, and seduces him with even greater enticements. Finally Satan assures the ambivalent youth that he may sin for as long as he wishes, that there will be plenty of time to repent when he reaches a more mature age.

Christ then gives the young man the same warning the ministers were delivering in church: "*Few shall be saved,* young man know, / *Most do unto destruction go.* / If righteous ones scarce saved be, / What will at last become of thee!" He provides one final chance for the sinner to convert and promises him that if he fails to do so, then he will never see God's kingdom. The youth still hesitates because he fears the derision of his friends if he abandons his merriments. He remains convinced that when he gets older Christ's benevolence will come forth. He responds, "Moreover, this I also know, / Thou can'st at last great mercy show. / When I am old, and pleasure gone, / Then what thou say'st I'll think upon." But Christ vows to cut his life short. Punishing the youth for clinging to his sporting ways, Christ tells him that he will have no more opportunities for repentance. The youth begs and pleads but the Lord will have none of it. "When I did call, you would not hear, / But did to me turn a deaf ear." The youth will have to pay dearly for this mistake. He appeals for at least one more year and promises to reform, but Christ maintains that if he grants another year, he is sure that the youth will nonetheless continue in his folly. On that merciless note Christ sends Death to the young man. The moral of the story, spelled out in the conclusion to the verse, is clear:

> Thus end the days of woful youth,
> Who won't obey nor mind the truth;
> Nor hearken to what preachers say,
> But do their parents disobey.
> They in their youth go down to hell,
> Under eternal wrath to dwell.
> Many don't live out half their days,
> For cleaving unto sinful ways.[60]

Puritan childhood lessons depicted a vengeful God, a persistent Satan, and an everlasting hellfire. By the time young sinners attended church and heard their ministers' sermons, they were long familiar with the dire message.[61]

Conversion narratives, the oral testimonies of Puritans seeking to enter the ranks of the visible saints, disclose an anxiety that perhaps the time for receiving grace had long passed. The portentous message delivered by Puritan ministers profoundly affected at least some of the churchgoing members of the community. The prospective converts—both male and female—shared a conviction that their souls, if left in the natural state, would ultimately reside among those pathetic unconverted souls groaning interminably in hell.[62]

60. Cotton, *Spiritual Milk for Babes,* emphasis added. All quotations on this children's verse have come from this source.

61. In 1678 Increase Mather addressed a portion of his sermon specifically to the younger members of his congregation. "Young men and young Women," he exhorted, "O be in earnest for Converting Grace, before it be too late. It is high time for you to look about you, deceive not yourselves with false Conversions (as many young men do to their eternal ruin). . . . Awake, Awake, and turn to God in Jesus Christ whilst it is called today, and know for certain that if you dy in your sins, you will be the most miserable of any poor Creatures in the bottom of Hell." See Mather, *Pray for the Rising Generation* (Boston, 1678), 22.

62. In this chapter I have drawn from the extant collection of fifty-one "Confessions" given at the First Church of Cambridge, Mass., between 1637 and 1645. Thomas Shepard, the minister of the church, recorded the narratives. They have been edited and published in *Thomas Shepard's Confessions,* ed. George Selement and Bruce C. Wooley, Publications of the Colonial Society of Massachusetts *Collections,* no. 58 (Boston, 1981). Conversion relations from the Wenham, Mass., congregation are recorded in Robert G. Pope, ed., *The Notebook of the Reverend John Fiske, 1644–1675* (Salem, Mass., 1974). I have also used McCarl, ed., "Thomas Shepard's Record of Relations," 432–66, and fourteen narratives from the First Church of East Windsor, Conn., from 1700 to 1725, recorded by pastor Timothy Edwards, father of Jonathan Edwards. Ten of them are from the years 1700–1702, two from 1722, and two from 1725. See Kenneth P. Minkema, "The East Windsor Conversion Relations, 1700–1725," *Connecticut Historical Society Bulletin* 51 (Winter 1986), 7–63.

Several conversion relations suggest that ministerial warnings were taken to heart. Abigail Rockwell told her minister that a particular sermon had precipitated her call to Christ. She recalled the text: "O young man in thy youth etc., and in particular such an expression as this being spoken to young ones, if you will not take warning by this I am afraid God will take you away next, were much awakening to me." [63] In her relation Hannah Bancroft professed her fear that she was already too old to convert, having heard in a sermon that people usually converted before they were thirty years old. In private counsel from her minister, however, she had learned that "though I was so old (for my age was ready to discourage me) yet there was hope for me." [64] Daniel Skinner may well have heard the same sermon, for he reported, "I heard that some thought there was a mercy for [those] that lived to thirty years of age before they was converted that ever was converted, afterwards which very much terrified me, for I thought I had out-stayed that time." [65] The idea that the opportunity for receiving grace had passed weighed heavily on many prospective converts. Some admitted that although they might have experienced awakenings in their childhood, they had always assumed that there would be plenty of time to change their sinful ways before they died. Samuel Pinne's wife confessed, "But my thinking that I was young and that it was time enough to mind my soul afterwards proved a great temptation to me to be negligent again and much unconcerned about my soul." [66]

Fear of eternal damnation provided the impetus to seek God. Daniel Skinner said, "I was in such distress at some times that I was afraid I should die and go to hell. I was afraid to go to sleep fearing that God would never let me wake more." Skinner vacillated between hopeful thoughts that God would show him mercy and the conviction that he would cast him "into ever lasting fire prepared for the Devil and his an-

63. "East Windsor Relations," Abigail Rockwell, March 18, 1701/1702; Eccles. 11:9.
64. Ibid., Hannah Bancroft, November 1700. It is difficult to determine the precise age of many confessors from the extant records. In Thomas Shepard's congregation most confessors gave their relation between the ages of twenty-five and thirty-five. See McGiffert, ed., *God's Plot* (1994 ed.), 138. Though such men and women heard a similar message, it is entirely possible that it *became* gendered as a result of different notions of what constituted "young" and "old" for men and women; was a woman of thirty joining the church and entering the community of saints, for example, viewed differently from a man of the same age?
65. "East Windsor Relations," ibid., Daniel Skinner, no date.
66. Ibid., Samuel Pinne's wife, May 28, 1701.

gels." Especially terrifying was the image of hell's perpetuity. Abigail Rockwell admitted that her first awakenings came from hearing a sermon delivered to unconverted sinners, "namely, can you bear to live half an hour in fire, and if not how can you bear to live in hell to all eternity."[67]

When Skinner was at the nadir of distress, he had remembered the comforting words of Christ which offered solace to those who would believe; he grieved for his sins, and he expressed hope that he would be able to sustain his newly found faith in the Lord. Other prospective converts, when they realized that their corrupt nature doomed them to everlasting perdition, decided to trust the Lord for their salvation. Not long after his marriage, Joshua Willis Jr. consulted his minister and heard that he "was in great danger of perishing forever." He "was advised to be earnest and diligent in the use of all means, for my soul's good." Ann Fitch knew she would be damned because, she remembered, a sermon had warned, "He that believeth not shall be damned," and she could not even believe in God, much less in Christ. Her apprehension was so pronounced that finally she sought private advice and learned that she was still in a state of nature and "stood in great need of an interest in Christ."[68]

The repentant sinners believed that God would have been completely justified in rejecting their penitence. Esther Bissell realized that her own heart condemned her, and she admitted that it was her own wickedness that had prevented her conversion. "God might justly cast me into hell," she proclaimed, "and that if ever He saved me it would be mere mercy . . . for I had nothing to commend me to God." Ann Fitch, although she desperately wanted to believe that Christ had died for sinners, saw herself as an irredeemable reprobate "and so vile that I could surely justify Him, if He should then have taken away my life and cast me into hell."[69]

Lay women and men feared hell equally, but lay women such as Ann Fitch and Esther Bissell tended to believe that it was their vile natures that would take them there rather than the particular sins they may have committed. Puritan conversion narratives have generally been seen as androgynous. According to Charles Cohen, for example, "The experience of grace submerges the peculiarities of gender"; women and men spoke with

67. Ibid., Skinner, Rockwell.
68. Ibid., Daniel Skinner, Joshua Willis Jr., December 24, 1700, Ann Fitch, March 1700–1701.
69. Ibid., Esther Bissell, July 24, 1700, Ann Fitch, February 26, 1700–1701.

"one tongue." Although I agree with Cohen's elegant and persuasive argument that "no one distinguished between the Spirit's operations in one sex or the other," I have nonetheless found that the narratives reflect disparity between men and women with regard to the sense of self.[70]

Women heeded their ministers' words in the strictest sense. In the state of sin they thought of themselves as completely worthless, virtually unredeemable, slaves of Satan. In her 1648 conversion narrative, Elizabeth Oakes described herself as "so unfit and unworthy that I was unfit." She admitted, "I saw I was dead and darkness, and Christ was peace and life and light." She mentioned she had "denied the Lord often" but did not list any more specific sins for which she now repented; instead, she recounted only a debased sense of her soul—the very essence of her being—as completely unworthy of Christ's advances. Neither did another female parishioner, Goodwife Jackson, speak of particular sins, other than mentioning deceit in a generic way. Calling herself a "poor silly creature," she sadly admitted, "I thought I was a rebellious wretch against God, and so I continued long."[71]

70. See Cohen, *God's Caress*, 222–23; Michael McGiffert, in the new edition of Shepard's diary and autobiography, accompanied by thirty-three of Shepard's extant "confessions" from 1630 to 1640, briefly mentions that spiritual depression was a "predominantly female affliction." See McGiffert, ed., *God's Plot* (1994 ed.), 141; Barbara Epstein, *Politics of Domesticity: Women, Evangelism, and Temperance in Nineteenth-Century America* (Middletown, Conn., 1981), 14; Murray G. Murphey, "The Psychodynamics of Puritan Conversion," *American Quarterly* 31 (Summer 1979), 135–47. Patricia Caldwell, *The Puritan Conversion Narrative: The Beginnings of American Expression* (New York, 1983), 9–15, notes the parallels between the conversion experience and female imagery of childbirth and weaning but does not emphasize gender differences in the relations. On the issue of spiritual equality between the sexes, see Margaret W. Masson, "The Typology of the Female as a Model for the Regenerate: Puritan Preaching, 1690–1730," *Signs* 2 (1976), 304–15; Laurel Thatcher Ulrich, "Vertuous Women Found: New England Ministerial Literature, 1668–1735," *American Quarterly* 28 (1976), 20–40; Mary Potter, "Gender Equality and Gender Hierarchy in Calvin's Theology," *Signs* 11 (1986), 725–39; and Amanda Porterfield, *Female Piety in Puritan New England* (New York, 1992). For a discussion of the gendered conversion narratives of the eighteenth century, see Susan Juster, *Disorderly Women: Sexual Politics and Evangelicalism in Revolutionary New England* (Ithaca, N.Y., 1994). Juster found gender distinctions emerging by the time of the Great Awakening; as I show later, women and men of the seventeenth and early eighteenth centuries experienced their social and spiritual worlds differently.

71. McCarl, ed., "Thomas Shepard's Record," 442, 446. The female narratives recorded in John Fiske's notebook sometimes mention specific sins, but these narratives were recorded in the third person, making it difficult to determine if the congregants themselves made the statements or if Fiske inserted these details later. In the case of Anne Fiske, the minister recorded, "Her particular sins were foolishness, vanity, and pride." See Pope, ed., *Notebook of John Fiske*, 6.

By contrast, their male co-religionist Abram Arrington did not mention the depravity of his soul in his conversion narrative. Instead, Arrington admitted that he "minded nothing but sin and my own pleasure and lusts." His compatriot Robert Browne confessed to the "evil of company keeping" as well as the "evil of Sabbath breaking and of not praying."[72] Oakes, Arrington, Browne, and Jackson all qualified for admission to Shepard's church, but their notions of sin and of their soul's relationship to themselves and Satan differed in subtle but significant ways. Women, like Oakes and Jackson, tended to identify their selves with their debauched souls, seen as completely under the devil's dominion in the natural state. Men, like Arrington and Browne, in contrast focused on particular sins, separating their natures from the sins they committed.[73]

In Chapter 3 we will see that, although Puritans conceived of the souls, whether women's or men's, as feminine, men were nonetheless able to own that part of their being which displayed "wifely" characteristics— that is, passivity and submissiveness—necessary to bond with Christ upon conversion. Margaret Masson has argued that men could safely participate in the drama of conversion because the rigid gender roles distinctive to the nineteenth century had not yet emerged.[74] My reading of the conversion narratives suggests that perhaps notions of masculinity were changing even earlier than Masson supposed. Men's increasing reluctance to convert in the late seventeenth and early eighteenth centuries may reflect an avoidance of the requisite "feminine qualities." And even in the men's relations of the mid-seventeenth century, there is a tendency to divorce the feminine soul from the male self. In the context of the meetinghouse, men seemed to differentiate what or who they *were* from what they *did*. They concerned themselves with the various sins they had committed, and they dutifully repented, but only rarely did they

72. Ibid., 442, 450.

73. Men's apparent ability to distinguish sinful behavior from a sinful essence may have had other ramifications, as Richard Godbeer has recently illustrated in "'The Cry of Sodom': Discourse, Intercourse, and Desire in Colonial New England," *William and Mary Quarterly*, 3rd ser., 52 (April 1995), 259–86. Godbeer argues that seventeenth-century men (and the communities they lived in) tended to distinguish sins they committed— specifically, sodomitical acts—from any essential identity they might have had (in this case, as "homosexuals"). Repentance was thus limited to specific acts, rather than, more expansively, to a transgressive being.

74. Masson, "Typology of the Female," 313–15.

take the further step of internalizing their ministers' words: sinful is as sinful does.[75]

The disjunction for New England Puritans between outward persons, presented through appearances and deeds, and inner selves, constituting the reality or essence of an individual's (redeemed or reprobate) nature, was troubling but inevitable. Though Puritans struggled to erect in America pure churches of visible saints, only God could truly know who was saved and who was damned. Hence, the visible church could never perfectly mirror the invisible church of God's elect, nor could outwardly righteous women and men, or their communities, ever be sure they were true saints.

"Secret sins" thus became a considerable problem for clergy and laity alike. They had covenanted not merely as individual women and men with their God but with one another collectively as godly communities. Committed to a common enterprise, they emphasized common, public action in building God's kingdom on earth and searching for signs of their salvation. Living closely, with great familiarity, and exerting themselves to monitor one another's behavior, these New Englanders emphasized openness and transparency while devaluing, indeed distrusting, pri-

---

75. For provocative reflections on the construction of gendered subjectivity, see Judith Butler, *Gender Trouble: Feminism and the Subversion of Identity* (New York, 1990). Butler challenges the notion that to be female (or male) is a "natural fact"; instead, she argues, gender is the result of "cultural performance," and the "naturalness" of gender is "constructed through discursively constrained performative acts that produce the body through and within the categories of sex" (viii). For a provocative counterargument to Butler, which privileges the "fact" of male and female bodies over the cultural and discursive nature of language about the body, see Lyndal Roper, *Oedipus and the Devil: Witchcraft, Sexuality, and Religion in Early Modern Europe* (New York, 1994). Recent scholarship on early America has focused particularly on the history of male subjectivity (see Godbeer, "The Cry of Sodom") and the formation of gender conventions in the late eighteenth and early nineteenth centuries, in the context of changing commercial relations. See especially Toby L. Ditz, "Shipwrecked; or, Masculinity Imperiled: Mercantile Representation of Failure and the Gendered Self in Eighteenth-Century Philadelphia," *Journal of American History* 81 (June 1994), 51–80; Carroll Smith-Rosenberg, "Domesticating 'Virtue': Coquettes and Revolutionaries in Young America," in *Literature and the Body,* ed. Elaine Scarry (Baltimore, 1988); Smith-Rosenberg, "Dis-Covering the Subject of the 'Great Constitutional Discussion,' 1786–1789," *Journal of American History* 79 (December 1992), 841–73; Jay Fliegelman, *Declaring Independence: Jefferson, Natural Language, and the Culture of Performance* (Stanford, Calif., 1993); John-Christophe Agnew, *Worlds Apart: The Market and the Theater in Anglo-American Thought, 1550–1750* (Cambridge, 1986). On female subjectivity, especially in the Revolutionary period, see Juster, *Disorderly Women.*

vacy. In such a world, privacy became secrecy, which itself became suspect; what remained secret was likely illicit, and secret sins were the most dangerous of all, both to individuals and communities.[76]

Thomas Shepard, in his autobiography, considered his wife's travail during the birth of their son Thomas to be a direct result of his secret sins. The immediate blame he accorded to an unskilled midwife, but he conceived of the ordeal as God's lesson (and a well-deserved one) for his violations. By his own admission, Shepard had begun to "grow secretly proud and full of sensuality," taking more delight in his wife than in his God. In addition, he conceded that he had become "secretly mindless of the souls of the people," presumably neglecting the needs of his congregation. For these sins that Shepard had committed secretly, that were known perhaps only to himself and to God, he was punished. His wife's afflictions taught him to "fear [God] more and to keep his dread in my heart."[77]

Sins that remained covert produced in the transgressor a sense of self-division, the outward appearance of righteousness masking inward and essential corruption. The secret sinner, though a reprobate, could dissemble—not ultimately before God, of course, but before the community. Only the rejection of secrecy through public disclosure, confession, and repentance could restore the possibility of grace. These public acts might realign the divided Puritan self, coordinating the presentation of the outward person with a more honest representation of the inner nature, or soul.

But women and men, because of their disparate conceptions of their essential natures, effected this realignment differently.[78] The conversion narratives suggest that Puritan men could distinguish between their innate selves (their souls) and the rest of themselves (mind and body) and thus could repent for particular sins without perceiving themselves as worthless. Men could achieve a kind of subjective transparency by reforming ungodly behavior, making their deeds reflect their desired regenerate selves, as Robert Browne tried to do: "And so I thought I would

76. See Hall, *Worlds of Wonder,* 173–78.
77. Shepard, *God's Plot,* 55.
78. For an insightful discussion of the way in which late seventeenth- and early eighteenth-century English Quaker women negotiated their "practical" and "mystical" selves, see Phyllis Mack, *Visionary Women: Ecstatic Prophecy in Seventeenth-Century England* (Berkeley, Calif., 1992), 351–402.

reform myself and endeavored to pray and to keep Sabbath, and so I
thought it would be better with me than others who had no regard." [79]
John Jones repented for what he knew angered God the most, "not so
much gross and open sins, especially in times of light and in these places
especially, but it was secret sins laid close to the heart under plentiful
means." Admitting his guilt and the difficulty he experienced in abandoning these hidden sins, Jones nonetheless searched and found "a remedy"—
the seeming contradiction of active resignation to Christ. Jones saw no unredeemable essential depravity in himself; his decision, rather, displayed a
freedom of action and an independence that were consistent with the
original "liberty [he took] in secret to commit those sins." [80]

Women, in contrast, more often achieved a darker wholeness that
equated their transgressive behavior with a perceived basic depravity:
repentance of particular sins was not sufficient to redeem their souls, for
a woman's sinfulness encompassed her entire being. If she were truly
sincere in her profession of faith, a woman found it necessary to confront her prescribed essential depravity. Ann Errington, for example,
could not easily elide her secret sins because they reflected her inner corruption. Even her marriage was based on false pretenses. Because her
sins were secret, her husband had mistakenly assumed that she was a
godly woman. She was convinced otherwise, but "I durst not tell my husband," she confessed, "fearing he would loath me if he knew me." [81] Her
secret sin was so great and so intrinsic to her nature that it virtually
defined her, making her marriage, indeed her entire life, a lie. Merely re-
penting would not be enough, for it was her soul, not simply her deed,
that was reprehensible.

Congregants, both women and men, distinguished between the states
of their souls and the actual sins they committed. In September 1648,
Captain Daniel Gookin conceded that, although he stayed away from
scandals, he remained "wedded to close wickedness," referring to a symbolic marriage between himself and the evil nature of his interior, feminine soul—as if these two were distinct entities. Clearly differentiating

79. McCarl, "Shepard's Record of Relations," 451.
80. Shepard, *Confessions*, 199–200.
81. Ibid., 185.

his self from the soul responsible for particular sins, Gookin made the specific point that finally the Lord let him see his "filthy nature and actual sins." Another of Shepard's congregants, Elizabeth Stone, drew a similar distinction between "nature" and deeds; yet unlike Gookin, she aligned herself with the state of her soul. Stone admitted she was in a "state of sin, such not troubled for particular sin but a state of sin." [82] Sarah Fiske, of the Wenham congregation, "prayed to God to show what sin was," all the while remaining convinced that she was "in a worse condition than any toad." [83]

This dichotomy in the way women and men related to sin was by no means rigid. There were women who confessed to particular sins (Goodwife Stevenson, for example, mentioned that she sinned against God and disobeyed her parents), and there were men, such as Robert Browne, who avowed that God had showed them their "vileness and wretchedness." By and large, however, the women identified more closely with their inner nature, the unregenerate (and feminine) soul.[84]

When women discussed their sins they took seriously the gravity of such transgressions; true to their ministers' teachings, confessing women equated the sins they had committed with a sinful and wretched heart. In a 1689 sermon, Samuel Willard spoke of the nature of sinfulness on the whole. "Sin and Holiness are directly opposite," he declared. Sinners, particularly the ones who "laugh at Fastings & Prayers, who ridicule those who are afraid of swearing, filthy communication, and profanation of God's Name & Day: certainly, these are impure, filthy Creatures, and must needs be enemies of an holy God." [85] Swearing and disdaining fast days and prayers were certainly sins, worthy of Willard's contempt, but

---

82. McCarl, "Shepard's Record of Relations," 452, 454, 466.

83. Pope, *Notebook of John Fiske*, 43.

84. Clergymen's attitudes coincided with women's on this point, perhaps anticipating the "feminization" of American Protestantism as sketched by Ann Douglas and others. For one example, see Thomas Shepard's autobiography. He called himself "a worthless instrument in his [Christ's] hand . . . and resolved to walk in sense of my weakness and vileness daily before him." Regarding what Shepard saw as the "abominations of my soul," he emphasized "my principal evil the root of my nature, whence so much sin came." See McGiffert, *God's Plot*, 39, 45. See also Ann Douglas, *The Feminization of American Culture* (New York, 1977).

85. Willard, *Compleat Body*, 74.

the minister painted the scope of sin more broadly, making the sinner—
the filthy creature—worse than the sin itself.

Echoing clerical teachings, Mistress Mary Gookin, for example, admitted, "I thought my sins were so great that I knew not what to say in
presence of God, but to lie at his feet. . . . I saw I could do nothing but sin
in all I did, sin in praying and hearing, and my sins appeared great in
God's sight." Mary Gookin seemed to herself the very personification of
sin, and she equated her self with her unregenerate soul. Employing the
common metaphor of the regenerate soul as a fruit-bearing tree, Gookin
sadly conceded, "I have been hitherto an unfruitful branch, and so lie
down at the Lord's feet." [86] Gookin's sins were so numerous, in her view,
that her very being must be at fault: she herself was the unfruitful branch;
she herself was the unregenerate soul, the filthy creature.

Whereas a female parishioner like Elizabeth Oakes would likely identify herself with the sinful soul ("he [Shepard] showed that the soul could
do nothing without Christ, and I saw it then that of myself I could do
nothing good"), a male congregant would, as far as possible, disassociate
himself from his soul. In his relation, John Shepard acknowledged that
"whatever a man did unregenerate was sinful, and plowing was sin, and
all what they did perform, and eating and drink and sleep, all was sinful." But unlike Mistress Gookin, who saw herself as the problem—the
unfruitful branch—John Shepard determined to set himself against his
sinful nature, as if it were a distinct part of himself which he had the
power to reform: "The Lord made me mourn for this sin of my nature,
and hence I set myself against this sin, whereas before it was against actual [sin]." [87]

Francis Moore's narrative similarly suggests a distinctively male attitude toward his nature and his sins. Distancing his reprobate soul from
his sins, he attributed his misdeeds to "the flesh resisting and contradict-
ing the Lord." Eventually he came to believe in his regeneracy, that he
was "a new creature"; yet he puzzled over the sins he continued to commit. He characterized these infractions—drunkenness, keeping "loose
company," profaning the Sabbath, security, and sloth—as "relapses,"

86. McCarl, "Shepard's Record of Relations," 460.
87. Ibid., 444.

rather than indications of hopeless depravity. By contrast, emphasizing original sin rather than willful sins of the flesh, Elizabeth Olbon "felt so much evil in her own heart she thought it impossible so poor a creature should be saved or received to mercy and so fell down in discouragements."[88] The wife of William Fiske, in the Wenham congregation, similarly emphasized the fundamental inability of her nature to avoid sins. Despite her "willingness" and "desire" to "turn from her sins," she was consumed with "fears" and convinced of her helplessness.[89]

Both sexes, however, recognized Satan's presence not merely as a tempter but as the ever-present force ready to possess the souls that veered from God's path. Even the best-intentioned convert or pious cleric knew that Satan's presence meant his or her own distance from God. And when sinners spoke of separation from Christ, implicitly they voiced their fears that they would be forever bound to the devil.[90]

Andrew Delbanco has argued that during the seventeenth century the notion of sin as the absence of God shifted to embody a sense of evil outside oneself. He has suggested that ministers could no longer sustain the focus on grace in their sermons and instead warned their congregations about the overwhelming presence of sin in the world.[91] Delbanco is certainly correct that early in the seventeenth century the ministers and the laity did speak of sin as the absence of God, but it is important to see that for New England Puritans this privation implied the presence of Satan. Satan loomed in their empty hearts not only as a tempter but, more

88. Shepard, *Confessions,* 35–36, 40.

89. Pope, *Notebook of John Fiske,* 30.

90. Richard Godbeer argues that Satan appears in these conversion narratives only in connection with the issue of responsibility for sin. Similarly, Charles Cohen maintains that although Satan appears uniformly in the narratives as the tempter, bent on destroying mankind, most of the references to sin omit reference to Satan and place the blame with the individual. My own reading of the sources suggests that these new church members had a much more expansive vision of Satan. Cohen makes a good point, however, when he notes, "rather than enticing to sin, he [Satan] dissuades from grace" (218). See Godbeer, *Devil's Dominion,* 102; Cohen, *God's Caress,* 216–18.

91. Andrew Delbanco, *Puritan Ordeal.* He maintains, "The journey to America was in part an effort to conserve what was left of the conviction that sin, rather than being an entity implanted in the soul, was something more abstract: a temporary estrangement from God" (79). See also 181–84 on the transition from grace to sin as the center of clerical attention.

important, as the lord of souls doomed to hell.[92] The emptiness left by God's distance was all too easily filled by Satan.[93]

Converts of Thomas Shepard's congregation frequently spoke of their apprehension of God's absence. Joanna Sill admitted that her "heart went after the world and vanities and the Lord absented Himself from her." Although she attended to her religious duties, still she "found no presence of God." Likewise, Robert Daniel, a husbandman and highway surveyor, claimed that he wanted "a heart to honor God" but found only "the casting of soul from presence of God." And Richard Cutter, a cooper, had heard that "one sin continued in with obstinacy and hardness will separate forever from Christ."[94]

While persistence in sin separated one from God, it just as fiercely bonded one to Satan. Elizabeth Cutter lived for several years with a family "where the people were carnal." She became ill with consumption and "after followed with Satan and afraid he would have me away."[95] John Jones disclosed that he had been perfectly content to continue in his sins until he heard "Mr. B[ulkeley] preaching about the covenant where he showed that everyone by nature was a prisoner in a pit and dungeon with no comfort to be found." Bulkeley painted the portrait of natural man "as in a dungeon sticking in his sins to be kept by Satan." At least one sinner was affected by this visual imagery. Jones admitted that the Lord had made him see that he "was a prisoner and kept by Satan. And no hope did appear of deliverance out of it."[96]

92. Thomas Shepard explained in his catechism how the void left by God was assuredly filled by Satan. Asked, "What is his present misery?" the catechumen was to answer: "He is departed from God by sin. God is departed from him in wrath for sin. He is full of all sin. . . . He is under the power of Sathan [sic] for sin. . . . He is an enemy to God. He may look for the everlasting fire of the wrath of God to break out upon him every moment in this condition." See Thomas Shepard, *A Short Catechism Familiarly Teaching the Knowledge of God and of our Selves* (Cambridge, Mass., 1654), 18.

93. If Puritan ministers in subsequent generations concentrated their sermons on the evil outside oneself, that is, the various sins and temptations that could pull sinners' hearts from God, rather than on the void itself, it was because the notion of Satan's presence had changed. There was indeed a shift in the concept of evil, but it was not complete until after the Salem witchcraft trials. After 1692, Satan seemed less visible in people's lives; he became merely the tempter, the seducer to evil. He was thus a far less threatening figure than he had been as the evil guardian of souls. This theme is developed in Chapter 5.

94. Shepard, *Confessions,* 51, 60, 179.

95. Ibid., 144.

96. Ibid., 200.

Converts knew that to sin was to forsake the Lord and become one with the devil, and that hell awaited them. Edward Hall granted that "he saw the want of Christ and that without Him he must perish." To be without Christ meant to expire with Satan. John Stansby conceded that in his natural state he was a "child of hell and if ever any a child of devil, I." Not only did he persist in his own lusts, but he encouraged others to do so as well. "Herein," he confessed, "I have been like the devil not only to hell myself but enticing and haling others to sin, rejoicing when I could make others drink and sin." Jane Wilkinson Winship "heard by T[homas] S[hepard] the evil of sin that separated from Christ. . . . And was afraid to die and should forever lie under wrath of God." [97]

In these expressions of fear, we can also see differences of gender. Stansby, having actively fostered sinfulness in others, called himself a "child of hell." Likewise, George Willows "saw nothing but hell due to him" because he had broken the Sabbath.[98] Jane Winship, on the other hand, was convinced simply that her own passivity and inherent evil would sentence her to an eternity in hell.

In expressing their separation from God, women more closely conformed to the models set by their male ministers. Thomas Shepard sounds much like his female congregants when he admits in his autobiography that in "prayer I saw my heart very vile, filled with nothing but evil, nay, mind and mouth and life, and void of God. Hence I prayed to the Lord to possess me again." [99] Shepard's use of "possess," a word more frequently associated with Satan's dominion, implied that a heart separate from God did indeed belong to the devil. When Michael Wigglesworth contemplated his "carnall sensuall heart that is apt to leav [its] rest in god," he was convinced that his soul would "seek it in the creature ever and anon." Later he realized gratefully that God had "quenched his lusts" and had "preserved [him] in so many fearful dangers, from the fury of so many raging devils." Most miraculous in Wigglesworth's view,

97. Ibid., 34, 86, 148. Ministers warned that Satan often worked through wicked men, enticing others to sin. Shepard, for example, wrote, "I saw also that as Satan by external means of wicked men labors to suppress and silence preachers and means, so by inward efficacy he silenceth and suppreseth any good motion, and spirit of prayer." See Shepard, *God's Plot*, 195.

98. Shepard, *Confessions*, 43.

99. Shepard, *God's Plot*, 83.

God "hath pluck't [him] out of sathans jaws and the belly of hell at last, when he finally leavs 1000s better." [100]

According to Wigglesworth, sinning meant breaching the promises he had made to the Lord. To persist in his "love of the creature," at the expense of the "love of christ," he acknowledged, would "break my covenant with the Lord Christ and prostitute my soul unto vanity." [101] Wigglesworth agonized over the possibility that he had indeed broken his covenant, and he seemed amazed that it should be so difficult to keep his promises. He wrote of the covenant "that if I would receiv his son whom he offered freely to me why he would enter into an Everlasting Covenant that should not be broken by himself: neither would he suffer it to be utterly broken by me." Though God's assurances were so generous and merciful, conforming, Wigglesworth lamented, was not easy, even though he wanted badly to "let christ be mine let me be his alone." Although he tried each day to "go away and sin no more," he admitted that such wishes were but "vain thoughts," and he was unable to overcome his pride. The most he could hope for was Christ's mercy on "so vile a sinner." [102]

Wigglesworth's fears embraced both "male" and "female" attitudes toward sin and Satan. Like many women, Wigglesworth was convinced of his innate depravity; like many men, he wrestled with the propensity to sin. He desperately desired to be near the Lord, and yet Satan and his own carnal heart lured him away again and again. Wigglesworth grappled with yet another Puritan dilemma: who bore the responsibility for sin, the devil or the self?

Ministers made it clear to their congregations that although Satan was constantly by their side, ready to assault them, the choice to withstand, defeat, or succumb to his devices was theirs. Satan had enormous powers, but he could not force his quarry to commit sin.[103] He did not have to compel his subjects, for their innate corruption inclined men and women to submit to Satan, as Samuel Willard warned: "The corruption

100. Wigglesworth, "Diary," 393, 421.
101. Ibid., 393.
102. Ibid., 344.
103. For a detailed treatment of the clerical views of Satan and sin, see Edward Trefz, "Satan as the Prince of Evil," *Boston Public Library Quarterly* 7 (1955), 3–22; Trefz, "Satan in Puritan Preaching," *Boston Public Library Quarterly* 8 (1956), 71–84, 148–59. See also Trefz, "A Study of Satan, with Particular Emphasis upon His Role in the Preaching of Certain New England Puritans" (Th.D. diss., Union Theological Seminary, 1952).

that is in men makes them fit subjects for Satan to work on." Willard believed that this inner concupiscence was to temptation "as tinder or gun powder is to fire, on which if a spark do but fall, it takes."[104] And Thomas Brooks, author of a widely read demonological treatise, declared, "Satan hath cast such sinful seed into our souls, that now he can no sooner tempt, but we are ready to assent; he can no sooner have a plot upon us, but he makes a conquest of us."[105]

Brooks reasoned that both Satan and the sinner were responsible for sin; Satan cast the seed, and the sinner ensured that it germinated. Historians have noted the seeming ambiguity in Puritan thought concerning the responsibility for sin. Ministers cautioned their flocks against abdicating personal responsibility for sin, but they recognized—indeed, emphasized—the part Satan played in leading sinners to their fate. Richard Godbeer has pointed to loopholes in the logic: "How could Satan himself pose a serious threat to the human soul if he had no power independent of God's will and human corruption? And if Satan was responsible for tempting men and women to sin, how was that different from being responsible for sin itself?"[106]

The clergy and the laity were not so troubled by the apparent paradox; to varying degrees they acknowledged both Satan's role and that of their own innate corruption.[107] Michael Wigglesworth noted in his diary that he often struggled "in combating with diverse temptations and prevailing

104. Samuel Willard, *The Christians Exercise by Satans Temptations* (Boston, 1701), 83. Once the devil acted upon his victims the snare was all the more difficult to escape. Increase Mather wrote of those who had fallen into Satan's embrace, "He [Satan] doth even what he will to them. If the devil put them upon doing this or that wickedness, they will do it." See Increase Mather, *Angelographia* (Boston, 1696), 85.

105. Thomas Brooks, *Precious Remedies against Satan's Devices* (1652; Edinburgh, 1987), 16.

106. Goodbeer, *Devil's Dominion*, 94. See also Dennis Edward Owen, "Satan's Fiery Darts: Explorations in the Experience and Concept of the Demonic in Seventeenth-Century New England" (Ph.D. diss., Princeton University, 1974), 48–52; and Trefz, "Satan as the Prince of Evil," 7–13.

107. Godbeer maintains that the ambiguity troubled some New Englanders so much that they found themselves possessed by Satan during the witchcraft trials. He says that the possessed girls were unable either to accept or to reject responsibility for sin; by claiming that they were possessed, they were able to blame both the devil for entering into their bodies and their own weakened spiritual condition for allowing it to happen in the first place. See Godbeer, *Devil's Dominion*, 113–14. Godbeer's explanation for possession is intriguing, but I question whether the issue of responsibility for sin was at the root of Puritan anxiety over evil.

corruptions of my own." [108] John Sill's conversion narrative, related by Thomas Shepard before his Cambridge congregation, typified the dual responsibility of one's own will and Satan: "And then when *sin or Satan* came to draw his heart from God, the Lord helped him to see it before it came as to be delivered from it." [109] Similarly, Nathaniel Eaton held his own degeneracy accountable, but he also confessed that Satan exacerbated the temptations and threw him into greater despair. For the sins he committed in "Sabbath breaking and company keeping," he blamed "the hidden corruption of my own heart," and when the temptations grew yet stronger he admitted that "Satan . . . found the house swept and I was worse." [110]

Eaton's reference to Luke 11:24–26 and Matthew 12:43–44 in which seven additional wicked spirits overtake a man who has rid himself of one indicates the particular arena in which the laity and the clergy found Satan most vexing. They appear to have understood that their own sinful natures contributed to their unregeneracy, but they were constantly amazed at Satan's determination to lure souls from God. They blamed themselves for specific acts of wrongdoing, but they knew that Satan worked tirelessly to possess their souls and keep them from entering into a covenant with God. Thomas Shepard placed greater blame on himself for his sins and considered his own heart to be the greatest foe. As he related in his autobiography, the Lord helped him to ask himself, "Why shall I seek the glory and good of myself who am the greatest enemy, worse than the Devil can be, against myself, which self ruins me and blinds me, etc.?" The devil may have tempted, but the self seized the opportunity to sin. As a sinner Shepard likened himself to Eve. "The Devil," he wrote, "overcame Eve to damn herself by telling her she should be like God." The devil instigated; Eve acted; sin prevailed. The three factors were in balance: "It was my misery to hold forth sin and Satan and self in my course." [111]

---

108. Edmund S. Morgan, ed., "The Diary of Michael Wigglesworth," in *Transactions, 1942–1946,* Publications of the Colonial Society of Massachusetts, no. 35 (Boston, 1951), 393.

109. George Selement and Bruce C. Wooley, eds., *Thomas Shepard's Confessions,* Publications of the Colonial Society of Massachusetts, *Collections,* no. 58 (Boston, 1981), 46, emphasis added.

110. Ibid., 54, 55.

111. Shepard, *God's Plot,* 44, 111, 112.

Shepard knew that Satan could do nothing without God's permission; hence, he believed that God arranged Satan's presence and his own subsequent sins for a divine purpose: "I saw also that the Lord let sin and Satan prevail there, that I might see my sin and be more humbled by it and so get strength against it." [112] John Cotton similarly acknowledged God's rationale for allowing sin: "Know that [God] hath had an hand in all our wickedness, he knows for what end he did it." God might have permitted the self to fall victim to Satan's temptations, Cotton reasoned, "to make us more humble, and holy, and gracious for ever after, which if we finde in our selves, we may for ever be comforted." [113]

Cotton recognized, too, that although Satan could not act without God's sanction, this constraint did not effectively diminish his capabilities. "It is true," he instructed, "Satan's worke was directed by God; but otherwise it is possible for Satan so to buffet our minds, by representing to us the number and burden of our sins, and so to hide the face of God from us . . . as that wee can see nothing but wrath and enmity in the presence of the Lord." Cotton felt it necessary to explain to his congregants why God, in his infinite goodness, would allow people to sin. He clarified that God himself was not responsible for making "the hearts of men hard, nor doth he encline them to sin, he tempts no man to evill, nor puts any habits of wickednesse into any mans heart." Although God did not make the unregenerate sin, according to Cotton, neither would he protect them from self, sin, and Satan: "First, he leaves men to themselves, he gives them up to the hardnesse of their hearts . . . and secondly, he leaves them to Satan." [114]

The temptations that people found most troubling, ministers frequently warned, were those which persistently reminded them of their own corrupt natures and tried to convince them that salvation would never be theirs. John Trumbull, a mariner in Thomas Shepard's congregation, confessed in his relation to a lifetime spent "fulfilling my own lusts." After a violent storm he came to the fearful realization of his woeful condition, and he decided that it was time to turn to God. But Satan sensed his hypocrisy. Trumbull recalled, "Satan told me: thou has no

112. Ibid., 83.
113. John Cotton, *The Way of Life* (London, 1641), 197.
114. Ibid., 151, 192.

interest in Christ because I had broken the Sabbath and that I must die in misery." [115] Trumbull himself was responsible for breaking the Sabbath; Satan tried to convince him that this transgression implied his utter lack of interest in Christ and his destiny to die in the devil's arms rather than in God's sweet embrace.

Penitent sinners such as John Trumbull were aware of Satan's delusions. In sermons and demonological treatises, ministers warned of one trick in particular, that of convincing sinners that they had no need or desire for Christ. Trumbull's Satan told him that his sins spoke for themselves; they proved his lack of faith. Shepard, his minister, experienced Satan's deceit in a similar way. As he explained, "When a man finds a loss of God, either he is wholly in the dark and cannot see him, or else Satan and his own natural abilities will be working and casting in light so that a man might be contented with that and seek no farther for the spirit's light nor feel such a need of it." [116] Satan and the soul's naturally sinful state worked together to keep the soul in the dark, far away from God's presence.

One of the members of Wigglesworth's Cambridge congregation, John Collins, expressed similar fears of his absence from God and subsequent possession by Satan. He deplored his "Christless condition," and realized that "everlasting wrath was my portion as being born an heir of and incapable of avoiding it by anything I was able to do." In addition to original sin, which no one could avoid, Collins regretted his particular neglect of prayer. "I thought I should go to hell," he said, "remembering how I had backslidden and forgotten God." Regardless of whether or not Satan had tempted Collins to neglect his reading and his prayers, Collins accepted responsibility for his own sinful mistakes. And his sins provoked fear because they demonstrated that Collins had broken his covenant with God. After hearing Thomas Hooker preach, Collins was

---

115. Ibid., 108.

116. Shepard, *God's Plot*, 138. Seventeenth-century conversion narratives reveal the frequency of this particular lure of Satan's. John Green, author of one of the relations included in Michael Wigglesworth's diary, spoke of the same device: "Hereupon," Green admitted, "I was assaulted with this temptation, why wilt thou pray? But do nothing but sin." See "John Green's Relation," in "Diary of Wigglesworth," ed. Morgan, 392. Jane Holmes, a member of Shepard's congregation and mother of nine children, fell victim to the same temptation. She said, "Satan set against me that I durst not go to prayer." See Shepard, *Confessions*, 77.

convinced that even Hooker "knew what a sinner I had been what covenants I had broke and seeing I had held the truth in unrighteousness I thought I was as good as in hell already." Under "the lash of Satan's terrors," having fled from God, Collins decided that God had "come out against [him] as an enemy"; in the battle between God and the devil, Collins believed that he was now fighting against the Lord.[117] The sinner's anxiety centered not on the question of blame but rather on the fact of privation from God, which signified and anticipated hell's eternal torments. Collins related, "I thought I was under the curse both of the law and covenant and that death spiritual everlasting would soon seize upon me. Satan told me it was too late to pray. My time was past. God had left me a long time and therefore there was little hopes he would return to me again."[118]

Fear of damnation and Satan's power in assisting sinners as they worked their way to hell pervaded experience and belief in Puritan New England. Ministers preached about the cosmic battle between God and Satan and subverted their promising message of Christ's open, loving arms with ominous threats of hell's wide, dark abyss. Lay people heard from their spiritual leaders that although they began their lives in a corrupt natural state under Satan's domination, they could struggle against the devil's hold and undergo conversion. But they also learned that conversion was not easy, nor did it bring an end to Satan's temptations. To the contrary, Satan pursued his victims even more vigorously after conversion, hoping to pull them back to his side before Christ could claim them at death.

The terror of Satan and anxiety over conversion could rage so wildly as to scare some Puritans literally to death. In despair over the impossibility of their own regeneracy, some people contemplated suicide (Satan was said to encourage such thoughts), and some of them actually accomplished the desperate act. In a 1675 sermon, Increase Mather reminded his listeners of the sorry demise of the young boy Abraham Warner, who drowned himself in 1660. The note young Warner left for his father revealed his utter dejection about his own fate and the example his life was setting for his younger brother: "O Father, I have kept my soul as long as

<hr />

117. "The Relation of Mr. Collins," "Diary of Wigglesworth," ed. Morgan, 426–28.
118. Ibid., 429.

ever I could; My ruin was pride and stubborness of my tender years. . . .
I have a younger brother that follows my steps, he is going the *wide* way
to destruction. I beseech you to take pains with him and correct him as
well as counsel him, that he may not be undone soul and body as well as
I."[119] Thomas Shepard himself was suicidal: "After grievous and heavy
perplexities," he wrote, "I was by then almost forced to make an end of
myself and sinful life, and to be mine own executioner." Happily, however, "the Lord came between the bridge and the water, and set me out of
anguish of spirit."[120] Anxiety about conversion could be so intense that a
person could be driven to deadly distraction even when divine assurance
finally appeared. Mrs. Thomas Whitteridge, in a state of great agitation
one night in 1673, cried out, *"He is come!"* and rushed out of her house
through the weeds and briars, only to be found the next morning lying
dead, face down in a shallow puddle.[121]

Though ministers extended the same message to all, without any conscious distinction of gender, women and men nonetheless embraced it—
and experienced it—differently. From their earliest years to their last
days, many Puritans took their ministers' words to heart; they lived with
the fear that their depraved selves (if they were women) or their persistent sins (if they were men) would indeed deliver them to Satan's clutches
and hell's fiery furnace.

Since the road to hell was wide and Satan was an ever-present guide
and relentless driver of women and men, his nefarious methods require
extensive examination. In Chapter 2, therefore, I explore beliefs about
the devil's wily ways, the devious methods he used to beguile his prey,
and the implicit acceptance of his physical as well as metaphorical presence during the witchcraft episodes.

119. Increase Mather, *The Wicked Man's Portion* (Boston, 1675), quoted in Elliott,
Power and the Pulpit, 42, emphasis added.
120. Shepard, *Spiritual Autobiography*, 44.
121. "Memoir of the Reverend William Adams of Dedham, Massachusetts," in *Collections of the Massachusetts Historical Society*, 4th ser., 1 (1852), 17–18, quoted in Elliott,
Power and the Pulpit, 42. On the relation between suicide and conversion, see John Owen
King, *The Iron of Melancholy: Structures of Spiritual Conversion in America from the Puritan Conscience to Victorian Neurosis* (Middletown, Conn., 1983), 49–54. The question
of whether suicide in Puritan New England was gendered deserves further study. I would
expect that women, more apt to be convinced of their essential depravity, would be more
likely to kill themselves, but I have not yet carried out the systematic research to argue such
a hypothesis.

POPULAR AND MINISTERIAL
VISIONS OF SATAN

THE clergy, magistrates, and laity in seventeenth-century New England held a common theological understanding of the devil's powers and how to defeat his suggestions and tortures. During the proceedings against Sarah Cole in 1692, Elizabeth Wellman testified that she "saw a black thing of a considerable bigness goe by her sid and as soon as Sarah Cole came against a tree that lay upon the ground This black thing was gon and be sene no more." Some may have doubted Wellman's testimony, but everyone in the courtroom would have assumed that the "black thing" mentioned was the devil and that his presence implicated Cole as a witch. Moreover, his presence would have validated Wellman's further testimony that Cole clasped her hands together, swung them twice over her head, and then mysteriously took flight. His sighting both incriminated Sarah Cole and corroborated what everyone knew: a witch was a person—usually a woman—who had made a pact with the devil. It made sense that the devil would lurk near one of his own.[1]

The medieval European legacy of witchcraft belief crossed the Atlantic, and many of its elements appeared in the colonial witchcraft liter-

---

1. Paul Boyer and Stephen Nissenbaum, eds., *The Salem Witchcraft Papers: Verbatim Transcripts of the Legal Documents of the Salem Witchcraft Outbreak of 1692*, 3 vols. (New York, 1977), 1:230.

ature.[2] Puritans deciphered and reproduced these various components in ways consistent with their religious ideology and, as we shall see especially in Chapters 3 and 4, their understanding of female and male characteristics. Satan's appearance beyond the meetinghouse was inextricably bound to his representation within the gendered and religious culture of Puritanism. In this chapter I emphasize the shared understanding of laity and clergy, women and men, regarding the devil's intrusion during witchcraft episodes. The devil appeared to seventeenth-century New Englanders in ways that made sense to them, in ways that were consonant with sermonic warnings, folk beliefs never articulated during church meeting, and people's own needs and desires.

My reading of the seventeenth-century witch trial documents emphasizes the centrality of the devil in the entire drama. Not all historians would agree. Some have noticed few direct references to Satan in the 1692 trials and have seen even those references as unrepresentative of folk belief. Rather, they have focused narrowly on the issue of maleficia, dissociating it from diabolical agency.[3] Historians have also underestimated the devil's presence in earlier witchcraft episodes. Yet, of the nine early cases (1638–51) cited by David Hall in his collection, seven contain references to Satan, either from "elite" or from "popular" sources. Many of the midcentury cases for which documents exist refer explicitly to Satan's tortures and the pressure some endured to sign his book;

2. For an extended discussion of the devil in the Middle Ages, see Jeffrey Burton Russell, *Lucifer: The Devil in the Middle Ages* (Ithaca, N.Y., 1984); idem, *Witchcraft in the Middle Ages* (Ithaca, N.Y., 1972). For other examples of European folk culture of the devil and witchcraft, including the British Isles, see Carlo Ginburg, *The Night Battles: Witchcraft and Agrarian Cults in the Sixteenth and Seventeenth Centuries* (New York, 1985); idem, *Ecstacies: Deciphering the Witches' Sabbath* (New York, 1991); David Warren Sabean, *Power in the Blood: Popular Culture and Village Discourse in Early Modern Germany* (New York, 1984); Norman Cohn, *Europe's Inner Demons: An Inquiry Inspired by Europe's Great Witch-Hunt* (New York, 1975); Stuart Clark, "Inversion, Misrule, and the Meaning of Witchcraft," *Past and Present* 87 (May 1980), 98–127; idem, "Protestant Demonology: Sin, Superstition, and Society (c. 1520–c. 1630)," in *Early Modern European Witchcraft: Centres and Peripheries,* ed. Bengt Ankarloo and Gustav Henningsen (Oxford, 1990), 19–82; Robert Muchembled, "Satanic Myths and Cultural Reality," in *Early Modern European Witchcraft,* ed. Ankarloo and Henningsen, 139–60; Keith Thomas, *Religion and the Decline of Magic* (New York, 1971); Alan MacFarlane, *Witchcraft in Tudor and Stuart England: A Regional and Comparative Study* (New York, 1970); Christina Larner, *Enemies of God: The Witch-Hunt in Scotland* (Baltimore, 1981).

3. See Richard Godbeer, *The Devil's Dominion: Magic and Religion in Early New England* (Cambridge, 1992), esp. 204–5.

even more allude to the devil indirectly, citing evidence of witches' teats (on which the devil or one of his familiars presumably sucked), strange lights, bizarre afflictions, or the appearance of evil dogs, all of which connoted the devil's involvement. In order to comprehend the full extent of the devil's perceived entanglement in all the witch trial episodes, we must understand the multiple meanings attached to Satan, both within the meetinghouse and outside it.[4]

Ministers and magistrates did not reject the various forms in which, according to popular belief, Satan might appear.[5] In fact, their vigorous determination to extract confessions of Satanic collusion from the accused women during the Salem trials might well have encouraged folk traditions. Yet there were significant differences in the way ordinary people and their ministers represented Satan. In the confines of the meetinghouse ministers preached about Satan as an ethereal and intellectual presence, but in the context of the witchcraft outbreaks or possession cases people perceived his presence as more physical and immediate. Nonetheless, there was no rigid division between elite and popular ideas about Satan. The laity absorbed what their ministers told them in church, and the ministers and magistrates, in turn, took seriously what the laity said about Satan during witchcraft and possession crises.[6]

Most seventeenth-century Puritans were as familiar with Satan's wily ways as they were with Christ's unfailing goodness. Ministers warned of Satan's devices well before any incidences of witchcraft appeared, and their congregations expected his intrusion into their daily lives. Satan the tempter or Satan the deluder was a close cousin of the Satan who facilitated Susan Cole's flight or, in the shape of a witch, choked, pinched, and terrorized unsuspecting victims.

4. David D. Hall, ed., *Witch-Hunting in Seventeenth-Century New England: A Documentary History, 1638–1692* (Boston, 1991), 10. See the early cases, including those of Jane Hawkins, Alice Young, Margaret Jones, Mary Johnson, Elizabeth Kendall, Widow Marshfield, Joan and John Carrington, and Alice Lake. Some of the references to Satan are found in the indictments; others in the testimony against the accused.

5. Religious and secular authorities showed some skepticism concerning the validity of spectral evidence in the courtroom, but most agreed that the devil could indeed appear in any shape he chose. Not all seventeenth-century colonists believed in the devil and witchcraft; see, for example, Richard Beale Davis, "The Devil in Virginia in the Seventeenth Century," in *Literature and Society in Early Virginia* (Baton Rouge, La., 1973), 14–42.

6. In possession, the devil took over people's bodies without their explicit consent; witches, by contrast, made a voluntary specific covenant with Satan, granting him permission to use their bodies to afflict others. Several historians have written about diabolical

Puritan ministers counseled churchgoers always to remain conscious of "Christ, the Scripture, your own hearts, and Satan's devices. . . . If any cast off the study of these, they cannot be safe here, nor happy hereafter."[7] Thorough knowledge of Satan was as important as knowledge of Christ, particularly because Satan was unrelenting in his assaults on humankind and would surely triumph if his foes were unprepared. Advising congregants to arm themselves spiritually, as if for war, Samuel Willard preached, "The Legions of darkness, all the powers of Hell, are engaged against the Christian: for, we wrestle not with flesh and blood; i.e. with that only, but with principalities, and powers, &c. And the main design of these enemies, is carried on by Temptations."[8]

Knowing one's enemy was a means to vanquish him, and so Puritan ministers often began their discussion of Satan by defining him as the evil angel and then describing the ways in which he lured souls from Christ. As a spirit, Satan enjoyed certain advantages in the ongoing battle for people's souls. His power, though not omnipotent, could exhaust even the most pious Puritan guarding against the temptation to sin, and it would overwhelm the spiritually lax. Since his fall, Satan had perfected his craft, mastering the most efficacious snares. Satan knew when people were particularly vulnerable to temptation and carefully chose those times to appear in their thoughts. He could tell, said Willard, when "the

possession in both Europe and America. For a detailed treatment of European possession cases, see Joseph Klaits, *Servants of Satan: The Age of the Witch Hunts* (Bloomington, Ind., 1985), 104–27; D. P. Walker, *Unclean Spirits: Possession and Exorcism in France and England in the Late Sixteenth and Early Seventeenth Centuries* (Philadelphia, 1981); and Richard Kieckhefer, *European Witch Trials: Their Foundations in Popular and Learned Culture, 1300–1500* (Berkeley, Calif., 1976). Historians of American possession have primarily adopted a psychological perspective. See especially John Putnam Demos, *Entertaining Satan: Witchcraft and the Culture of Early New England* (New York, 1982), 57–96; Carol F. Karlsen, *The Devil in the Shape of a Woman: Witchcraft in Colonial New England* (New York, 1987), 222–51. Demos argues that the possessed girls were acting out psychological deficiencies in their upbringing, and Karlsen contends that the possession derived from the girls' dissatisfaction with colonial gender and class roles. Accounting for the colonists' spiritual beliefs, Godbeer (*Devil's Dominion,* 109) says that possession expressed a fundamental ambiguity in Puritan theology concerning responsibility for sin.

7. Thomas Brooks, *Precious Remedies against Satan's Devices* (London, 1652), 15. For the most detailed demonological treatise, which outlines Satan's temptations, cruelties, and powers, see Richard Gilpin, *Daemonologia Sacra; or, A Treatise of Satan's Temptations* (1677; London, 1867).

8. Samuel Willard, *The Christians Exercise by Satans Temptations: or, An Essay to discover the methods which this Adversary, useth to Tempt the Children of GOD; and to direct them how to escape the mischief thereof* (Boston, 1701), A2.

eyes are full of Adultery, by their wanton and lascivious glaunces, when the *ear is enchanted* with vain discourses." [9] Slyly attuned to the imagination, Satan waited with the appropriate temptations whenever Puritans relaxed their will and piety. "The devil is like an archer," Henry Smith preached; "man is his mark, and temptations are his arrows." [10]

John Davenport warned that "a froward discontented Frame of Spirit was a Subject fitt for the Devill to worke upon in that way." [11] And indeed, the devil appeared to Elizabeth Knapp precisely because she was dissatisfied with her life. According to Willard, Knapp confessed that Satan appeared to her and "that the occasion of it was her discontent, that her condition displeased her, her labor was burdonsome to her, shee was neither content to bee at home nor abroad." [12] Earlier Knapp had admitted that the devil offered her things that "suted her youthfull fancey, money, silkes, fine cloaths, ease from labor to show her the whole world." [13] Quite frequently Satan tried to lure people into his service by tempting them with offers of riches, an easy life, and ultimately, salvation.

Satan suited his bait to the particular weaknesses of his quarry. And his temptations were often matched to the sex of his prey. Cotton Mather wrote of one victim, Mercy Short, that her devil tormentors "used a thousand Flatteries and Allurements to induce her into a compliance with the Desire of the Divel. They showed her very splendid garments, and thence proceeded unto greater glories, which they promised her if shee would sign to Their Bok [book]." [14] Mather's accounts of both Mercy Short and Mary Johnson, the first woman to confess to witchcraft in New England, in 1648, illuminate how the devil's temptations were

9. Ibid., 90.

10. Thomas Fuller, ed., *The Works of Henry Smith; including Sermons, Treatises, Prayers, and Poems,* 2 vols. (Edinburgh, 1867), 2:23.

11. Quoted in Samuel G. Drake, *Annals of Witchcraft in New England* (Boston, 1869), 90. In a 1653 witchcraft case in New Haven colony, Goodwife Larrimore testified against the accused, Elizabeth Godman, that after hearing Davenport's sermon, "she looked upon Mrs. godman to be of such a frame of spirit." See Hall, *Witch-hunting in Seventeenth-Century New England,* 62. See also Deodat Lawson, *Christ's Fidelity the Only Shield Against Satan's Malignity* (Boston, 1704).

12. Samuel Willard, *A Briefe Account of a Strange & Unusuall Providence of God befallen to Elizabeth Knap[p] of Groton,* in *Groton in the Witchcraft Times,* ed. Samuel Green (Groton, Mass., 1883), 16. Willard wrote the details of this case in a letter to Cotton Mather in 1671. The original letter is in the "Mather Papers" at the Boston Public Library.

13. Ibid., 8.

14. Cotton Mather, "A Brand Pluck'd Out of the Burning" (c. 1693), in *Narratives of the Witchcraft Cases,* ed. George Lincoln Burr (New York, 1914), 263.

seen to work in a gendered way. Johnson had said, according to Mather, "that a devil was wont to do her many services. Her master once blamed her for not carrying out the ashes, and a devil did clear the hearth for her afterwards." [15]

Men, too, were presented with attractive enticements, consonant with their earthly roles as men. The devil told the accused witch William Barker that he would pay off all Barker's debts if only he would sign in blood his covenant with Satan.[16] Perhaps articulating his own financial concerns, Andrew Carrier similarly confessed that the devil offered him a house and land in Andover if he would only capitulate to the devil's wishes. When the devil visited twenty-seven-year-old Joseph Ring of Salisbury, Massachusetts, he offered him the "p[ro]mise of any thing that he woold have & ther wear presented all delectable things p[er]sons and places Imaginable." And Samuel Wardwell, executed for witchcraft in September 1692, confessed that the devil had appeared to him twenty years before, taking advantage of his discontent "because he was in love with a maid named Barker who slighted his love." Wardwell admitted that he was lured by "the appearance of a man who called himself a prince of the aire & promised him he should live comfortably and be a captain." [17]

Popular tradition blended a diabolism as old as the eleventh century with knowledge gained from learned treatises on witchcraft and the devil and from the European witch trials of the fifteenth and sixteenth centuries. Riding to meetings at night, flying through the air, succumbing to the devil's lures, signing pacts in blood—these elements were common to the understanding of witchcraft in the Middle Ages. In 1477, for example, a woman in the Savoyard town of Villars-Chabod finally confessed to authorities that eleven years before she had been discontented and financially burdened, and so a friend had taken her to a festive gathering where she had encountered a demon named Robinet. Appearing in the form of a black man, Robinet promised her that her desires

15. Hall, ed., *Witch-Hunting*, 24.

16. *Salem Witchcraft Papers*, 1:65. Carol Karlsen has argued that the accused witches tended to be women who were discontented with their material lives. Many of them admitted during testimony that they turned to Satan because he offered them a way to improve their lots in life. I agree with Karlsen in substance, but her particular focus on women may shift attention away from the broad powers that Puritans ascribed to Satan; allurement was one of Satan's many snares for *both* men and women. See Karlsen, *Devil in the Shape of a Woman*, 128–30.

17. *Salem Witchcraft Papers*, 2:565, 3:783.

would be fulfilled if she promised to renounce God and worship him instead. Initially hesitant, the woman capitulated to Robinet's offers of gold and silver. The demon also gave her a stick on which she flew through the air to a meeting where there was more feasting and dancing, and where the people worshiped Robinet, who had now turned into a black dog.[18]

Colonial New Englanders drew from a long tradition of tales and witchcraft trials that described Satan's temptations and crafty ways. Although the ministers refrained from recounting such stories, they said and did nothing to challenge the received notions of the European folk narratives. Children's verses, for instance, taught that Satan, not confining his seductions to prospective witches, loomed ever ready to entice young people with his promises to satisfy all their wants and desires. In John Cotton's *New England Primer,* in the "Dialogue between Christ, Youth, and the Devil," a persevering Satan tries to lure a boy with permission to skip school and play all day long. "When others read, be thou at play," he suggests. "Think not on God, don't sigh nor pray / Nor be thou such a silly fool, / To mind thy book or go to school; / But play the truant; fear not I / Will straitway help you to a lie." [19]

Benjamin Keach in his *War with the Devil: or the Young Man's Conflict with the Powers of Darkness* told the tale of the young man who was convinced he could live his life as he pleased, oblivious to any counsel that his preachers might offer concerning salvation. At the beginning of the story he resolves: "At Cards and Dice, and such brave Games I'le play, / And like a Courtier, deck my self most gay; / With Perriwig, and Muff, and such fine things, / With Sword and Belt, Goloshoos and Gold Rngs, / Where Bulls and Bears they Bait, and Cocks do fight / I do resort with speed, There's my delight / To drink and sport, amongst the jovial crew / I do resolve, whatever doth ensue." His conscience tries in vain to convince him that unless he forsakes these wicked ways and turns to Christ, he will perish in hell, but the Youth is temporarily swayed by the devil's promises. Once again, the devil chooses his lure to fit his victim's particular weakness: "I'll make his mind run after things below, / And

18. Kieckhefer, *European Witch Trials,* 25. See also Russell, *Lucifer,* 62–91. On the folklore of black dogs, see Katharine M. Briggs, *British Folk Tales and Legends: A Sampler* (London, 1977), 115–20.

19. "A Dialogue between Christ, Youth, and the Devil," in John Cotton, *The New England Primer* (c. 1691; Boston, 1777).

raise up trouble which he did not know: / . . . His Breast is tender, apt to entertain / The sparks of Lust which long he can't refrain."[20]

Perhaps the devil's most serious trickery was his offering anxious sinners the assurance of salvation. Religious authorities taught that repentance and sanctification could be taken as signs that God had chosen a person to have faith and thereby stand among the elect. The abandonment of sin and the living of a godly life, though not an infallible indication, could signal a person's faith in God and thus his or her ultimate salvation. Satan's favorite ploy was to convince fearful sinners that their behavior merited God's grace and that they would indeed be chosen on Judgment Day. In one demonological treatise, Satan is portrayed assuring sinners that they need not concern themselves with minor indiscretions: "If there must be a resurrection, and a judgement, yet God is not so rigid an Exactor, as to call thee to account for every petty sin; Those great Sessions are for haynous malefactors: God is too mercyfull to condemne thee for small offenses."[21]

In their religious training lay people learned to beware Satan's devices for convincing his potential recruits that life after death would be better with him than with God. Indeed, the devil's appearance during the witchcraft episodes resonated with the ministers' words, and the lures his victims recalled frequently paralleled and mocked the heavenly rewards described in their lessons. During the largest witch hunt in the colonies before the Salem incident—in Hartford, Connecticut, 1662–65—a Mrs. Miggat testified that Elizabeth Seager had met her at the river and told her "that god was naught, god was naught, it was very good to be a witch and desired her to be one, she should not ned fare [need fear] going to hell, for she should not burn in the fire."[22] Similarly, during the Salem trials, the devil tried to assure Mary Lacey Jr. that "she would

20. Benjamin Keach, *War with the Devil: or the Young Man's Conflict with the Powers of Darkness* (London, 1676). This lengthy poem was also printed in the colonies. William Bradford published the twelfth edition in New York in 1714.

21. Joseph Hall, *Satan's Fiery Darts Quenched* (London, 1647), B4.

22. Charles Jeremy Hoadley, Collection of notes and papers relating to witchcraft, chiefly transcripts from early court record, Samuel Wyllys Papers, Connecticut Historical Society. See also John Taylor, *The Witchcraft Delusion in Colonial Connecticut* (New York, 1908), 82. Taylor's book contains verbatim excerpts of the Connecticut trials. Documents for the Hartford witch hunt can also be found in Hall, ed., *Witch-Hunting*, 147–63.

obtain glory with him. He would set up his Kingdom and there would be happy days and better times for her if she obeyed him."[23]

Another of Satan's ploys was to insist that there was no such thing as heaven and that Judgment Day was merely the invention of zealous ministers. In one discourse Satan mocked, "In how vain and causeless awe art thou held, of dangers threatned to thy soule; and horrors of punishment after this life; whereas these are nothing but politique bugs, to affright simple, and credulous men? Sinne freely," he recommended, "and feare nothing; Take full scope to thy pleasures; After this life there is nothing. . . . There is no further reckoning to be made."[24] The devil used this strategy on William Barker Sr., promising "that there should be no day of resurection or of judgement, and neither punishment nor shame for sin."[25] Rebecca Eames told the Salem court that the devil promised to keep her crime of adultery a secret, thus enabling her to avoid damnation. And during Elizabeth Knapp's possession, Satan tried to scare her by showing her the horrors she would endure in hell if she were not faithful to him; but he also aimed to convince her that "heaven was an ougly place, & that none went thither but a company of base roagues whom he hated."[26]

Sometimes the lay witnesses did not explicitly mention the devil in their testimony; instead, they referred to incidents that clearly implied his presence. John Cole, for example, husband of the accused witch Sarah Cole, described being troubled by cats and dogs and a "ball of fire." While he was at prayer with his family, he "heard something like a great thing flung against the house & on a sudden it was at him & struck him on the head . . . so that I was forced to break of prayer for about a quarter of an hour." Later he resumed praying but the devil stalked him still; eight days later he saw a "great Cat of an unusuall bignes," and when he pursued it into the cornfield near his house, "tho it was very calm all the stalks did wave as if there had been a strong wind." Ever since, Cole maintained, his children

---

23. *Salem Witchcraft Papers,* 2:522.

24. Hall, *Satan's Fiery Darts,* B3

25. *Salem Witchcraft Papers,* 1:66. David Hall maintains that some spiritually confused lay people, unable to find solace from their ministers, sought relief from the devil. See David D. Hall, *Worlds of Wonder, Days of Judgment: Popular Religious Belief in Early New England* (New York, 1989), 139–47.

26. *Salem Witchcraft Papers,* 1:282; Willard, *Briefe Account,* 14.

Frontispiece to the third edition of Joseph Glanvill, *Sadducismus Triumphatus*, 1689 (courtesy of the Beinecke Rare Book and Manuscript Library, Yale University, New Haven, Conn.). Following Glanvill, Cotton Mather and other Puritan ministers used Christian theology to argue that a belief in God implied a belief in devils and witches. Blending theology with folklore, New England clergy and laity both heard and told stories about the devil's machinations.

had been afflicted with witchcraft.[27] The strange wind, the large animals, the ball of fire—all spoke clearly of Satan's involvement. That all the commotion began when he was praying sealed the case: obstructing the godly from worship was one of Satan's better-known snares. In John Cole's chronicle the devil's presence was understood and unmistakable.

In the didactic treatises Satan appeared not as a metaphorical character but as an actual embodiment of worldly and spiritual attractions; he was cunning, manipulative, and above all, persistent. Satan's presence in poems and sermons was undoubtedly a literary tool meant to elucidate the Puritan theology of temptation versus repentance, but the vivid portrayal may have been all too realistic. His personification may have inspired people to think of the devil as a more literal agent than ministers intended: as the genuine, living creature of folklore, capable of entering people's homes as well as their minds.

Satan's grand design, the clergy taught, was to overthrow God's kingdom. Cast from heaven with his followers and furious with God for his lot, Satan roamed the lower world "seeking whom he may devoure . . . , ever intent to assault mankind and above all, the most godly: for his opposition and hatred . . . is most against God, and for his cause, against his children, especially Christ."[28] Satan's opposition to God found expression in his wrath against God's children. As one Puritan writer explained in an exhaustive study, Satan's malice derived from a "desperate madness and revenge against God, wherein he shews his rage against heaven, and hunts after our blood as for a little water to cool his tongue; and when he finds his hand too short to pull the Almighty out of his throne, he endeavors, panther-like, to tear his image in man."[29] Satan labored to draw people away from godly pursuits; if they were unregenerate, he tried to keep them languishing in their sins, and if they were converted he worked even harder to force them to forsake their covenants.

The raging battle between God and Satan filled Puritan sermons. Ministers portrayed a ferocious and relentless foe, almost, but not quite, as strong as the Almighty. Both Christ and Satan needed soldiers. Every true believer, declared Urian Oakes, "is engaged on Christs side against the world, the flesh, and the devil . . . and is prepared for battle," and every

27. *Salem Witchcraft Papers*, 1:232.
28. Robert Baylie, *Satan the Leader in Chief to all who Resist the Reparation of Sion* (London, 1643), 32.
29. Gilpin, *Daemonologia Sacra*, 13.

wicked man is a soldier who fights against God: "He puts on the whole armour of the devil . . . and fight[s] it out to the last with the Infinite majesty." [30]

Satan endeavored to draft God's children into his army. Puritans believed that Satan was most interested in persuading the godly to join his ranks—thus his exceptional attention to the Bible Commonwealth. Samuel Willard explained that "Satan hath a peculiar malignity against the People of God. . . . Indeed, he is an Enemy to all Mankind; but he hath a more special pick at Gods People." [31] Increase Mather told his readers in 1679 that if succeeding generations of colonists turned from the Lord it would be tragic but not unimaginable, because "the Devil seeketh to corrupt those places especially, which once were famous for Religion." And "what Land under Heaven," Mather asked, "hath been more noted for profession and Religion, than New-England?" [32]

Mather's concern may have been merely rhetorical. [33] He and several other ministers frequently bemoaned what they saw as the declension of religious belief and moral behavior in New England. Yet the manner in which they expressed their concern spread the image of Satan as the leader of an insidious, invading army of devils.

Ministers saw the onslaught of witchcraft in New England as a punishment for the colonists' sins as well as an evil omen of what would come if confession and repentance did not ensue. [34] Deodat Lawson had been minister at Salem just before the outbreak of accusations. In the midst of the trials, he delivered a fiery sermon at Salem Village, attribut-

30. Urian Oakes, *The Unconquerable, All Conquering and More than Conquering Souldier: or the successful warre which a believer wageth with the enemies of his soul* (Boston, 1674).

31. Willard, *Christians Exercise*, 4.

32. Increase Mather, *A Call from Heaven* (Boston, 1679), 66–67.

33. See also Increase Mather, *The Day of Trouble is Near* (Cambridge, Mass., 1674); and idem, "Enquiry: What are the Evils which have provoked the Lord to bring his Judgments on New England," n.d., American Antiquarian Society, box 2, folder 4.

34. For the clerical view that the devil (and God) was punishing Massachusetts, see especially Cotton Mather, *Wonders of the Invisible World,* 74–80. For a discussion of the various ordeals the colonists faced—including warfare with Native Americans, the loss of their charter in 1684, and the immigration of Quakers into the colony—all generally interpreted as (diabolical) threats to their safety and order, see Godbeer, *Devil's Dominion,* 181–203. On the Quaker threat in particular, see Carla Gardina Pestana, *Quakers and Baptists in Colonial New Massachusetts* (Cambridge, 1992).

ing the uncommon rage of Satan there to the severe displeasure of God: "The Lord doth Terrible things amongst us, by lengthening the Chain of the *Roaring Lyon,* in an Extraordinary manner; so that the *Devil is come down in Great Wrath."* And while on earth, Satan was "Endeavoring to set up his *Kingdom,* and by Racking Torments on the *BODIES,* and Affrightning Representations to the *Minds* of many amongst us, to Force and Fright them to become his Subjects."[35] Cotton Mather agreed that "an Army of Devils" had broken into the English settlement, and it was the community's duty "to deliver our distressed Neighbours, from the horrible Annoyances and Molestations with which a dreadful Witchcraft is now persecuting of them."[36] Satan's extraordinary effort to destroy New England and set up his own kingdom constituted an unprecedented attack, according to Mather, one "more snarl'd with unintelligible Circumstances than any that we have hitherto Encountred."[37]

The image of a sinner in metaphorical bondage to Satan, serving the devil rather than God, took on a more literal meaning outside the meetinghouse. Sinners who battled Satan in a spiritual sense confessed during the witchcraft crisis that they also confronted him physically.[38] Witnesses insisted that the devil had accosted them and tried through persuasion and violence to make them join his army and worship him. William Barker testified at his trial that "Satan's design was to set up

35. Deodat Lawson, *Christ's Fidelity the Only Shield Against Satan's Malignity* (Boston, 1704), 53.

36. Cotton Mather, *Wonders of the Invisible World* [Boston, 1693], in *The Witchcraft Delusion in New England,* ed. Samuel Drake, 3 vols. (Roxbury, Mass., 1866), 1:16, 33.

37. Ibid., 15. For a recent compelling defense of declension, see Delbanco, *Puritan Ordeal,* esp. chap. 7.

38. Lyndal Roper's provocative book *Oedipus and the Devil: Witchcraft, Sexuality, and Religion in Early Modern Europe* (New York, 1994), esp. 199–225, examines the meaning of witchcraft fantasies and images of the devil from a psychoanalytic perspective. Roper insists, and I agree, that accusations and confessions are not merely scripted, nonsensical ravings of people in a world so far removed from our own that we cannot possibly understand them. Her discussion of the deep antagonisms between women in sixteenth- and seventeenth-century Germany, focusing on the relation of witchcraft confessions to the issue of motherhood and child-mother separation, highlights the psychic anxieties our world shares with theirs. Never merely reductive, however, Roper's analysis is contingent on historical circumstances that change. My argument, though not specifically psychoanalytic, similarly recognizes the close connection between a particular worldview and what we might see now as irrational belief.

his own worship, abolish all the churches in the land, *to fall next upon Salem* and soe goe through the countrey." Elizabeth Johnson, one of the accused in the Salem trials, conceded that she herself had agreed to "pull down the kingdom of Christ and to sett up the devils kingdom."[39]

Worried about the inroads Satan was making into their community, the Salem magistrates took such confessions very seriously. Repeatedly those charged as witches informed the court that the devil planned to set up his own kingdom, and that they had participated in his operations.[40] William Barker went so far as to describe for the court some of the devil's weapons that he had seen not far from Salem Village: "There being a little off the Meeting-House about an hundred five Blades, some with Rapiers by their side, . . . and might be more for ought I know."[41] Some lay people believed that God could overpower Satan under any circumstances. During Elizabeth Knapp's possession, some spectators tried to talk through her body to Satan about his armor against God. Willard recorded, "One told him, God had him in chaines, hee replyed, for all my chaine, I can knocke thee on the head when I please. . . . Another Answered, but God is stronger than thou, He presently rejoyned, that's a ly, I am stronger than God."[42] Satan tried to convince the audience that he could dominate God's forces; only in the end, when Knapp rid her body of Satan, was it clear that God had won this battle.

Satan used his physical strength as a last resort; his primary strategy in the war against God was to gather as many recruits as possible by more insidious means, especially through deception. Yet during the witchcraft episodes the laity described Satan's snare as a literal, rather than metaphorical, trap. Witnesses and people accused of witchcraft told of meetings with the devil attended by over two hundred people, partaking of the devil's sacrament, professing allegiance to him, and forsaking their covenants with the Lord. Under examination Mary Bridges confessed that "they Drank Sack at the witch meeting at Andover: it stood there in

39. *Salem Witchcraft Papers*, 1:66, 100, emphasis added.

40. See, for example, the confessions of Ann Foster and Elizabeth Johnson Sr., among others, *Salem Witchcraft Papers*, 2:343, 501.

41. Ibid., 1:68.

42. Willard, *Briefe Account*, 18.

potts & they drawed it out of a barrill."[43] She claimed that she knew only two of the other people there, Goodwives Foster and Carrier, but that more than one hundred others participated.

The court anxiously listened to this sort of testimony, hoping to find out who else in their midst belonged to the devil. Mary Toothaker told eager listeners that eight others signed the devil's book at the Salem witch meeting and that she heard the beating of a drum at the meeting as well as the sound of a trumpet, perhaps signaling others to come and join the devil's party. One witness, Robert Moulton, testified that he saw one of the accused, Susannah Sheldon, carried through her yard and over a stone wall by some witches. He claimed, "I heard her say that she Rid Upone a poole [pole] to Boston and she said the divel Caryed the poole." And Susannah Sheldon claimed that she "was siting on the inside of the dore sill and goody buckly came and stoped my mouth and caried mee awai I know not how an near a mile."[44]

What might sound preposterous to twentieth-century ears suggested to the ministers and magistrates that evil had indeed descended physically upon the residents of Massachusetts. Mary Bridges claimed, for example, that she got to the meeting by riding with the "black man" upon a pole, up and away over the tops of the trees.[45] Ann Foster declared that she and Martha Carrier both rode upon the pole "& that the stick broak: as they ware caried in the aire above the tops of the trees & they fell but she did hang fast about the neck of Goody Carier." She exclaimed that she had heard from some of the other witches that "their was three hundred & five in the whole Country, & that they would ruin that place the Vilige."[46]

43. *Salem Witchcraft Papers*, 1:135. On the ritual significance of the Lord's Supper and laity's fears about partaking of this sacrament, see Hall, *Worlds of Wonder*, 156–62. When Ann Putnam Sr. cried out against the accused Rebecca Nurse at her examination, "How oft have you eat and drunk y'r own damaon [damnation]," she articulated lay worries— reinforced by ministers' reiteration of 1 Cor. 11:28–29—that unworthy partakers of the Lord's Supper would surely be damned. See *Salem Witchcraft Papers*, 2:585.

44. Ibid., 3:769, 3:731, 1:321.

45. Ibid., 1:135. Mary Bridges's "black man" may have been a reference to demonic imagery often ascribed to Native Americans. See William S. Simmons, "Cultural Bias in the New England Puritans' Perception of Indians," *William and Mary Quarterly*, 3rd ser., 38 (1981), 56–72.

46. *Salem Witchcraft Papers*, 2:343.

During the Salem trials accused "witches" and witnesses had the opportunity to disclose their encounters with the devil in a public forum. In
fact, the court encouraged detailed descriptions of Satan. From the surviving court transcripts, it is clear that many lay people believed Satan capable of assuming any shape he chose in order to torture and capture his
prey. And although the ministers never actually described Satan physically to their congregations in the meetinghouse, they did not question
lay people's representations of him in the context of the trials.

The devil appeared to colonists in all shapes and guises. In 1671 Satan
came to Elizabeth Knapp at her bedside and in her cellar in the shape of
an old man. On an earlier occasion, Knapp confessed, the devil had accompanied her on a journey between Groton and Lancaster in the form
of a "blacke dog with eyes in his back, sometimes stopping her horse,
sometimes leaping up behind, & keeping her . . . 40 rod at least behind,
leading her out of the way into a swampe."[47] In 1692, John Louder told
the court that after a confrontation with Bridget Bishop, an accused
witch, he had been plagued by a black creature that "looked like a
Munky only the feet ware like a Cocks feete w'th Claws and the face
somewhat more like a mans than a Munkiey." The creature had said to
him, "I am a Messenger sent to you for I understand you are trobled in
mind, and if you will be Ruled by mee you shall want for Nothing in this
world." Louder had tried to attack the demon and shouted out, "You
devill I will kill you," before it disappeared. When it reappeared mysteriously through locked doors, Louder had cried out, "the whole armor of
god between mee and you," and the creature had sprung back and finally
flown away over an apple tree.[48]

There may have been some skeptical ministers, but credulity prevailed.
Elizabeth Knapp insisted that during her strange and violent possession,
she had seen a witch in the shape of a dog with a woman's head climb up
the chimney of her home. Willard carefully examined the scene and reported that there was indeed an impression in the clay of the chimney, although he hesitated to own her claims. His circumspection was limited,
however, and he conceded to his readers, "Something there was, as I my-
selfe saw in the chimney in the same place where shee declared the foot
was set to goe up."[49]

47. Willard, *Briefe Account*, 7, 10.
48. *Salem Witchcraft Papers*, 1:100.
49. Willard, *Briefe Account*, 13.

The examination of Tituba, Samuel Parris's West Indian slave, reveals how anxious were the magistrates and ministers that the accused recount every detail of their trysts with the devil. The following testimony betrays the court's belief in the devil's physical reality:

Q. whatt familiarity have you w'th the devill, or w't is itt if you Converse w'th all? tell the truth whoe itt is that hurts them.

A. the Devill for ought I know.

Q. w't appearanc or how doth he appeare when he hurts them, w'th w't shape or what is he like that hurts them.

A. like a man. . . . I saw a thing like a man, that tould me Searve him & I tould him noe I would nott doe Such thing. . . .

Q. w't Other likenesses besides a man hath appeared to you?

A. Sometimes like a hogge Sometimes like a great black dogge, foure tymes. . . .

Q. w't other Creatures have you seene

A. A bird

Q. w't bird?

A. a little yellow Bird.

Q. where doth itt keep?

A. w'th the man whoe hath pretty things there besides. . . .

Q. w't other Creatures did you see?

A. I saw 2 Catts, one Red, another black as bigge as a little dogge. . . .

Q. what Service doe thay Expect fro[m] you?

A. they Say more hurt to the Children. . . .

Q. how doe you hurt those that you pinch? doe you gett those Catts? or other thing to doe it for you? tell us, how is it done? [50]

Rather than deny the possibility that Satan had adopted these bizarre guises, the Salem court accepted the laity's visions. Behind the language of the witchcraft trial records are certain assumptions. Laity and magistrates, women and men alike shared the belief that the devil could intrude in various costumes and demand that his victims serve him.

Although descriptions of the devil's horrific appearance seem heavily influenced by medieval folklore, accounts of Satan's powers corresponded

50. Ibid., 3:750–51.

to those detailed by ministers and remained consistent with biblical tradition. The devil's guile stands out in the trial records, as it does in the sermon literature. He was repeatedly said to have squeezed through tiny cracks in walls and doors or appeared unexpectedly, catching his victim off guard, just as the ministers warned he might catch one's soul unarmed if vigilance lagged.[51] Whether the devil displayed himself physically in a recognizable shape or materialized in the subtler form of a persistent temptation, his goal remained the same—to capture the souls of God's children in order to destroy God's kingdom.

The Salem court listened and often prodded its witnesses to reveal more but never publicly questioned the validity of their eyewitnesses' testimony.[52] Witnesses were not challenged on the presumed efficacy of Satan and his witches. Though some ministers queried the extent of the devil's powers, their questioning was not immediately decisive in undermining the construction of fabulous images of the devil during the witchcraft episodes. Could Satan carry his victims through the air? Could Satan actually possess a person's body? And most important, did Satan have the ability to take over someone's body without her or his permission and use it to assault others?

The discourse between the laity and the clergy, between popular and elite belief, is important for those seeking a fuller understanding of the colonists' actions during the witchcraft episodes. The accused, the victims, the courts, and the clergy explicitly voiced their impressions of the crises at hand and in the process represented for us their beliefs and the meanings they attached to their experience. In these discussions we see the supernatural landscape of early New Englanders, not just in the realm of abstract ideas but concretely manifested in the course of their lives. For many, Satan was a real presence. What could be more ethereal—and at the same time more real—than the invisible specters that brutally tor-

51. In Joseph Safford's testimony against Elizabeth How, for example, he described his wife's affliction "by the aparishtion of good how," which "apeard to her throug a crevie of the clambouerds which she knew no good person could do." See ibid., 2:452.

52. On the seventeenth-century criminal justice system more generally, see Gail Sussman Marcus, "'Due Execution of the Generall Rules of Righteousness': Criminal Procedure in New Haven Town and Colony, 1638–1658," in *Saints and Revolutionaries: Essays on Early American History,* ed. David D. Hall, John M. Murrin, and Thad W. Tate (New York, 1984), 99–137; and John M. Murrin, "Magistrates, Sinners, and a Precarious Liberty: Trial by Jury in Seventeenth-Century New England," in ibid., 152–206.

tured the innocent townspeople and villagers, ministers and common folk alike, of Puritan New England?

For several months of the Salem trials, religious and secular authorities believed that the appearance of a specter, or the devil in a human shape, indicated that the accused had actually made compacts with Satan, thus granting the devil permission to appear in their shapes and torment others. The important implications of such a covenant are explored in the next chapter; for now it is enough to know that the compact signified a deal willingly struck with Satan. Satan offered the victim both worldly and spiritual rewards (although many of the accused complained that Satan never fulfilled his promises), and in return he extracted permission to use his victim's shape to afflict others.[53]

The victims of a witch's violence or of the devil's seduction were usually the only observers of the mysterious shapes. In the courtroom, accusers might claim that the shape of an accused "witch" molested them, and often such tortures, carried out by an invisible agent, continued before the court in the course of the examination. The questioning of Martha Corey in March 1692 illustrates the credence given spectral evidence and the severity of its ramifications. Early in the witchcraft proceedings, twelve-year-old Ann Putnam named Corey as one of her tormentors. Corey's examination included many of the tactics that the magistrates used in later inquiries as well as many of the antics used by the accusers to incriminate those accused.[54] In court the afflicted girls claimed that the shape of Martha Corey tortured them. In fact, Corey's mere presence seemed to affect the girls' behavior in public. When she bit her lip several of the girls appeared bitten; when her hands were free, the girls claimed that they had been pinched. During her questioning the accusers exclaimed that they saw both a yellow bird and a man whispering in her ear. The magistrates saw nothing, but begged Corey to explain "all these thing[s] that are apparent." Corey laughed at the accusations, no

---

53. Satan's failure to keep his promises is considered in Chapter 4. As mentioned earlier, the key difference between a possessed person and a witch was that of complicity. The English physician John Cotta wrote, "The possessed and the witch, are both the habitacles of Divels; with this onely difference, that the witch doth willingly entertaine him." See John Cotta, *Infallible True and Assured Witch: or The Second Edition, of the Tryall of Witchcraft* (London, 1624), 118.

54. See Martha Corey's examination, *Salem Witchcraft Papers*, 1:244–66.

doubt further implicating herself, and continued to profess her ignorance of any such matters.[55] Disturbed by what they witnessed in court, the magistrates implored, "Why do not you tell how the Devil comes in your shape & hurts these?"[56]

The magistrates were forced to scrutinize and evaluate mysterious and invisible afflictions as evidence. No one could see the tormentors, and yet here were the accusers undergoing all sorts of tortures in plain view. It appeared to the court as well as to the spectators that shapes indeed harmed the victims. If no shapes were visible, it was because the devil was exceedingly cunning.

At first the court admitted "spectral evidence"—that is, attestation by those afflicted that the specter of an accused person was torturing them. John Jackson Jr. swore that the devil appeared to him in the shape of a woman; when asked what woman, he named his Aunt Howe.[57] Some of the witnesses were not able to tell if their tormentor was the accused or the *shape* of the accused. William Stacy testified that one night, after a series of bizarre incidents involving Bridget Bishop, he awoke suddenly, freezing cold, and felt that something was in his room. According to the court record, "He gott up and sat upon his beed [bed]: he at the same time seeing the said Bridgett Bishop sitting at the foot of his bed . . . or one in the said Bishops shape; she having then a black cap & a black hat, and a Red Coat." He further related that "the said Bishop or her shape clapt her coate close to her Leggs & hopt upon the bed and about the Roome and then went out: and then it was Dark."[58] A few days later John Louder corroborated Stacy's accounts. He said that one night he felt a great weight on his chest and was able to see from the moon's bright light that Bishop, "or her likeness," was sitting on his stomach torturing him.[59]

Other, more alarming testimony that Bishop's shape had tormented several victims convinced the court that Bishop was indeed a witch and had made a compact with Satan. In exchange for her covenant, many believed, Satan now had Bishop's permission to assume her shape and tor-

55. See Chapter 4 for a discussion of gendered responses to witchcraft accusations.

56. *Salem Witchcraft Papers*, 1:253.

57. Ibid., 2:469.

58. Ibid., 1:93. Implicit in many of these tortures was a sexual aggression also described in Karlsen, *Devil in the Shape of a Woman*, 134–44.

59. *Salem Witchcraft Papers*, 1:99.

ture people. On the strength of spectral evidence, the Salem Court of Oyer and Terminer hanged Bridget Bishop for witchcraft on July 10, 1692.

Bishop's hanging disturbed some of the ministers and magistrates involved in the Salem trials. Nathaniel Saltonstall, one of the magistrates, resigned from the court, and Governor William Phips turned to the leading ministers in Boston for counsel. The "Return of Several Ministers Consulted" is an important document because it signaled a major difference between the magistrates and the clergy concerning the types of evidence that should be used in the court to convict. The Mathers, Cotton and Increase, and other ministers had come down strongly against the use of spectral evidence.[60]

The clergy's reluctance to admit spectral evidence was not due to any doubt that specters existed. On the contrary, the ministers fully believed that the devil was capable of claiming a person's body for his own and torturing others in that shape. In fact, the ministers were so convinced of Satan's immense powers that they were sure he could perform his feat regardless of the person's intentions. It was not necessary for the accused witches to give the devil permission to claim their bodies for his own. If the devil needed someone's body to afflict another, it was in his power to commandeer it; consent may have been involved, but Satan did not necessarily require complicity.

Whether or not the devil could assume a person's shape was not a new question; as early as the sixteenth century clergymen had written about the devil's ability to appropriate another's body.[61] In the seventeenth

60. See Chadwick Hansen, *Witchcraft at Salem* (New York, 1969), 117–31, for a narrative of events following Bishop's hanging. On the Mathers' position on spectral evidence, see David Levin, "Did the Mathers Disagree about the Salem Witchcraft Trials?" *Proceedings of the American Antiquarian Society* 95 (April 1985), 19–37. Other scholars, notably Perry Miller and Kenneth Silverman, have argued that Increase Mather urged the court to refrain from relying on spectral evidence, whereas Cotton Mather broke with his father and the other leading ministers to defend the court's procedures. On the contrary, Levin concludes, and I agree with his reading of the evidence, both Cotton and Increase Mather recognized the liabilities of spectral evidence based on their understanding of the devil's powers as overwhelming. Cotton Mather believed that the judges acted in good faith and was reluctant to cast aspersions on their previous convictions, whereas Increase emphasized the need for an immediate change in the policy. See also Increase Mather, *Cases of Conscience Concerning Evil Spirits Personating Men* (Boston, 1693); and Cotton Mather, *Wonders of the Invisible World* (Boston, 1693), reprinted in *The Witchcraft Delusion in New England*, ed. Samuel Drake, 3 vols. (Roxbury, 1866), vol. 1.

61. See for example, Bartolommeo Spina, *Quaestio de Strigibus* (Venice, 1525; Rome, 1576).

century, physicians and clergymen concerned themselves with the issue of Satan's visibility. The English physician John Cotta, whose texts on witchcraft were widely read on both sides of the Atlantic, turned to the Bible to prove that the devil could disguise himself in one's shape. "Did not Saul contract with [the Witch of Endor], and she promise unto Saul to bring up Samuel untohim [*sic*]?" Cotta asked. "Did not Saul see the vision raised by her, or at least speak thereto, and receive answer therefrom, I. Sam. 28.8? Were not then his eyes and eares (those two outward senses) certain witnesses of her Sorcerie?" So strong was the association of witchcraft with diabolical agency in the popular imagination that Cotta connected the Witch of Endor with the devil, even though the latter does not appear in this biblical scene.[62]

Cotta always relied on God and the Bible for explanations of Satan's powers. He believed that although the devil could appear in someone's shape using "false shadowes and outward induced shapes covering those things which are created of God," the trickster could not create the shape by himself. That power would be against "the generall power of Nature," in other words, against the almighty power of God. Since the devil was still a creature of God, "these seeming transmutations of Men into Cattes, and the like, are swift and sodaine, in a moment, and without preparation: and therefore are not true, but seeming and juggling transmutations."[63] Satan could not create, but he could enter into another's body.[64]

New England ministers never doubted that Satan could assume various shapes. Samuel Willard pronounced, "That [fallen angels] can assume a bodily shape is in vain questioned by any."[65] Generally, though, the debate among the ministry over Satan's guises arose in connection

62. Cotta, *Infallible True and Assured Witch,* 32. For a persuasive reevaluation of the Witch of Endor, see Pamela Tamarkin Reis, "Eating the Blood: Saul and the Witch of Endor," *Journal for the Study of the Old Testament* 73 (1997), 3–23.

63. Cotta, *Infallible True and Assured Witch,* 35–36. Cotta believed that physicians rather than ministers should ascertain whether a person was truly possessed by Satan or if their symptoms merely reflected a serious illness caused by natural disease. See Robert Middlekauff, *The Mathers: Three Generations of Puritan Intellectuals* (New York, 1971), 156–57.

64. Increase Mather commented, "But to imagine that spirits shall really generate bodies, is irrational." See Increase Mather, *Remarkable Providences Illustrative of the Earlier Days of American Colonisation* (Boston, 1684), 125.

65. Willard, *Christians Exercise,* 51.

with the Genesis story. Here the issue of whether the devil could assume shapes merged with the related concern of whether that metamorphosis implied consent. Was the serpent merely an instrument of Satan, as John Davenport avowed, or was it "the Devil [himself] in the Serpent's form," as Benjamin Colman preached?[66] Ministers debated the occasions on which Satan might assume shapes, but they always agreed that it was well within his power to do so.

The spectral evidence issue raised by the laity's accusations during the Salem witchcraft trials forced the ministers to confront the implications of the devil's capabilities. Never before had they had cause to outline the devil's powers in such detail. Sermons that warned of Satan's subtleties had not ventured into this speculative arena with any frequency. But when the laity, some of them regular churchgoers, began claiming that Satan assumed people's shapes—even those of pious people—the clergy had to determine the extent of Satan's powers and take a stand.[67]

"The Return of Several Ministers Consulted" did just that. The essay, probably written by Cotton Mather, acknowledged the difficulties faced by the court in dealing with the witchcraft cases and requested that the "discovery of these mysterious and mischievous Wickednesses, may be perfected." The ministers counseled caution, however, "lest by too much Credulity for things received only upon the Devil's Authority, there be a Door opened for a long Train of miserable Consequences, and Satan get an advantage over us, for we should not be ignorant of his Devices." Carefully and judiciously avoiding criticism of the court's previous convictions, the "Return" discreetly intimated that the proceedings had not

66. John Davenport, *Ancient Waymarks* (London, 1642); Benjamin Colman, *A Brief Dissertation on the Three First Chapters of Genesis* (Boston, 1735), 50. See also Edward K. Trefz, "Satan as the Prince of Evil," *Boston Public Library Quarterly* 7 (1955), 3–22. Although he maintained that the devil could not generate shapes, Cotta allowed, rather ambiguously, that "there are many supernaturall workes of the divell manifest to sense, wherein man doth not participate in knowledge, contract or consent with him. Did not the Divell in the body of a Serpent miraculously reason, dispute, speak and conferre with Eva, Gen. 3?" See Cotta, *Infallible True and Assured Witch*, 27.

67. During the summer of 1692 one of the victims accused Samuel Willard of witchcraft. Other prominent citizens who were incriminated included Nathaniel Saltonstall, the judge who had resigned from the court after Bishop's death; Dudley Bradstreet, the Andover justice of the peace; the wives of Governor Phips and Increase Mather.

perhaps been handled in the most prudent way possible; some convictions may have been precipitous, and in the future the court should act with "exceeding tenderness towards those that may be complained of; especially if they have been Persons formerly of an unblemished Reputation." [68]

As the accusations spread beyond Salem and spectral evidence threatened to destroy previously pious reputations, the ministers sought an end to the whole business. But they could not dismiss the laity's testimony out of hand because they believed in witchcraft and credited the devil with enormous power. The "Return," then, merely called for more stringent rules of evidence; the ministers urged the court to treat witchcraft cases as they would any other criminal case. The evidence, they concluded, ought to be more considerable than simply the sight of a specter representing the accused person. Trusting the visible afflictions and contortions of the victims in court was no better. According to the document, this kind of testimony was "frequently liable to be abused by the devil's Legerdemains." [69] Mather put the ministers' position succinctly: the devil was capable of appearing in anyone's shape, even that of the innocent and the virtuous. Here the ministers clearly departed from the court's procedures but nonetheless "recommend[ed] unto the Government, the speedy and vigorous Prosecution of such as have rendered themselves obnoxious." [70]

If spectral evidence could no longer be trusted as conclusive, then something had to be put in its place. The ministers advised the court to follow the guidelines set forth by the English Puritans William Perkins and Richard Bernard.[71] The New England clergy had consulted the works of these men both before and during the Salem trials. Their recommen-

68. The document appeared on June 15, 1692, five days after Bridget Bishop's hanging. "The Return of Several Ministers Consulted," in *What Happened in Salem: Documents Pertaining to the Seventeenth-Century Witchcraft Trials,* 2nd ed., ed. David Levin (New York, 1977), 111. "The Return" is also reprinted in the London edition of Cotton Mather's *Wonders of the Invisible World* (1693; London, 1862).

69. Ibid.

70. Ibid. Stephen Foster has aptly characterized Mather's "Return" as "schizoid." See Stephen Foster, *The Long Argument: English Puritanism and the Shaping of New England Culture, 1570–1700* (Chapel Hill, N.C., 1991), 259.

71. See Richard Bernard, *Guide to Grand-Jury Men,* 2nd ed. (London, 1629); and William Perkins, *Discourse on the Damned Art of Witchcraft* (London, 1608). For an interesting discussion of the legal struggle to reconcile the folk culture with the theology, see Richard Weisman, *Witchcraft, Magic, and Religion in Seventeenth-Century Massachusetts* (Amherst, Mass., 1984), 98–105.

dations included dividing the evidence into two categories, convictive and presumptive. Convictive evidence established a direct link between the accused witch and the devil. If the suspect did not confess such collusion, then Perkins allowed two reputable witnesses to testify that the accused had indeed made a compact with the devil or had entertained one of the devil's familiars. Bernard believed that witches' marks, visible proof that the devil had conferred with the victim, would also verify complicity with Satan. According to these authorities, a witch could not be condemned unless an explicit pact had been made with the devil.

Proof of misdeeds and malefic actions constituted presumptive evidence. A witch could not be convicted on the basis of presumptive evidence alone; more substantial verification, such as the signing of a pact, had to be ascertained.[72]

Richard Weisman has written extensively about the tension between the official response to witchcraft by court and clergy, on the one hand, and the more popular demands of the laity, on the other. He argues that the laity grew dissatisfied with the court's insistence upon a strict theological interpretation of the law requiring proof of a pact made with the devil. They would have been satisfied, he maintains, had the court convicted the accused solely on the evidence of maleficent activity which was so abundantly presented.[73] If we extend Weisman's point, it seems clear that the voluminous accounts of maleficium warranted conviction in the laity's view precisely because such evil was unimaginable *except* as the result of a diabolical covenant. In this popular theology, malefic acts incriminated those associated with their perpetration because they could be committed only with Satan's assistance, and Satan collaborated only with those who signed his pact.[74]

The laity, not only the court and clergy, spoke of witchcraft in a reli-

72. Perkins, *Discourse*, 204–13; Bernard, *Guide*, 212–24. On the problem of finding the "truth" about witches, see Katharine Eisaman Maus, "Proof and Consequences: Inwardness and Its Exposure in the English Renaissance," *Representations* 34 (Summer 1991), 29–52.

73. Weisman, *Witchcraft, Magic, and Religion*, 96–114.

74. Richard Godbeer maintains that the popular focus on maleficium made it difficult for the court to convict because the witnesses' testimony focused on evil deeds perpetrated by the witch, rather than on diabolical activity. See Godbeer, *Devil's Dominion*, 155–63. My interpretation allows for a more expansive definition of maleficium, which presupposes (among the laity as well as the court and clergy) a sense of the devil's involvement. Convictions resulted when the link between the witch's behavior and the devil's presence was made clearly.

gious discourse. At the start of her examination before the justices of Salem on August 25, 1692, the defendant Sarah Bridges denied the accusations of witchcraft against her and expressed her hope that "God would Clear her Inocencey." But when pressured and confronted with incriminating evidence, particularly the confession of her own sister, Hannah Post, Bridges admitted that "she had been in the Divels Snare, . . . that the Divel Came to her like a man[,] would have her Signe to his book & told His name was Jesus & that She must Serve & worship him." The devil, she continued, pricked her finger, forced her to sign his book in blood, and demanded that she "renounce god & Christ,"[75] Bridges's covenant with the devil made her a witch in the eyes of the religious and secular authorities, just as it incriminated her before the community that testified against her.

Lay people may have been frustrated by the court's deliberate measures, but they agreed with Perkins and Bernard that detection of a witch must be based on the theological definition of witchcraft. Witchcraft entailed far more than mischievous and maleficent sorcery; a witch was a person in league with the devil, fighting on his side in what the Puritans believed to be the ongoing battle between God's army and Satan's legions. Cotton Mather's sermon *A Discourse on Witchcraft,* delivered in the winter of 1688–89, exemplified the Puritan understanding of witchcraft. "*Witchcraft,* is a Renouncing of *God* and Advancing of a filthy *Devil* into the Throne of the Most High," Mather proclaimed. "*Witchcraft* is a Renouncing of *Christ,* and preferring the Communion of a loathesome lying *Devil* before all the Salvation of the Lord Redeemer."[76] Lay witnesses during the witchcraft trials presented alarming, but nonetheless theologically orthodox, statements that incriminated the accused by their association and collusion with Satan. One witness gave evidence, for example, that two of the accused witches, Giles Corey and Goody Oliver, "kneeled doune befour the black man and went to prayer."[77] As this testimony suggests, the folk culture and the folk theology of the laity did not separate common people from other members of their communities who occupied positions on the court and among the clergy.

Theological interpretation merged with folk versions of witchcraft;

75. *Salem Witchcraft Papers,* 1:139.
76. Cotton Mather, *A Discourse on Witchcraft,* in Levin, *What Happened in Salem,* 97.
77. *Salem Witchcraft Papers,* 1:105.

Mocking convention and defying prescriptions, women dance with devils, in a woodcut from R.B. [Nathaniel Crouch], *The Kingdom of Darkness* (London, 1688), popular on both sides of the Atlantic (courtesy Connecticut Historical Society, Hartford, Conn.). Such representations both reflected and encouraged the idea of women as witches.

the participants in the witchcraft episodes held a common belief about Satan. Even if there were two separate conventions—one focused on proving the pact with Satan, the other more willing to construe the existence of a pact without direct evidence—during the trials they encouraged and reinforced each other. Eager to exact confessions, perhaps so as to avoid relying on spectral evidence alone, neither the court nor the clergy discredited the various popular forms in which the laity described Satan. The tales of the night rides and accounts of Satan's rapiers were rendered

credible—perhaps inadvertently—and validated so that the court could
determine if the accused had actually signed a pact with the devil.

For their part, lay witnesses and victims were willing to accuse and convict witches based on observed, if "presumptive," maleficence alone. But
woven into their stories and accusations, of course, was the understanding that the accused were capable of such transgressions only with the aid
of the devil's power. When forty-five-year-old John Allen testified against
Susannah Martin, he told the court of his refusal to use his tired oxen to
cart something for Martin, of a perceived threat from her in retaliation,
and of an incident that followed which linked her to the devil. The oxen,
exhausted after a long day's work, had strayed from a safe grazing area
to one perilously close to the Merrimack River. At first Allen presumed
his oxen had drowned, but then after seeing their tracks and locating
them, he tried to lure them very gently back from danger. All of a sudden,
he recounted, "thay all run with such violence as if thay their mosion had
ben dyabolical." Thus he encouraged the prosecution, declaring "the s'd
Susana martin in the case being undoubtedly confident that shee was
a wich." [78]

The blending of folk culture and theology was not unique to Salem.
Witchcraft cases in seventeenth-century Connecticut reveal a similar
worldview. Mercy Desborough had been charged with witchcraft and
countless acts of maleficence; it was alleged that she had bewitched Henry
Grey's oxen, making them jump over a fence, and had caused beer to
jump out of a barrel. During the trial in Fairfield, Ann Godfree testified
that Mercy "answered yt there was a woman came to her & reuiled [re-
viled] her & asked what shee was doing she told her she was praying to
her God, then she asked her who was her god allso tould her yt her god
was ye deuill." [79] Having renounced God and taken up with the devil in-

78. Ibid., 2:570. Similar examples abound in the transcripts. The references to the
devil, which we might overlook, were clear to seventeenth-century audiences. Joseph Safford, in his testimony against Elizabeth How, said that his wife had initially been favorably
disposed toward How but changed her mind "becaus shee apeard to her throug a crevie of
the clambouerds which she knew no good person could do." Later that morning, as his
wife kindled the fire, he heard her shriek out, "Ther be the evill one take tham," conflating
the devil's presence with the two accused women, How and Goody Oliver (Bridget Bishop).
See Ibid., 2:452. On the various myths surrounding Bridget Bishop's mistaken identity,
see Bernard Rosenthal, *Salem Story: Reading the Witch Trials of 1692* (Cambridge, 1993),
71–75.

79. Taylor, *Witchcraft Delusion,* 71.

stead, Mercy was now expected to afflict others in order to recruit them into the devil's service. The accusations from the laity may have focused on the ordeals inflicted and endured, but implicit was the notion that the accused had been in league with Satan.

The laity, the magistrates, and the clergy all assumed that maleficium was rooted in complicity with Satan, and that is why spectral evidence was so thorny an issue. When victims entered into a pact with Satan and hence became witches, they granted the devil permission to enter their bodies in order to torment others. If the devil could have appropriated someone's body without permission, then it would have been nearly impossible to distinguish who had covenanted with Satan and who was an innocent victim of his deception.

In the fall of 1692 two unidentified authors, "P.E." and "J.A.," wrote and published the first widespread discussion of spectral evidence in the form of a dialogue between two similarly unnamed characters, "S" and "B." Contemporaries knew that Reverend Samuel Willard was, in fact, the author; the editors of his *Compleat Body of Divinity* list it as one of his publications, and the Boston merchant Robert Calef also attributed the work to him.[80] "S" and "B" may have stood for William Stoughton, the chief justice of the Court of Oyer and Terminer, and Thomas Brattle, a Boston minister; or the initials may have stood simply for Salem, representing the position of the Salem court, and Boston, representing the position of the Boston ministry.[81] In either case, the debate between the court and the clergy was spelled out in simple, direct, and often sarcastic language.

The style and the tone of the imaginary dialogue suggests that Willard was trying to explain the issues to a wide audience. By the time the pamphlet appeared, the court had already heeded the advice of the ministers; it had lost its credibility and had stopped the vigorous prosecution of the

80. Chadwick Hansen has pointed out that the pamphlet was not published in Philadelphia as the title page showed, for Willard feigned its publication outside of Massachusetts because of Governor Phips's ban on witchcraft publications, implemented in order to quell the hysteria. "P.E." (Philip English) and "J.A." (John Alden) were suitable choices for pen names since they had earlier left the colony. See Hanson, *Witchcraft at Salem*, 187. Stephen Foster concludes that Willard's authorship of the piece has been amply demonstrated. See Foster, *Long Argument*, 365n68.

81. Samuel Willard, *Some Miscellany Observations On our present Debates respecting Witchcrafts, in a Dialogue Between S. & B.* (1692; Boston, 1869). See the editors' introduction.

accused.[82] Willard's *Miscellany Observations*, then, was a way to present the controversy to the public; following a classical model, in a method designed to appear evenhanded, the conversational format allowed him to elucidate the positions of both the court and the clergy, while ultimately it permitted him to vindicate the ministers' case against spectral evidence.

The inflection of the dialogue was quick and sometimes mocking. S and B debated not only whether the devil could assume the shape of an innocent person but also whether the court should accept testimony from the afflicted. The two sides were far apart on these matters, but both agreed that witches existed and that they needed to be punished. B, speaking for the ministerial view, tried to establish that innocent people could be accused of witchcraft mistakenly and that this travesty should be avoided at all costs. He was appalled that the court would convict someone of witchcraft with evidence weaker than that required in other capital cases, such as murder. S, on the other hand, complained about the obstacles faced by the prosecution. Few people actually witnessed the signing of pacts with the devil; to require such witness or other sorts of unattainable evidence, S contended, could result in acquital and freedom for heinous criminals.[83]

Speaking for the court, S argued that the afflicted were quite capable of submitting reliable testimony—as they had, in his view, at Salem. But the clergy had questioned whether such witnesses had been bewitched at all and, by implication, whether their words were sound. Perhaps, B offered, the afflicted had also been victims of Satan's devices and were themselves possessed. As objects of possession rather than witchcraft, the afflicted may have experienced their torments directly from Satan, without a witch's intervention.

The court found this hypothesis difficult to accept and defended its policy of accepting testimony from the afflicted. S asserted that there were seven signs of bewitchment, and that the afflicted at Salem had fit six of

---

82. According to Bernard Rosenthal, Mary Easty, one of the executed women, played a major role in ending the affair by suggesting that the court separate the accusers from the accused and from each other to see if their stories would hold up when they were questioned individually. She also wanted the court to try the confessing witches, thus eliminating their incentive to confess and save their lives by so doing. See Chapter 4 for a discussion of Easty's petition and the meanings of confession. See also Rosenthal, *Salem Story,* 178–82.

83. Willard, *Some Miscellany Observations,* 7–8.

the descriptions. B countered that it was not unusual for bewitchment to precede possession. And if the devil himself was causing their tortures, how then could the court possibly accept the testimony of such witnesses? Their words were not their own but Satan's. B was being too "streitlaced" on the issue of evidence, S complained; but B concluded, "Whatever comes from them is to be suspected; and it is dangerous using or crediting them too far." [84]

The clergy's position stated that even if the afflicted were to be trusted, no specific accusations based on spectral evidence should be allowed. Fantastic tales of the tormenting specters were not sufficient for conviction. Bewildered, S asked, "Do you not believe that his Spectre is seen afflicting by the person afflicted?" The clergy, not willing to say so unequivocally, contended that even if it were true, there was no proof that the body behind the specter was a witch. S declared that "it is the Devil in the Spectre," and he had gotten permission from a witch to use her body to afflict others; therefore the accused was guilty of witchcraft. B simply would not concur: "I know you all said so, and tell us that the Devil cannot represent an innocent person doing mischief, but [you have] never proved it; nor can we believe you." [85]

The court was reluctant to concede that the devil had the ability to use an innocent person's body for his mischief; it was frightening for S to contemplate the possibility that Satan might be allowed to roam freely. But B insisted that such unusual things had happened, and not just to godly persons but to those "famous for extraordinary Piety." [86] When S countered, "Who knows but they were Hypocrites and Witches for all?" B retorted sarcastically, "True, and so are you for ought I certainly know." [87]

Willard's acrimonious hypothetical conversation between the court

84. Ibid., 16.
85. Ibid., 17.
86. Ibid., 18. Increase Mather also addressed this concern in *Cases of Conscience*. He concluded that "it is not usual for Providence to permit the Devil to come from Hell and to throw Fire on the Tops of Houses, and to cause a whole Town to be burnt to Ashes thereby. There would be (it must be confessed) no living in the world if Evil Angels should be permitted to do thus when they had a mind to it. Nevertheless, Authors worthy of Credit, tell us that this has sometimes happened." See Increase Mather, *Cases of Conscience Concerning Evil Spirits* (Boston, 1693), 18.
87. Willard, *Some Miscellany Observations*, 18.

and the clergy was not the only document that admonished the court for its eagerness in using spectral evidence and the testimony of the afflicted in condemning accused witches.[88] Thomas Brattle authored a searing indictment of the trials in a letter to an unknown minister, dated October 1692.[89] Brattle's letter makes clear that he was not an isolated skeptic; he castigated those who merely wanted to contradict the authority of the judges and presented himself as one who simply wanted to point out the many instances in which the judiciary had erred. Distinguishing between "reason and religion," Brattle thought it absurd to believe that the afflicted could actually be cured by the touch of the accused, as had been "demonstrated" in court. Anticipating negative reaction from the world outside Puritan New England—and indeed, our own modern world—Brattle claimed they "will laugh at the demonstration, and conclude that the said S.G. [Salem gentlemen] are actually possessed, at least, with ignorance and folly." He went so far as to accuse the afflicted of fraud and blamed the chief justice of the court, William Stoughton—along with "this poor land"—for the tragedy.[90]

In 1693 Increase Mather published, and other ministers endorsed, *Cases of Conscience Concerning Evil Spirits,* which denounced spectral evidence and questioned the credibility of the afflicted. Mather's reasoning echoed Willard's and Brattle's as well, although his tone was not so caustic. "And is it not then possible," he asked, "for the Dogs of Hell to poyson the Imaginations of miserable Creatures, so as that they shall believe & swear that such Persons hurt them as never did so?"[91] Mather

88. According to Richard Weisman, the court and the clergy tried to conceal their disagreements from the public. Anyone who read Willard's debate, however, would not have been fooled. See Weisman, *Witchcraft, Magic, and Religion,* 154.

89. Stephen Foster has pointed out that Brattle's letter—which included footnotes and an appendix—was not intended for private correspondence and may have circulated in manuscript. See Foster, *Long Argument,* 258, 365n68.

90. "Letter of Thomas Brattle, F.R.S.," in *Narratives of the Witchcraft Cases, 1648–1706,* ed. George Lincoln Burr (New York, 1914), 170, 171. For a helpful discussion of Brattle's letter, see Rosenthal, *Salem Story,* 186–93.

91. Increase Mather, *Cases of Conscience,* 26. Mather agreed with the recommendations put forth by Perkins and Bernard. Of Perkins, Mather wrote, "Nor do I know any one that has written on the case of Witchcraft with more Judgment and Clearness of Understanding." He referred to Bernard's book as a "solid and wise Treatise" (31). See Foster, *Long Argument,* 256–60, for an incisive treatment of Increase Mather's thoughts on the spectral evidence issue and his hesitancy to denounce the court's procedures.

believed that this scenario was indeed feasible. He stated unequivocally "that the Devil may sometimes have a Permission to Represent an Innocent Person as tormenting such as are under Diabolical Molestations." Mather insisted that "to take away the life of any one; meerly because a *Spectre* or devil, in a Bewitched or Possessed person does accuse them, will bring the Guilt of Innocent Blood on the land." [92]

The court's vigorous prosecutions and convictions precipitated a rethinking of the issues among the clergy and laity alike.[93] It made perfect sense, according to Puritan theology, to accord great power to Satan, and to believe that he was capable of extraordinary things, including assuming the shape of an innocent person. Skeptics may have already doubted the immediacy of Satan's intrusion, as we have seen, but ironically, at least among believers, it was a renewed wariness of Satan and his powers, rather than abandonment of belief, that effectively ended the 1692 witchcraft episode. In part as a result of "The Return of Several Ministers Consulted," Increase Mather's *Cases of Conscience,* and Willard's S and B debate, tales of Satan's specters were no longer heeded in court, but belief in Satan's frightful talents remained undiminished, at least among some.

As if to reaffirm his own faith, and perhaps the faith of Massachusetts Bay's inhabitants as well, Cotton Mather published *Wonders of the Invisible World* in October 1692. A detailed examination of five of the witchcraft trials, Mather's attempt to defend and justify the proceedings has been read as a reconciliation with the court. Stephen Sewall, the court clerk, aided Mather in the book's planning stages, and William Stoughton included an introduction.[94] Ironically, in his valiant attempt to harmonize

92. Mather, *Cases of Conscience,* 32, 34.

93. The timing of Willard's pamphlet is crucial in understanding its implications. By the fall of 1692, 141 women and 44 men had been accused of witchcraft; a total of 59 had been tried; 31 had been convicted; and 19 had been executed. See Karlsen, *Devil in the Shape of a Woman,* 51. For a fascinating account of the publishing history of Willard's pamphlet and the Mathers' books, see Mary Rhinelander McCarl, "Spreading the News of Satan's Malignity in Salem: Benjamin Harris, Printer and Publisher of the Witchcraft Narratives," *Essex Institute Historical Collections* 129 (January 1993), 39 61. On the confluence of lay and clerical belief at the end of the trials, see Mark A. Peterson, "'Ordinary' Preaching and the Interpretation of the Salem Witchcraft Crisis by the Boston Clergy," ibid., 84–102.

94. Weisman, *Witchcraft, Magic, and Religion,* 129. See also M. Wynn Thomas, "Cotton Mather's *Wonders of the Invisible World*: Some Metamorphoses of Salem Witchcraft," in *The Damned Art: Essays in the Literature of Witchcraft,* ed. Sydney Anglo (London, 1977), 202–26.

relations between the clergy and the court, the minister became the court's chief apologist.[95] Mather may have had another motive in writing *Wonders of the Invisible World,* however. In effect, he was defending Puritan theology. If belief in Satan wavered, then so might belief in God, and this the minister could not countenance. If, as Brattle had proposed, one might draw a dichotomy between "reason and religion," Mather wanted to prove otherwise; he sought to establish how unreasonable—indeed heretical—it was to deny Satan's powers. "That there is a *Devil,*" he emphatically proclaimed, "is a thing Doubted by none but such as are under the Influence of the *Devil.* For any to deny the Being of a *Devil* must be from an Ignorance or Profaneness, worse than Diabolical."[96] Mather's discourse on the evils of Satan was unrestrained. He emphasized the devil's pervasive and implacable nature, and he warned his readers of circumstances, such as those during the Salem trials, in which neighbors accused one another and invited the devil's intrusion.

Mather's treatise focused on the devil's wrath rather than on the technical problems with evidence during witchcraft trials.[97] He clearly affirmed that the devil would appear not only during witchcraft episodes but at all other times as well. Indeed, Mather cautioned, "there are very few Humane Affairs whereinto some Devils are not Insinuated; There is not so much as a *Journey* intended, but *Satan* will have an hand in *hindering* or *furthering* of it." He emphasized the devil's ubiquity and explained that the devil was able to threaten and abuse people constantly because he had aides in his endeavors. Mather detailed the devil's origin as an angel fallen from the love of God, and he said that there were actually thousands of such fallen angels, or devils, of whom the famed Beelzebub was the leader and the rest were his soldiers. To comprehend the enormity of Satan's army, "Think on vast Regiments of cruel and bloody

95. See Hansen, *Witchcraft at Salem,* 169–71, for a discussion of how historians have interpreted Mather's participation in the witchcraft trials. See also David Levin, "Did the Mathers' Disagree?"

96. Mather, *Wonders of the Invisible World,* 55.

97. M. Wynn Thomas says that Mather's *Wonders of the Invisible World* was the last major work to use the language of the devil's wrath descending upon God's chosen people. "It was a great Jeremiad," Thomas contends, "that powerful mixture of lament, rebuke, and exhortation so characteristic of the preaching of the second and third generations of Puritan settlers." See M. Wynn Thomas, "Mather's *Wonders,*" 213. See also Kenneth Silverman, *The Life and Times of Cotton Mather* (New York, 1985), 111–14.

French Dragoons," Mather suggested, "with an *Intendant* over them, overrunning a pillaged Neighbourhood, and you will think a little, what the Constitution among the Devils is." He conjectured that since there were so many devils, some were more suited to or qualified in certain areas of deceit than others. He suggested, "It is not likely that every Devil does know every *Language;* or that every Devil can do every *Mischief.* Tis possible, that the *Experience,* or, I may call it so, the *Education* of all Devils is not alike, and that there may be some difference in their *Abilities.*"[98] It was not surprising to Mather that the devil's rage should descend upon New England; Satan had an army, and the people had let down their defenses.

Mather's *Wonders of the Invisible World* did not depart significantly from other Puritan treatises. Ministers often described Satan to their congregants as not just one devil but the composition of all the fallen angels. The seventeenth-century English minister Henry Smith, for example, had written of Satan's vast numbers and power. Satan was not called merely "a liar, nor a tempter, nor an accuser, nor a slanderer, nor a deceiver, nor an adversary, nor a viper, nor a lion. . . . But when Christ asked him his name, he called himself Legion, which imports a multitude, as if he should brag of his number."[99] Jonathan Mitchel also catechized, "By Satan is meant the company (or regiment) of fallen (apostate) Angells united & combined under our Head as sworne enemies (adversaries) to (oppose) the glory of God in the Salvation of men." He explained that just as the proper name of a nation signifies all its inhabitants, so too "that by Satan or Devill (in the singular number) the meaning is not that there is only one Evill Angell or Devill; no there are an exceeding multitudes [*sic*] of these evill spirits."[100] Satan connoted all of the devils, but he was also "the ringleader of the rest called the prince of Devills."[101]

On this issue the laity concurred. The poet Anne Bradstreet also understood that there were many devils for different purposes: "The skillful fisher hath his several baits for several fish, but there is a hook under all;

98. Mather, *Wonders of the Invisible World,* 57, 58.

99. Thomas Fuller, ed., *The Works of Henry Smith; including Sermons, Treatises, Prayers, and Poems,* 2 vols. (Edinburgh, 1867), 2:19.

100. Jonathan Mitchel, "Continuation of Sermons Concerning Man's Misery," unpublished sermons, Massachusetts Historical Society, August 1655.

101. Ibid.; see also Samuel Willard, *The Child's Portion* (Boston, 1684), 29–30.

Satan, that great Angler, hath his sundry baits for sundry tempers of men, which they all catch greedily at, but few perceives the hook till it be too late." [102]

If Mather's *Wonders* presented no new information about Satan's wrath, it was nonetheless far more alarmist and provocative than conventional sermonic cautions against Satan's devices because Mather made the explicit connection between Satan and witchcraft. As Satan's agents, eagerly gathering recruits for the devil's legions, witches were capable of undermining individual resistance to sin and might even deliver an entire community into Satan's clutches and hell's dark furnace. In the past the devil had tried to lure the people of New England into his snare, as he was wont to do with the godly, but according to Mather, "now there is a more than ordinary *affliction,* with which the *Devil* is Galling of us: and such an one as is indeed Unparallelable." Mather wrote, "The *Devil,* Exhibiting himself ordinarily as a *Black man,* has decoy'd a fearful knot of proud, froward, ignorant, envious and malicious creatures, to lift themselves in his horrid Service, by entring their Names in a *Book* by him tendred unto them." [103] With such references to the physicality of the devil, and the concreteness of his actions, *Wonders of the Invisible World* blended the theology of Satan with the folk culture of witchcraft.

Mather's book was published just after the last trials ended under the special Court of Oyer and Terminer and before the new trials in which spectral evidence was not credited; it was a time when many people harbored suspicions about the court's methods in obtaining convictions, and some doubted that the accused had ever been guilty at all. In this climate, Mather's provocative work was not favorably received. If the rest of New England now seemed ready to relegate the devil to the realms of rhetoric in ministers' sermons, to discrete religious discourses within the confines of the meetinghouse, Mather still saw Satan breaking out of this separate sphere, ranging more widely and physically as the dark man or black dog throughout New England.[104]

---

102. Jeannine Hensley, ed., *The Works of Anne Bradstreet* (Cambridge, Mass., 1967), 276.

103. Cotton Mather, *Wonders of the Invisible World,* 102.

104. See Thomas, "Mather's *Wonders,*" 202–9; Silverman, *Life and Times of Cotton Mather,* 111–18; Middlekauff, *The Mathers,* 159–61. Foster (*Long Argument,* 257) maintains that Mather's reputation was destroyed "by a defense of the trials little short of frenetic." The subtle changes in attitudes toward Satan in ministers' sermons and lay conversion narratives after Salem are discussed in Chapter 5.

A measure of Mather's increasing isolation from the current of opinion about Satan and his devices came in the form of Robert Calef's stinging *More Wonders of the Invisible World*, published in 1700.[105] The first historical account of the witchcraft trials, Calef's book portrayed Mather in a singularly unflattering light. Just after the trials, for example, Cotton and his father, Increase, had visited a young woman, Margaret Rule, who had been either bewitched or possessed by Satan. Calef attended the session in which the Mathers sought to rid Rule of Satan's trespasses, and he insinuated that Mather's attempts were licentious and inappropriate. He reported that Mather "rubbed her stomach (her breast not covered with the bed-clothes) and bid others do so too, and said it eased her. Then she revived. . . . [Upon her falling into another fit] he rubbed her breast, etc." [106] Mather responded angrily that in fact Rule had been fully clothed, although not in bed-clothes, and that he and his father did not encourage her to implicate others in her ordeal, as Calef had suggested.[107] But Mather's reputation never recovered, for the worldview had altered. In post-Salem New England, Satan no longer appeared able to make such tangible intrusions.

Until 1692, however, the living folk traditions concerning the shapes in which the devil appeared, the caches of weapons seen at meetings, the violent attacks upon unsuspecting victims worked in concert with the theology preached by New England clergy. And the clergy, inheritors of the same folk culture as the laity—and perhaps more eager to see New England return to God's good graces—held their own visions of the devil, which, in turn, may have encouraged the laity's fantastic representations. Likewise, folk beliefs in Satan served to reinforce Puritan theology. Although leery of the court's procedures, ministers ultimately insisted on Satan's power, not his impotence, and encouraged those who covenanted with Satan to confess and return to the Puritan fold. Thus they endorsed such conceptions of the devil and renewed their own and the community's covenant with God.

105. Robert Calef, *More Wonders of the Invisible World: or The Wonders of the Invisible World Display'd in Five Parts* (London, 1700), in *Narratives of the Witchcraft Cases, 1648–1706*, ed. George Lincoln Burr (1914; New York, 1968). Robert Middlekauff has argued that some of Mather's obsessive views about Satan's powers "bordered on irrationality even in the seventeenth century." See Middlekauff, *The Mathers*, 327.

106. Calef, *More Wonders*, 324–41.

107. Cotton Mather to Robert Calef, January 15, 1694, in *Selected Letters of Cotton Mather*, ed. Kenneth Silverman (Baton Rouge, La., 1971), 50–52. Mather responded to

In this chapter I have emphasized the commonalities among New Englanders—between clergy and laity, and women and men, particularly— regarding their belief in the devil, witches, and their powers. Yet common participation in a single social and intellectual world also involved some dissonances, especially between the sexes, along gender lines established and negotiated in Puritan New England. And as will become clear, Satan's assaults, even if commonly understood, afflicted women and men differently. In chapter 3, I explore how the laity and the clergy interpreted Satan's possession of souls. With the implicit understanding that the souls of both men and women were feminine, participants and observers of the witchcraft episodes accordingly conceived of Satan's possession in gendered terms.

Calef's charges written and circulated prior to publication.

3

THE DEVIL, THE BODY,
AND THE FEMININE SOUL

Puritans regarded the soul as feminine and characterized it as insatiable, in consonance with the allegedly unappeasable nature of women. If historians have noticed the New England Puritans' feminized representation of the soul, they have failed to comment on it or accord it much significance.[1] Yet such representation is crucial to understanding how the soul could unite with Christ on regeneration or, alternatively, with the devil through sin.

The body, for its part, also entangled women. Puritans believed that Satan attacked the soul by assaulting the body. Because in their view women's bodies were weaker, the devil could reach women's souls more easily and breach these "weaker vessels" with greater frequency. Not only was the body the path to the soul's possession; it was the very ex-

---

1. Several scholars have studied the Puritan conception of the soul, but none has commented on gender distinctions. See, for example, Sargent Bush Jr., ed., *The Writings of Thomas Hooker: Spiritual Adventure in Two Worlds* (Madison, Wis., 1980); Charles Lloyd Cohen, *God's Caress: The Psychology of Puritan Religious Experience* (New York, 1986); Edmund S. Morgan, *The Puritan Family: Religion and Domestic Relations in Seventeenth-Century New England* (New York, 1944); Kathleen Verduin, "'Our Cursed Natures': Sexuality and the Puritan Conscience," *New England Quarterly* 56 (1983), 220–37; Margaret W. Masson, "The Typology of the Female as a Model for the Regenerate: Puritan Preaching, 1690–1730," *Signs* 2 (Winter 1976), 304–15. For an interpretation of the gendered soul and its relationship to corporeal women which differs from mine, see Richard Godbeer, "'Love Raptures': Marital, Romantic, and Erotic Images of Jesus Christ in Puritan New England, 1670–1730," *New England Quarterly* 68 (1995), 355–85.

pression of the devil's attack. A witch's body clearly manifested the soul's acceptance of the diabolical covenant.

Women were in a double bind during the witchcraft episodes. Their souls, strictly speaking, were no more evil than men's, but the representation of the vulnerable, perpetually unsatisfied, and yearning female soul, passively waiting for Christ but always open to the devil as well, implicated corporeal women themselves.[2] The representation of the soul in terms of worldly notions of gender and the understanding of women in terms of the characteristics of the feminine soul, led by circular reasoning to the conclusion that women were more likely than men to submit to Satan. A woman's feminine soul, jeopardized in a woman's feminine body, was frail, submissive, and passive—qualities that most New Englanders thought would allow her to become either a wife to Christ or a drudge to Satan.

Witches, unlike commonplace sinners, took a further damning step. Their feminine souls made an explicit and aggressive choice to conjoin with the devil. By defining a witch as a person whose (feminine) soul signed a pact with Satan rather than wait quiescently for Christ, Puritans effectively demonized the notion of active female choice. A woman was damned if she did and damned if she didn't. If her soul waited longingly for salvation in Christ, such female yearning could evoke the image of an unsatisfied woman vulnerable to Satan; if, on the contrary, a woman's soul acted assertively rather than in passive obedience, by definition it chose the devil. Although theoretically they were no more inherently evil than men, the process of defining the soul and the body in the context of life in Puritan New England made them seem so.[3]

In this chapter I examine the cultural construction of gender in early

2. Since both men and women possessed feminine souls, ministers would have contended that the sexes were spiritually equal. Yet Carol Karlsen has shown that women's discontent with their lot in life opened them to witchcraft accusations. She has demonstrated that the sins for which women were punished—pride, deceit, envy—signified women's overall unhappiness, and as John Davenport suggested, Puritans knew that "a froward discontented frame of spirit was a subject fitt for the Devill to work upon." See Carol F. Karlsen, *The Devil in the Shape of a Woman: Witchcraft in Colonial New England* (New York, 1987), 125. I suggest that the gender distinction cut even deeper.

3. For the prevailing European view that women were more evil than men, see the influential Heinrich Kramer and James Sprenger, *Malleus Maleficarum,* ed. and trans. Montague Summers (1486; New York, 1971), esp. 41–47, which appeared in various languages in almost thirty editions.

America to understand the intersection of Puritan theology, Puritan eval-
uations of womanhood, and the seventeenth-century witchcraft episodes.
The Puritans' earthly perception of women's bodies and souls corresponded to their otherworldly belief in Satan's powers. Here I explore
how New Englanders considered women more vulnerable to Satan because their image of the soul and its relation to the body allowed them to
associate womanhood with evil and sin.[4] During the witchcraft episodes,
the learned and the common people alike molded belief and interpreted
circumstances, in the end cooperating in the construction of their natural
and supernatural world.[5] Of course, this seventeenth-century worldview
was influenced by considerations of gender. The gendered nature of the
Puritans' social universe was not only reflected in their understanding of
women's and men's bodies and souls; it was echoed in images of the supernatural behavior and power that they believed the devil conferred on
his female and male witches.[6]

4. One index of New Englanders' propensity to link womanhood with witchcraft is the
disproportionate number of women among those accused of this crime. Approximately
78 percent of the seventeenth-century "witches" who could be identified by sex were female. See Karlsen, *Devil in the Shape of a Woman,* 48. On English perceptions of the
female body and feminine spiritual imagery, see Phyllis Mack, *Visionary Women: Ecstatic
Prophecy in Seventeenth-Century England* (Berkeley, Calif., 1992), 15–43. Marilyn J.
Westerkamp suggests a similar Puritan characterization of women as evil. See Westerkamp,
"Puritan Patriarchy and the Problem of Revelation," *Journal of Interdisciplinary History*
23 (Winter 1993), 571–95. For an earlier example of the association of womanhood with
evil, see Amy Schrager Lang, *Prophetic Woman: Anne Hutchinson and the Problem of Dis-
sent in the Literature of New England* (Berkeley, Calif., 1987), 15–51.
5. Although some historians perceive a sharp division between the clergy and the laity,
like David D. Hall and others I see a consensus between elite and popular thought concerning matters of religion and the supernatural. See David D. Hall, *Worlds of Wonder,
Days of Judgment: Popular Religious Belief in Early New England* (New York, 1989), esp.
3–20. See also Richard Godbeer, *The Devil's Dominion: Magic and Religion in Early New
England* (Cambridge, 1992), 154–57.
6. For other explanations of New England witchcraft which consider the issues of
women and gender in different ways, see Karlsen, *Devil in the Shape of a Woman;* and John
Putnam Demos, *Entertaining Satan: Witchcraft and the Culture of Early New England*
(New York, 1982). See also Ann Kibbey, *The Interpretation of Material Shapes in Puritanism: A Study of Rhetoric, Prejudice, and Violence* (New York, 1986). For a discerning
discussion of the gendered nature of bodies and souls in European witchcraft cases, see
Lyndal Roper, *Oedipus and the Devil: Witchcraft, Sexuality, and Religion in Early Modern
Europe* (New York, 1994), esp. 171–98. Roper looks particularly at the way in which exorcism and magic in sixteenth-century Germany highlighted the question of the relationship between the body and the soul in Protestant and Catholic communities.

Lay and clerical views of the tortures that Satan's victims endured during the witchcraft episodes paralleled the sermon literature, which discussed the relationship among the body, the soul, and Satan. The body was the most vulnerable part of a person's total being, its Achilles' heel. Succumbing to Satan's assaults and temptations, the body could become the Puritan's own worst enemy. It was the primary battleground in the struggle between the devil and the individual soul.[7] The Reverend Henry Smith characterized the body as a betrayer. "So soon as we rise in the morning," he lamented, "we go forth to fight with two mighty giants, the world and the devil; and whom do we take with us but a traitor, this brittle flesh, which is ready to yield up to the enemy at every assault?"[8] Sinful temptations devised by Satan, such as carnality, drunkenness, and licentiousness, provoked the body and threatened to lead it astray, thus giving Satan an inroad to the soul.

Puritan sermons asserted that the body and the soul were both essential to human beings; each had its specific purpose, though the soul reigned supreme. The Reverend Samuel Willard explained that all the various parts of the body were made "to be at the Command and under the Government of the Nobler Part [the soul]." For example, "Here are the *Hands,* Organs suited to perform the Devices of the Soul, wherewith many Works are wrought. . . . And here are the *Feet* which carry the Body according to the Direction of the Soul."[9] The body did the soul's bidding; a weak body, unable to withstand the devil's attacks or seductions, rendered the soul vulnerable to Satan's extortion. The Reverend Joshua Moodey referred to the body as "a close Enemy because within thee, and the more dangerous because so close . . . , an Enemy that lurks in thine own bosome, and thence is advantaged to do thee the more harm."[10]

It seems ironic that Puritans envisioned the body as protecting the soul rather than the reverse, so that a strong body rendered a person's soul

7. On the struggle between body and soul, see John Downame, *The Christian Warfare Against the Devil, World and Flesh* (London, 1634).

8. Thomas Fuller, ed., *The Works of Henry Smith; including Sermons, Treatises, Prayers, and Poems,* 2 vols. (Edinburgh, 1867), 2:18.

9. Samuel Willard, *The Compleat Body of Divinity* (Boston, 1726), 123.

10. Joshua Moodey, *Soldiery Spiritualized or the Christian Soldier Orderly, and Strenuously Engaged in the Spiritual Warre, and So Fighting the Good Fight* (Cambridge, Mass., 1674), 8.

less vulnerable to Satan's exertions. The body, after all, was usually seen as the weaker link in the soul-body relationship. However illogical, the belief was nonetheless common that the body became the path to the soul. A strong body was less likely to submit to the devil's temptations and thus better able to protect the soul from the devil's domination.

The body's duty was to protect the soul, but more often than not it failed. Clergy and laity alike knew all too well that the body's lustful desires frequently overwhelmed the will, which resided in the soul. And although the body may have committed the sins, ultimately the soul bore the responsibility. It was the soul that Satan held in bondage. "It is true, the body is employed in it, and all the members of it are engaged in this drudgery," Willard admitted, "but the bondage of it lies on the inward man." [11]

Willard's use of the term "inward man" as a synonym for the (feminine) soul drew on biblical precedent and Puritan speculation that used the names of bodily things to designate spiritual entities. The metaphor carried more connotation of femininity in the seventeenth century than it had earlier. Quoting the source of the trope, the seventeenth-century English minister Richard Sibbes blurred the lines between the physical and the spiritual, writing that the heart is not "the inward material and fleshy part of the body; but that spiritual part, the soul and affections thereof . . . all the powers of the soul, the inward man, as Paul calleth it, 2 Cor. iv. 16 is the heart." Paul's phrase gained new currency from seventeenth- and eighteenth-century ideas of physical anatomy which perceived women's sexual organs as identical to men's, except insofar as they were contained within the body. If inwardness meant femaleness, the term suggests that the soul was feminine; it, or "she," ultimately carried the burden of the body's weaknesses. [12]

11. Willard, *Compleat Body*, 229. On the relationship among the understanding, the will, the body, and the soul, see Cohen, *God's Caress*, 34–46. On the will and the soul, see also Perry Miller, *The New England Mind: The Seventeenth Century* (Cambridge, Mass., 1939), 181–85, 256–66.

12. Cohen, *God's Caress*, esp. 37, 39. Galen wrote, "turn outward the woman's, turn inward, so to speak, and fold double the man's, and you will find the same in both in every respect." These audiences remained convinced of Galen's account at the same time that they began to embrace newer interpretations of sexual anatomy. See Thomas Laqueur, "Orgasm, Generation, and the Politics of Reproductive Biology," *Representations* 14 (Spring 1986), 5, and see 14–16. For a fuller discussion of the ways in which two genders corresponded to one sex—the male—see Laqueur's *Making Sex: Body and Gender from the Greeks to Freud* (Cambridge, Mass., 1990).

Puritans conceived of body and soul as integral parts of the self, yet distinct in function and prestige. As a result of the Fall, the body and soul suffered punishments that had to be endured. Willard explained the distinction to his congregation. Although the body was merely the instrument of the soul, the pair fit together to form a complete person, and so the body as well as the soul had to suffer for sin. The suffering, Willard reasoned, came in two forms, "privative" and "positive." Creatures could be denied things that would otherwise make their lives more comfortable, or they could actually undergo manifest miseries, both emotional and physical.[13]

As a consequence of original and subsequent sin, the body endured the punishment of ill health. The privative suffering manifested itself in the lack of vivacity and the disposition to illness, the positive suffering, in physical ailments that afflicted the human body. "These evils," according to Willard, "meet the man in the womb before he is born, and they follow him to his grave; and every affliction gives a chop at the tree of the life of the outward man, till at last it falls, and he dies."[14]

And yet, "if a man had a thousand bodies," postulated Willard, "he had better lose them all, than one soul." Willard admitted that a person could endure all sorts of corporal miseries and still be content; spiritual punishment mattered more. Spiritual miseries, Willard explained, included "all those evils to which the Soul is subjected in this life." The soul constituted "the most excellent part in Man," and so the miseries it suffered had to be significantly greater.[15] A strong body could endure enormous suffering, but the agony of the soul imposed a more lasting effect on a person's life.

The soul's most excruciating misery resulted when the divine union with Christ, expected upon conversion, was cruelly subverted, and instead a diabolical union was concluded with the devil as a result of sin. Puritans believed that this was exactly the devil's intention; Satan aggressively pursued souls, persuading them to join his minions instead. Deodat Lawson (preaching in the midst of the 1692 witchcraft crisis in Salem) proclaimed, "when he [Satan] *touches* the life of the Body, he *Aims* at the Life of the Soul."[16] Willard (in more ordinary times) warned his congre-

13. Willard, *Compleat Body*, 224–28.
14. Ibid., 224.
15. Ibid., 227.
16. Deodat Lawson, *Christ's Fidelity the Only Shield Against Satan's Malignity* (Boston, 1704), 23. This sermon was originally delivered in Salem Village on March 24, 1692.

gation, "It is the Souls destruction the Devil mainly aims at: it is the precious Soul that he hunts for." Both Lawson and Willard illustrated their point with the biblical example of Job; the devil tortured Job's body, but his aim was to devastate the soul. "He little regards the Body in comparison of that," said Willard.[17] Cotton Mather made the same point. The devil's goal, he wrote, was to "seduce the souls, torment the bodies."[18]

Prior to conversion, the soul, corrupt and degenerate in its natural state, inevitably succumbed to Satan's ploys and surrendered to his domination. Upon conversion the soul cleaved to Christ, "as moulded into one loafe."[19] The regenerate souls of both men and women were united with Christ as if in marriage. Because the soul was inherently feminine, both Satan and Christ could possess the soul in a sexually specific way. Whether the soul fell victim to Satan's temptations or enjoyed Christ's protection upon conversion, the bond was heterosexual since it was literally the soul, and only metaphorically the body, that Puritans believed converged in the union.

The marriage between God and a believer was the most common metaphor of regeneration because it closely approximated the relationship between husband and wife, for Puritans the most important human relationship.[20] Puritan ministers drew on a long Christian tradition in describing the union, in which the soul took the place of the wife and Christ that of the husband.[21] Thomas Shepard explained, "The soul hence gives

17. Willard, *Compleat Body*, 229.

18. Cotton Mather, *Wonders of the Invisible World* (Boston, 1693), reprinted in *The Witchcraft Delusion in New England*, ed. Samuel Drake, 3 vols. (Roxbury, Mass., 1866), 1:101.

19. John Cotton, *The Way of Life* (London, 1634), 375.

20. On the roles of Puritan women as wives and mothers, see Amanda Porterfield, *Female Piety in Puritan New England: The Emergence of Religious Humanism* (New York, 1992). See also Morgan, *Puritan Family*, especially the chapter titled "Puritan Tribalism." Of course, Puritans were not the first to use matrimonial and sexual imagery to describe their love for Christ. For a discussion of the medieval tradition, see Caroline Walker Bynum, *Fragmentation and Redemption: Essays on Gender and the Human Body in Medieval Religion* (New York, 1991), 151–79; and Ann E. Matter, *The Voice of My Beloved: The Song of Songs in Western Medieval Christianity* (Philadelphia, 1990). On the metaphor of maternal love, see Caroline Walker Bynum, *Jesus as Mother: Studies in the Spirituality of the High Middle Ages* (Berkeley, 1982), 110–69.

21. For the Puritan understanding of marriage, see John Cotton, *A Meet Help: or, a Wedding Sermon, Preached at New-Castle in New England, June 19, 1694* (Boston, 1699);

itself, like one espoused to her husband, to the Lord Jesus."[22] The betrothal metaphor extended to consummation, which ministers insisted
sacred marriages required, no less than profane ones. As Increase Mather
explained, "In this Life Believers are Espoused to Christ. At his Second
coming will be the Consummation of the Marriage. Christ will then
come as a Bridegroom."[23] Jonathan Mitchel agreed: "Our present state
is but an Espousal, the consummation of the Marriage is at the day of
Judgment; thence follows the full enjoyment each of other in Heaven,
when Christ hath carried his Spouse home to his Fathers house."[24] The
layman John Winthrop wrote, "God brought me by that occasion in to
such a heavenly meditation of the love betweene Christ and me, as rav-
ished my heart with unspeakable ioye [joy]; methought my soule had as
familiar and sensible society with him as my wife could have with the
kindest husbande."[25] The mystical union between the believer and Christ
was analogous, consummation and all, to the relationship between wife
and husband, female and male. For both men and women, the soul was
the female part that bonded spiritually, emotionally, and physically with
Christ.

If the feminine soul was to merge with Christ upon regeneration, then
it must have possessed certain attributes that prepared it for this union.
Margaret W. Masson has described the regenerate Christian as a passive
and submissive convert who exemplified "wifely" traits.[26] The convert

---

Samuel Willard, *Compleat Body*, 610–20; Benjamin Wadsworth, *The Well-Ordered Family* (Boston, 1712); Alexander Niccholes, *A Discourse of Marriage and Wiving* (London,
1615); Thomas Gataker, *Marriage Duties* (London, 1620). For the historians' view of the
relationship between men and women in marriage, see Morgan, *Puritan Family*, 29–64;
James T. Johnson, "The Covenant Idea and the Puritan View of Marriage," *Journal of the
History of Ideas* 32 (1971), 107–18; Karlsen, *Devil in the Shape of a Woman*, 160–68;
Laurel Thatcher Ulrich, *Good Wives: Image and Reality in the Lives of Women in Northern New England, 1650–1750* (New York, 1980), 35–50.

22. *The Works of Thomas Shepard,* ed. John Albro, 3 vols. (Boston, 1853; repr. New
York, 1967), 2:31.

23. Increase Mather, *Practical Truths Plainly Delivered* (Boston, 1718), 54.

24. Jonathan Mitchel, *A Discourse of the Glory to Which God hath Called Believers by
Jesus Christ* (London, 1677), 30.

25. Robert C. Winthrop, *Life and Letters of John Winthrop,* 2 vols. (Boston, 1869), 1:105.

26. Masson, "Typology of the Female," 304–15. On the relationship between sin and
female imagery, see David Leverenz, *The Language of Puritan Feeling: An Exploration
in Literature, Psychology, and Social History* (New Brunswick, N.J., 1980), 148–56.
Leverenz argues that sin was more often associated with anal than with sexual imagery.

was supposed to wait patiently for Christ's overtures of grace.[27] According to Shepard, the soul had an obligation to be quiescent. When the lover is Christ, said Shepard, "it is no presumption now, but duty to give *her* consent."[28] At regeneration, Cotton Mather exhorted, "in this Act of *Resignation* there must and will be nothing less than thy very *All* included. *Resign* thy *Spirit* unto Him, and say, *O my SAVIOUR, I desire that all the Faculties of my Soul may be filled with thee, and used for thee. Resign* thy *Body* unto Him."[29] The convert's object was to surrender completely to Christ's domination.

Masson investigates the apparent paradox that conversion required men to act not like dominant and assertive husbands but like passive "female" converts. She argues that men were able to assume such passivity because the fluid gender identities of the seventeenth and eighteenth centuries allowed men to adopt typically female attributes while retaining their masculinity. This apparent role ambiguity was possible, she contends, because the more rigid sexual differentiation characteristic of the nineteenth century had not yet emerged. I argue instead that the gender role fluidity was made possible by the gendered split between the body and the soul. Men were not required to adopt outwardly feminine traits and risk compromising their masculinity; but man's soul, his inner self, could safely display female virtues. Passivity and receptivity to Christ's advances resided in mens' (female) souls, but their bodies—and sense of themselves—remained masculine.[30]

The ministers' use of the marriage metaphor to explain the bond between Christ and saints imposed worldly gender divisions on the most important spiritual process. And the analogy worked so well precisely because the institution was so basic. Puritan women and men understood what was expected of them in marriage. Because the image of sacred

27. Joshua Moodey described the passive soul waiting for Christ: "Christians, let your Souls be silent and still before the Lord, *Commune with your own Hearts & be still,* that you may listen to what God has to say to you. . . . Keep in a still, quiet posture, then sit to hear and obey." See Moodey, *Soldiery Spiritualized,* 43.

28. Shepard, *Works,* 1:197. See also Verduin, "Our Cursed Natures," 220–37.

29. Cotton Mather, *Glorious Espousal: A Brief Essay to Illustrate and Prosecute the Marriage, Wherein Our Great Saviour Offers to Espouse unto Himself the Children of Men* (Boston, 1719), 26.

30. Masson, "Typology of the Female," 313–15. See Chapter 5 for further discussion of male and female attitudes toward sin and one's soul.

marriage had many of the components of profane marriage, the metaphor and the institution reinforced each other. The wife submitted to her
husband, just as a female soul would give herself up to Christ. Indeed,
the feminine soul's very happiness depended on Christ's protection, just
as a woman's contentedness was thought to depend, ideally, on her prov-
idential betrothal.[31]

The relationship between the unregenerate soul and the devil paralleled conjugality with Christ, although in submitting to Satan men and
women were enslaved rather than joined in a respectful and benevolent,
if necessarily hierarchical, relationship.[32] Both slavery and matrimony implied perpetual and powerful connections, and interestingly, ministers employed the metaphor of possession for both bonds—with Christ and
with Satan. Thus, William Adams could declare: "If thou are none of
Christs, thou art the Devils. The possession of men in the world is divided betwixt *Christ* and *Satan*. What *Christ* possesses not are under *Satans power* and tyranny. Know therefore that if Christ hath no possession of thee, thou art possessed of the Devil."[33] Although both Christ
and the devil possessed souls, the nature of the possession differed dra-

31. Ulrich, *Good Wives,* 110–23. Ulrich suggests that because marriage was such an
important event in one's life, the decision could not be left entirely up to the man or woman
involved and required parental approval. Although divorce was available in the seventeenth
century, it was rare.

32. The metaphor is a reminder that, although Puritan marriages may have aspired to
spiritual equality, reality dictated a power imbalance between husband and wife. In some
marriages, at least, the wife felt herself to be a virtual slave to her husband. See Mary Beth
Norton, *Liberty's Daughters: The Revolutionary Experience of American Women, 1750–
1800* (Boston, 1980), 41–51. In 1694 London, Mary Astell anonymously published a defense of women titled *Reflections upon Marriage.* She bemoaned the fate of "poor Female
Slaves" who "groan under Tyranny" and grew unavoidably weary of the "matrimonial
yoke." Quoted in Margaret George, "From 'Goodwife' to 'Mistress': The Transformation
of the Female in Bourgeois Culture," *Science and Society* 37 (Summer 1973), 152–77.

33. William Adams, *The Necessity of the Pouring Out of the Spirit from on High Upon
a Sinning Apostatizing People, set under Judgment, in order to their Merciful Deliverance
and Salvation* (Boston, 1679), 38. One could also argue that possession characterized the
legal relationship between husbands and wives. When a woman married she became *feme
covert,* literally covered by her husband. She could not own property or sign contracts, and
legally she did not own any wages she may have earned. See Norton, *Liberty's Daughters,*
45–47; Marylynn Salmon, *Women and the Law of Property in Early America* (Chapel Hill,
N.C., 1986); Joan R. Gunderson and Gwen V. Gampel, "Married Women's Legal Status in
Eighteenth-Century New York and Virginia," *William and Mary Quarterly,* 3rd ser., 39
(1982), 114–34; Norma Basch, *In the Eyes of the Law: Women, Marriage, and Property in
Nineteenth-Century New York* (Ithaca, N.Y., 1982), 19–26.

matically: possession by Christ assured freedom and salvation; posses-sion by the devil meant perpetual terror and degradation.[34]

Ministers preached that Satan held the unconverted soul in bondage; natural man, in other words, came completely under Satan's control. Jonathan Mitchel urged his congregation to emerge from the corrupt state of nature, "wherin men are before conversion, which is here said to be a state of darkness & bondage to Satan & consequently of perdition."[35] Samuel Willard likewise equated Satan's possession with man's natural state. "The first possession of the heart is held by the Strong man," he ex-plained, "whether by him we understand Satan, who is called the God of the world, and rules in the Children of disobedience; or the *body of death*, or the corrupt nature in man."[36] "How fearfull a thing is it to be serving the devill!" exclaimed Robert Baylie. Those who resist God in sin "lie cap-tive like Gally-slaves, but a part with their master for ever in his horrible portion."[37]

The analogy to slavery allowed ministers to speak of the devil's mas-tery as complete and inescapable. Thomas Hooker said of the wicked, "the Devill rules in them; he speaks their tongues, and works by their hands, and thinks and desires by their minds, and walks by their feete."[38] The union merged the devil with the soul not in marital bliss but in ever-lasting unhappiness. Willard stated unequivocally: "This slavery is a Soul misery."[39]

---

34. John Winthrop argued that the authority a husband had over a wife paralleled Christ's authority over a believer, and this subjection brought freedom: "This liberty is maintained and exercised in a way of subjection to authority; it is of the same kind of lib-erty wherewith Christ hath made us free. The woman's own choice makes such a man her husband; yet being so chosen, he is her lord, and she is to be subject to him, yet in a way of liberty, not of bondage." See John Winthrop, *The History of New England from 1630 to 1649*, quoted in *Puritan Political Ideas, 1558–1794*, ed. Edmund S. Morgan (Indianapolis, Ind., 1965), 139.

35. Jonathan Mitchel, *Continuation of Sermons Concerning Men's Misery*, November 9, 1653–November 7, 1655, "From the Power of Satan unto God," August 15, 1655, Massa-chusetts Historical Society, Boston. See also Edward Trefz, "Satan as the Prince of Evil," *Boston Library Quarterly* 7 (1955), 3–22.

36. Willard, *Compleat Body*, 170.

37. Robert Baylie, *Satan the Leader in Chief to all who Resist the Reparation of Sion* (London, 1643), 37.

38. Thomas Hooker, *The Soules Humiliation* (London, 1637), 35.

39. Willard, *Compleat Body*, 229.

Of course, this connubial metaphor implicitly presumed an unregenerate feminine soul and an unrelenting masculine devil. Although they rarely drew explicit attention to the female nature of the soul, clergy and laity alike used feminine adjectives, such as barren or fecund, to describe it and used the feminine pronoun for it. In addition, the soul was described as insatiable—a negative characterization more often ascribed to women than men. The soul was forever seeking happiness that it could never attain unaided.[40] Indeed, Urian Oakes spoke of the natural propensity to sin, original sin, in feminine terms. "Indwelling sin," he explained, was a "home-bred enemy, that mother of all the abominations that are brought forth in the lives of men, that adversary that is ever molesting the peace, disturbing the quiet, and endangering the people of GOD."[41] Bearing within it the "mother" of all sin, the unregenerate, natural soul submitted willingly to Satan's domination.

John Cotton described the unrepentent soul as a female entity. Depicting the "ungracious frame of nature" with which humankind entered the world, Cotton recounted the process of regeneration: "So as now the poor soule begins presently to stand amazed at her former condition, and looks at it as most dangerous and desperate; and now the soule begins to loathe itself, and to abhor itselfe, and to complaine and confesses its wickednesse before God."[42] Cotton's soul is thus ungracious, wicked, self-hating, and—as the possessive pronoun implies—female. Enveloped

40. When Elizabeth Godman was accused of witchcraft, for example, in 1653, one male witness suggested she had caused the death of Mrs. Bishop's children to revenge Mr. Bishop's lack of affection toward her. Godman agreed she pined for Mr. Bishop but blamed Mrs. Bishop herself for excessive yearning. Of the mother, Godman is alleged to have said, "She kills her children with longing, because she longs for everything she sees." See David D. Hall, ed., *Witch-Hunting in Seventeenth-Century New England: A Documentary History, 1638–1692* (Boston, 1991), 65.

41. Urian Oakes, *The Unconquerable, All Conquering and More than Conquering Souldier: or the successful warre which a believer wageth with the enemies of his soul* (Boston, 1674), 2. The English minister Obadiah Sedgwick saw the womb as the bearer of sin; "so sin is truely sin; though it never gets out beyond the wombe which did conceive and enliven it." See Obadiah Sedgwick, *The Anatomy of Secret Sins* (London, 1660), 9. Sedgwick lived c. 1600–1658. These sermons were published posthumously.

42. John Cotton, *Way of Life,* 5. The Reverend Samuel Parris also employed the feminine pronoun to refer to the soul. In October 1692 in Salem, Parris delivered a sermon on kisses as the manifestation of Christ's love: "O when wilt thou come unto me, sais the Soul. She desires to dwell in the house of the Lord, & there to behold his beauty." See James F. Cooper Jr. and Kenneth P. Minkema, eds., *The Sermon Notebook of Samuel Parris, 1689–1694,* Publications of the Massachusetts Historical Society, no. 66 (Boston, 1993), 210.

in Satan's embrace, she is yet eager to confess so that she can be coupled with Christ instead.

Feminine images of the soul frequently punctuate Puritan sermon literature. In 1679 William Adams described the minister's work in preparing souls for conversion as "travailing in birth with Souls till Christ be formed in them." [43] He compared the soul in its natural state to a wilderness, "barren and unfruitful, bringing forth no fruit to God, but wild fruits of sin." Once these unregenerate souls shifted their devotion from Satan to Christ upon conversion, they "shall be changed, tilled, converted and made fruitful, to bring forth fruits of holiness unto God." [44] "Fertile and fruitful" described the converted soul; the reprobate soul, possessed by Satan, remained "barren of all grace and goodness." [45]

The representation of the soul as a woman invited metaphors of fecundity and sexuality. Anne Bradstreet portrayed the eyes and ears as the doors of the soul, "through which innumerable objects enter," but the soul is never satisfied. Borrowing an image from the book of Proverbs, she likened the soul to "the daughters of the horseleach"; it "cries, 'Give, give'; and which is most strange, the more it receives, the more empty it finds itself and sees an impossibility ever to be filled but by Him in whom all fullness dwells." [46] In Bradstreet's vision, the feminine soul needed a virile Christ to satisfy her otherwise insatiable desires.

An English minister named Simmons used similar sexual imagery. Like

43. Adams, *The Necessity of the Pouring Out of the Spirit*, A4. Samuel Willard also used the metaphor of birth. "They are in travailing pain," he said of the sinner whose soul remained reprobate. See Willard, *Compleat Body*, 230.

44. Adams, *Necessity of the Pouring Out*, 4. For an interesting discussion of landscape description in terms of female sexuality and motherhood, see Annette Kolodny, *The Lay of the Land: Metaphor as Experience and History in American Life and Letters* (Chapel Hill, N.C., 1975).

45. Adams, *Necessity of the Pouring Out*, 18. The laity conceived of sin and the soul similarly. Robert Daniel, one of Thomas Shepard's congregants, found his soul empty of all goodness and admitted in his conversion narrative: "I find myself barren and fruitless." See *Thomas Shepard's Confessions*, ed. George Selement and Bruce C. Wooley, Publications of the Colonial Society of Massachusetts, *Collections*, no. 58 (Boston, 1981), 61.

46. Anne Bradstreet, "Meditations Divine and Moral," in *The Works of Anne Bradstreet*, ed. Jeannine Hensley (Cambridge, Mass., 1967), 282. The "daughters of the horseleach" comes from Proverbs 30:15: "The leech has two daughters; / 'Give', says one, and 'Give', says the other. / Three things there are which will never be satisfied, / four which never say, 'Enough!' / The grave and a barren womb, / a land thirsty for water / and fire that never says, 'Enough!'"

Bradstreet, he conceived of the eyes as the "port-holes" of the soul, through which "sin and Satan creep in at." He cautioned, "If those doors stand wide open for all comers and goers, either your soul, Dinah-like, will be gadding out, or Satan will be getting in, by which the poor soul will be defiled and defloured."[47] Simmons recalled Dinah, the daughter of Jacob, who left the protection of her father and brothers and was raped by Shechem, son of Hamor the Hivite.[48] Like Dinah, the soul left unguarded would fall victim to Satan's invasion; his potent intrusion was best described in sexual terms, as a rape.

The feminine soul thus was insatiable, driven by almost physical desires, as Samuel Willard argued in his *Sacramental Meditations:* "The soul of man must have something to live upon, that is the great want, and for this want the creature hath no supply." Like a growling stomach, Thomas Shepard suggested, the soul "must have something to quiet and comfort it."[49] Ironically, the active pursuit of sustenance and spiritual fulfillment was not only futile, given the soul's unrelenting appetite but invited Satan's abuse, conceived as rape and possession.

Christ and Satan, then, were viewed as aggressively masculine warriors, battling for the feminine soul's fidelity. Unconverted souls, ministers warned, unwittingly conspired with the forces of Satan and "spen[t] all their days in *Continual Rebellions*" against God.[50] As general, Satan showed little regard or mercy for his own troops. The soul thus occupied a dangerous position; even if she were an unwitting conscript in Satan's legion, she had to defend herself against the devil himself. As Bradstreet

47. Rev. Mr. Simmons, "How may we get rid of spiritual sloth, and know when our activity in duty is from the spirit of God?" in *Puritan Sermons, 1659–1689: Being the Morning Exercises at Cripplegate, St. Giles in the Fields, and in Southwark by Seventy-Five Ministers of the Gospel In or Near London,* ed. James Nichols, 6 vols. (Wheaton, Ill., 1981), 1:439. Samuel Willard similarly described the eyes as "the Soul's *Looking-Glasses,* to take in Visible Objects, and to turn every way." See Willard, *Compleat Body,* 123.

48. See Genesis 34. Although Shechem later wanted to marry Dinah, her brothers avenged their sister's dishonor by killing all the males in the city.

49. Samuel Willard, *Some Brief Sacramental Meditations, Preparatory for Communion, at the Great Ordinance of the Supper* (Boston, 1711), 21–22; Shepard, *Works,* 2:28. Kathleen Verduin notes the nearly physical desires of the soul in its pursuit of happiness in "Our Cursed Natures," 236.

50. Cotton Mather, *Triparadisus,* pt. 3, sec. 8, unpublished manuscript, Mather Family Papers, 1613–1819, octavo volume no. 49, American Antiquarian Society, Worcester, Mass.

and Simmons cautioned, the soul had to shield herself from Satan's advances so that she would not be "defiled and defloured." [51]

During the witchcraft trials the unfulfilled feminine soul, quick to succumb to the devil's possession, became equated with dissatisfied women, subjects primed for the devil's intrusion. The ministers taught that Satan tortured and weakened the body in order to dominate the soul, and the laity interpreted that message quite literally; that interpretation affected the understanding of sin, the soul, and the body in unanticipated ways. To lay people's minds it seemed that the weaker bodies of women rendered their souls more accessible to Satan. The clergy did not disagree. John Cotton succinctly described how sin, the soul, and Satan were related: "When a man wittingly and willingly commits any knowne sinne, he doth as actually give his Soule to the Devill, as a Witch doth her body and soule; we thereby renounce the covenant of God, and Satan takes possession of us." [52] Cotton made a distinction between sinners and witches; Satan possessed the souls of all sinners alike, but witches, whom he assumed were women, compounded their crime.

The witch's surrender was explicit; not only did her body falter and her soul submit, but in addition the witch explicitly enlisted to promote the devil's purpose. The witch acted aggressively. Her soul specifically chose the devil, instead of passively waiting for Christ, and she purposely allowed the devil to use her body. She presumably gave the devil permission to commandeer her body—her shape—in order to recruit more witches and perform maleficium. Thus, the assertive witch contrasted with the passive fallen sinner.

In both old and New England, Puritans conceived of women as the weaker sex. [53] In seventeenth-century England some debated whether this

51. Michael Wigglesworth also bemoaned the impurities of a sinful soul: "that I should break my covenant with the Lord Christ and prostitute my soul unto vanity." See Edmund S. Morgan, ed., "The Diary of Michael Wigglesworth," Publications of the Colonial Society of Massachusetts, no. 35 (Boston, 1946), 393.

52. Cotton, *Way of Life*, 5. See Chapter 4 for a discussion of the relationship between sin and witchcraft. Sinners knew that every sin implicitly forged a covenant with Satan, which would ultimately cast them into hell. The implicit covenant with the devil was made literal and explicit during the witchcraft episodes.

53. For an interesting discussion of seventeenth-century English attitudes toward women's weaknesses, see Antonia Fraser, *The Weaker Vessel* (New York, 1984), 1–5. On the liminal, spiritual state of pregnancy, see Mack, *Visionary Women*, 35–44. For the New England experience, see Lyle Koehler, *A Search for Power: The 'Weaker Sex' in Seventeenth-Century New England* (Urbana, Ill., 1980).

weakness extended to women's spiritual or moral state as well. Joseph Swetnam argued in *The Arraignment of Lewd, Idle, Froward and Unconstant Women* that women were inherently evil. He wrote, "Then who can but say, that Women spring from the Devil, whose heads, hands, hearts, minds, and souls are evil?" His book came under attack, but it nonetheless went through six editions between 1615 and 1702.[54] Meric Casaubon, an English scholar with a special interest in witchcraft and possession, disagreed. It was not, he contended, that women were evil but that their brains were weaker, and so they were more likely to be caught in Satan's traps. He wrote of women, "all men know [them] to be naturally weaker of brain, and easiest to be infatuated and deluded."[55] Swetnam blamed all of woman—her body as well as her soul—for her evil nature; Casaubon blamed specific physical limitations. A weaker brain was quite distinct from an evil soul; seventeenth-century opinion considered the brain a part of the physical anatomy, like the liver or the spleen, whereas the soul was an immortal entity.[56]

New Englanders may have shared some of Swetnam's sentiments, but publicly they confined their notions of women's weakness to their physical states. The colonists shared with their English brethren the belief that women's bodies were physically weaker than men's and subject to more debilitating illness. An English midwife, Jane Sharp, wrote in a 1671 midwifery manual "that the Female sex are subject to more diseases by odds than the Male Kind are, and therefore it is reason that great care should be had for the cure of that sex that is the weaker and most subject to infirmities in some respects above the other."[57] New Englanders concurred. Cotton Mather explained in his *Angel of Bethesda*, the only complete colonial medical guide, that "the Sex that is called, *The Weaker Vessel,* has not only a share with us, in the most of our Distempers, but also is liable to many that may be called, Its *Peculiar Weaknesses.*" He

54. Joseph Swetnam, *The Arraignment of Lewd, Idle, Froward, and Unconstant Women* (London, 1634), 15, quoted in Fraser, *Weaker Vessel,* 2.

55. Meric Casaubon, *A Treatise Concerning Enthusiasme, As it is an Effect of Nature: but is Mistaken by Many for Either Divine Inspiration, or Diabolical Possession* (London, 1655), 119.

56. See Cohen, *God's Caress,* 39.

57. Jane Sharp, *The Midwives Book. Or the Whole Art of Midwifry Discovered. Directing Childbearing Women how to Behave Themselves In their Conception, Breeding, Bearing, and Nursing of Children* (London, 1671), 250.

The devil embraces a woman, from Ulrich Molitor, *De Lamiis et Phitonicis Mulieribus,* 1490. Although their theology challenged earlier images of the carnal, lustful woman, Puritans nonetheless believed that Satan attacked the soul by assaulting the body—as in this fifteenth-century image—and that the devil more easily and frequently breached the "weaker vessels" of women (courtesy Beinecke Rare Book and Manuscript Library, Yale University, New Haven, Conn.).

reported that women's "Tender and Feeble Constitutions" were subject to a "Variety of Distempers."[58]

As we have seen, the feminine souls of women *and* men were responsible for sinfulness and were all too likely to fall into Satan's deadly embrace. During the witchcraft episodes, however, the devil consistently and disproportionately seemed to torture women, trying to obtain their signatures in his black book, win their souls, and use their bodies to molest and recruit others. Given the gendered social and theological arrangements of seventeenth-century New England, we should not find this bias surprising.

Applying the teachings of their ministers rather literally, the laity expected that women's weaker bodies would suffer more severely than men's in a world besieged by Satan's wrath. Because women's bodies lacked the strength and vitality of men's, according to popular thought, the devil could more frequently and successfully gain access to and possess women's souls, thus bringing them, according to Deodat Lawson, "into *full* Submission, and entire *Resignation* to his Hellish Designs."[59]

The devil pursued souls with particular vigor and success during witchcraft outbreaks; yet he did not display any new methods or depart in any significant way from his well-known devices. Satan perhaps asserted himself more physically and immediately in these incidents. Indeed, the evocative language in which the clergy expressed God's wrath toward those who refused to convert may have led the laity to interpret God's anger and the devil's torments so literally. But the powers of Satan nevertheless corresponded to those detailed by Puritan ministers.[60] The

58. Cotton Mather, *The Angel of Bethesda* (1724; Barre, Mass., 1972), 233. Women's lives were threatened by the dangers of childbirth. It is estimated that one woman died for every 150 births until as late as 1930. Today in the United States one woman out of 10,000 dies in childbirth. See Laurel Thatcher Ulrich, "'The Living Mother of a Living Child': Midwifery and Mortality in Post-Revolutionary New England," *William and Mary Quarterly*, 3rd ser., 46 (1989), 27–48. See also Ulrich, *A Midwife's Tale: The Life of Martha Ballard, Based on Her Diary, 1785–1812* (New York, 1990).

59. Lawson, *Christ's Fidelity*, 27.

60. William Adams, for example, said of the unconverted, "their miseryes and sorrows will be like to grow more intense and sharp, pinching and distressing, to have more and more of divine anger in them." He described God's spiritual punishments as if they were physical afflictions: "The Lord will make *more and more* wrath appear in his Judgments upon such a People, make his Arrows in their hearts sharp, cuting and piercing." See Adams, *Necessity of the Pouring Out*, 10.

laity saw Satan in various guises, often in the accused witch's bodily shape. As we have seen, civic and religious leaders disputed whether the specter was a sign that the one impersonated had actually compacted with Satan or whether Satan could simply assume the bodily shape of an innocent person. Either way, the clergy and the laity believed that the devil, in any form, meant to molest the bodies of potential recruits in order to capture their souls.

Anxious to dominate their souls, Satan harassed his victims' bodies first. The language of the indictments brought against the accused illustrates the extent of the agonies; its nearly formulaic repetition attests to the ubiquitous belief in Satan's physical powers. The indictments read that the victims were "Tortured Afflicted Consumed pined Wasted and Tormented."[61] Presumably, Satan had already possessed the body and soul of his primary victim, the witch, and so with her permission, and through her body, he attacked yet more victims. The accused woman Mary Bridges testified that "the way of her afflicting was by sticking pins into things and Clothes & think of hurting them."[62]

Those claiming such affliction described their tortures more graphically. One woman, Mary Walcott, swore that the apparition of Goody Buckly came and "hurt me and tortord me most dreadfully by pinching and choaking of me and twesting of my nick several times" in order to persuade her to sign a covenant with Satan and renounce God. Likewise, Susannah Sheldon told the court, "I have very often ben most greviously tortored by Apperishtion of Sarah Good who has most dredfully afflected me by bitting pricking and pinching me and almost choaking me to death." Sheldon recalled that on June 26, 1692, Good "most violently pulled down my head behind a Cheast and tyed my hands together with a whele band & allmost Choaked me to death."[63] The court records abound with women testifying that the devil, usually but not always in the shape of the accused, brutally tormented their bodies and tempted them to sign his book in blood, signifying his possession of their souls.

61. Paul Boyer and Stephen Nissenbaum, eds., *The Salem Witchcraft Papers: Verbatim Transcripts of the Legal Documents of the Salem Witchcraft Outbreak of 1692*, 3 vols. (New York, 1977), 1:57. This indictment is found in most of the trials.
62. Ibid., 1:135.
63. Ibid., 1:149, 2:374.

The devil's victims usually tried to endure his torture of their bodies and to resist relinquishing their souls, though with mixed results. Mercy Lewis told the court that the devil came to her in the shape of the accused George Jacobs Sr. and urged her to join his minions. "Because I would not yeald to his hellish temtations," she surmised, "he did tortor me most cruelly . . . and allmost redy to pull all my bones out of joynt . . . but being up held by an Allmighty hand . . . I indured his tortors that night." The devil could damage her body but not ultimately master it, and so he would not have her soul. The possessed Mary Warren, however, owned that she "yeilded," and "was undon body and soul," and that she did it "for eas to her body: not for any good of her soul." [64]

The devil often appeared directly to his prospective converts, and he could be so persuasive that some women confessed to giving themselves completely to him. Sarah Bridges testified that "the Divel Came Somtimes like a bird Som times like abare Sometimes like aman," and she admitted "Renouncing God and Christ & Gave her Soul & Body to the Devil." [65] Bridges acknowledged that the devil threatened to kill her if she confessed, but still she told the court that she used to "afflict persons by Squezing her hands & Sticking pins in her Clothes." Mary Barker also confessed that she was "afrayd She has Given up her Self Soul & body to the Divel." [66] These two and many others admitted that the devil had urged them to inscribe his book and that they had capitulated. Once they signed over their souls, they were expected to inflict harm on others, while the devil seized their shapes to attack, entrap, and recruit additional witches for his service. The devil's victims endured affliction either from the devil directly or from the shape of a witch.

Women suffered afflictions particular to their sex. It was not unusual, Puritans believed, for a witch who had given herself body and soul to Satan to have suckled familiars, or imps. These little creatures, often animals or small, strange beasts, were thought to have received nourishment in the form of blood from the witch's body. Often the familiars sucked at the breasts, but they were as likely to latch onto any unusual marking, or

64. Ibid., 2:483, 3:797.
65. Ibid., 1:139, 141. Giving oneself "soul and body" did not necessarily have a sexual meaning, although as I suggest below, the devil was considered capable of using the witch's sexual body. See Chapter 4 for a fuller discussion of the meanings of confession.
66. Ibid., 60.

witch's teat.[67] The West Indian woman Tituba told the court that she saw a small yellow bird "suck [Sarah] Good betwene the fore finger & Long finger upon the Right Hand." She added that sometimes she saw a cat along with the bird, and one time she noticed Good with two kinds of bizarre creatures. One, which had wings and two legs and a head like a woman, subsequently turned into a woman; the other was "a thing all over hairy, all the face hayry & a long nose & I don't know how to tell how the face looks w'th two Leggs, itt goeth upright & is about two or three foot high & goeth upright like a man."[68] In Connecticut the authorities searched the body of Mercy Disbrough and found "on her secret parts growing within ye lep of ye same a los [loose] pees of skin and when puld it is near an Inch long somewhat in form of ye fingar of a glove flatted."[69]

The creatures signified that the devil had taken possession of these women's bodies, and now they, as well as the devil himself, had the right to suck their blood. Susannah Sheldon, an eyewitness against Bridget Bishop, testified that Bishop "puled out her brest and the black man gave her a thing like a blake pig it had no haire on it and shee put it to her brest and gave it suck and when it had sucked on brest shee put it the other and gave it suck their then she gave it to the blak man." Although Sheldon claimed this creature suckled at her breasts, Bishop still underwent a court-appointed search for likely spots where an imp might nurse.

67. On the relationship between the humoral theory of medicine and breast feeding during the colonial period, see Paula A. Treckel, "Breastfeeding and Maternal Sexuality in Colonial America," *Journal of Interdisciplinary History* 20 (Summer 1989), 25–51. Treckel explains that menstruation was believed to be the elimination of bad humors from the body. During pregnancy the menstrual blood was thought to nourish the fetus until birth and then to change color in the womb and flow into the breasts after birth to feed the baby. Presumably, a witch suckling an imp would be providing the familiar with blood rather than milk, unless she also was breast-feeding an infant.

68. *Salem Witchcraft Papers*, 3:752. John Putnam Demos has commented on the implications of women's apparently unique ability to nurture Satan and his imps, maintaining that the witch and her imp presented a perverted picture of human motherhood. See Demos, *Entertaining Satan*, 179–81. Lyndal Roper says that witchcraft accusations in sixteenth- and seventeenth-century Germany most often involved motherhood motifs, including giving birth, lying-in, feeding, child death, and anxieties involving child separation. See Roper, *Oedipus and the Devil*, 202–18.

69. John Taylor, *The Witchcraft Delusion in Connecticut, 1647–1697* (New York, 1908), 45.

The witch's familiar signified that the devil had taken possession of a woman's body; creatures such as the one in this seventeenth-century woodcut, as well as the devil himself, were
thought to receive nourishment in the form of blood from the witch's body, usually, but not
always, from her breasts (from Cotton Mather, *On Witchcraft* [Mt. Vernon, N.Y.: Peter
Pauper Press, Inc., 1950]. Reprinted with permission).

Five women found on her body "a preternathurall Excresence of flesh
between the pudendum and Anus much like to Tetts & not usuall in
women." [70] The testimony, together with spectral evidence, damned her.
Despite her repeated protestations of innocence, Bishop was hanged as
a witch.

The witch might also be expected to yield her body sexually to the
devil's imps. In medieval folklore, the witch's familiar, or incubus, had
intercourse with the witch. The learned tracts on witchcraft written in
the colonies, however, such as Increase Mather's, were skeptical: "What
fables are there concerning *incubi* and *succubae* and of men begotten by

70. *Salem Witchcraft Papers,* 1:106, 107.

daemons! No doubt but the devil may delude the fancy, that one of his vassals shall think (as the witch at Hartford did) that he has carnal and cursed communion with them beyond what is real." Mather admitted, "Nor is it impossible for [the devil] to assume a dead body, or to form a lifeless one out of the elements, and therewith to make his witches become guilty of sodomy." Later in the text he reconsidered this point: "But to imagine that spirits shall really generate bodies, is irrational." [71] In the colonial witchcraft trials, this traditional element was not emphasized, although the possibility of such behavior was certainly intimated. The creatures that sucked at women's breasts and at other sexually sensitive areas of their bodies may have been sucking for sexual pleasure rather than nourishment.

Witches' bodies no longer belonged to themselves; Satan could take them wherever he pleased to use as he wished. The devil appeared in the forms of both men and women witches, but when a specter assaulted a victim in a sexual way, it was always in the shape of a woman. Men (and occasionally women as well) told of waking at night to find the specter of a witch sitting on top of them in bed. References to sexual activity were veiled but unmistakable. When Samuel Gray woke to see Bridget Bishop's apparition standing between the baby's cradle and his bed, he testified, "he said to her in the name of God what doe you come for. then she vanished away soe he Locked the dore againe & went to bed and between sleepeing & wakeing he felt some thing Come to his mouth or lipes cold, & there upon started & looked up & againe did see the same woman." In a similarly suggestive tale, Bernard Peach claimed that Susannah Martin "drew up his body into a heape and Lay upon him about an hour and half or 2 hours, in all which taim this deponent coold not stir nor speake." [72] New Englanders did not typically interpret the devil's intrusion in sexual terms; yet they sometimes understood his interaction with women witches in particular ways in light of their sexuality and their female bodies.

Satan also tried to capture men's souls, but his torture of their bodies was markedly different and less drastic than that of women. Men were not as likely to be seen suckling imps, although their bodies were searched

71. Increase Mather, *Remarkable Providences Illustrative of the Earlier Days of American Colonisation* (Boston, 1684), 124–25.
72. *Salem Witchcraft Papers*, 1:94, 2:562.

during the trials, and the investigations occasionally found evidence of such activity. During the examination of two accused men, George Burroughs and George Jacobs, both of whom were eventually hanged, the examiners found nothing unusual on Burrough's body, but Jacobs was not so lucky. The four men reported "3. tetts w'ch according to the best of our Judgement wee think is not naturall for wee run a pinn through 2 of them and he was not sinceible of it." As far as the court was concerned, the three abnormal markings, one in Jacob's mouth, one on his shoulder blade, and one on his hip, signified the devil's possession of his body and soul.[73]

But the devil's possession of men contrasted with his domination of women because New Englanders expected that men's heartier bodies were more difficult and less tempting objects of the devil's attacks. The assumption that the devil had a different relationship with men was never explicitly articulated, but the incidents recounted at the trials can provide us with some insight into Puritans' thinking about gender and the affliction of evil. First, witches were less likely to seduce men than women into the devil's service.[74] And when men described their encounters with the accused, their testimony centered on bizarre acts of maleficence, rather than the physical harm allegedly caused by the witch's shape. Samuel Endicott charged Mary Bradbury with selling the captain of his ship butter that turned rancid after he and his crew were at sea for three weeks. She was at fault whether she had been negligent or fraudulent or had used magic to transform good butter into bad, and he did not doubt that she was a witch. As additional evidence, Endicott described a violent storm that cost the ship its mainmast, its rigging, and fifteen horses. The ship sprang a leak and took on four feet of water, and its crew was forced to unload the cargo. When they came upon land, Endicott saw "the appearance of a woman from her middle upwards, haveing a white Capp and white neck-cloth on her, w'ch then affrighted him very much."[75] Mary Bradbury's shape frightened Endicott, and her misdeeds plagued him, but he suffered no direct, violent, physical abuse.

73. Ibid., 1:159.
74. For an explanation that emphasizes sexual seduction, see Karlsen, *Devil in the Shape of a Woman*, 135. Karlsen notes that 86 percent of possession cases in colonial New England were women.
75. *Salem Witchcraft Papers*, 1:122–23, 2:368.

Often the male victims focused on harm to their personal property. Samuel Abbey told the court that after Sarah Good left his house, he began to lose cattle "after an unusuall Manner, in drupeing Condition." He lost seventeen cattle in two years, in addition to sheep and hogs, and he believed that the devil and Sarah Good were responsible. John Roger testified that after an argument with Martha Carrier seven years before, two of his sows were lost and one of them was found dead near the Carriers' house with both of its ears cut off.[76]

Even more often it was men's families who suffered, their wives and their children.[77] Although William Beale testified that he awoke one morning because "a very greate & wracking paine had seized uppon my body," his primary piece of evidence against Philip English was that his son, who had been expected to recover from smallpox, died later that day after Beale saw English's shape upon the chimney.[78] Samuel Perley complained against Elizabeth How that she stuck his ten-year-old daughter and his wife with pins. Astonished at the brutality, he claimed, "i could never aflict a dog as goode how aflicts mi wife." Perley's daughter "Pine d a wai [pined away] to skin and bone and ended her sorrowful life."[79] The devil, in the shapes of the accused, tortured these two men, but not by destroying their own bodies.

When men were direct victims of physical violence at the hands of the accused, the scenes were far less dramatic. Samuel Smith, for example, heeded a threat from the alleged witch, Mary Easty, and as he walked

76. Ibid., 1:190. Thieves would sometimes cut off sows' ears so that they could no longer be identified, but Roger interpreted this incident differently.

77. Cotton Mather's account of the sufferings that the Goodwin children endured at the hands of Satan are particularly poignant. Six of the family's seven children experienced extraordinary misery. Mather recorded, "They would at times ly in a benummed condition; and be drawn together as those that are ty'd Neck and Heels . . . and presently be stretched out, yea, drawn Backwards, to such a degree that it was fear'd the very skin of the Bellies would have crack'd. They would make most pitteous out-cries, that they were cut with Knives, and struck with Blows that they could not bear." See Cotton Mather, *Memorable Providences, Relating to Witchcrafts and Possessions* (1689), in *Narratives of the Witchcraft Cases,* ed. George Lincoln Burr (New York, 1914), 102.

78. *Salem Witchcraft Papers,* 1:317–18. There were exceptions; a few men testified to bodily harm. Benjamin Abbott, for example, suffered a painful sore and was scheduled to have it lanced by a doctor, but it disappeared when the accused woman, Martha Carrier, was led away by the constable. See 1:189.

79. Ibid., 2:439.

past a stone wall on his way home he "Received a little blow on my shoulder with I know not what and the stone wall rattleed very much which affrighted me." [80] In that same situation a woman might have suffered untold bodily fits and injuries.

On the rare occasions when male victims complained of severe physical abuse, it was generally at the hands of another man. Apparently, even with the aid of the devil, women were not physically capable of doing great harm to the bodies of men. The aforementioned William Beale accused Philip English of causing the great pain that seized his body. Similarly, Benjamin Gould testified that Giles Corey, who was later pressed to death, induced "shuch a paine in one of my feet that I Cold not ware my shoe for 2: or 3.days." [81] Eighty-one-year-old Bray Wilkins likewise was convinced that it was John Willard who had brought on a painful urinary tract obstruction. He told the court, "I continued so in grievous pain & my water much stopt till s'd Willard was in chains." After Willard pleaded his innocence, Bray Wilkins testified that he "was taken in the sorest distress & misery my water being turned into real blood, or of a bloody colour & the old pain returned excessively as before." [82]

Characteristically, Satan granted extraordinary power to his accomplices, either clairvoyance or great bodily strength.[83] In keeping with seventeenth-century notions, Satan bestowed unequal powers on men and women. He endowed his male witches with unusual strength, and so made even other men vulnerable to the male witches' physical violence. Women's bodies he gave only enough strength to torture their female victims, often, apparently, through their mere presence and without any particular bodily force. Female witches seemed able only to abuse other women, whereas male witches could torture naturally weaker women as well as typically robust and potent men.

George Burroughs, a former minister at Salem and a condemned witch, epitomized the strength that Satan could contribute to male collaborators. After the trial, one eyewitness, Thomas Greenslit, revealed that he

80. Ibid., 1:301.
81. Ibid., 244.
82. Ibid., 3:848.
83. For a discussion of the powers Satan bestowed, see D. P. Walker, *Unclean Spirits: Possession and Exorcism in France and England in the Late Sixteenth and Early Seventeenth Centuries* (Philadelphia, 1981), 9–17. Also see Increase Mather, *Cases of Conscience Concerning Evil Spirits* (Boston, 1693); and Increase Mather, *Remarkable Providences*.

had seen Burroughs exhibiting strength so extraordinary that it could only have come with the devil's assistance. Greenslit saw Burroughs "lift and hold Out a gunn of Six foot barrell or thereabouts putting the forefinger of his right hand into the Muzle of s'd gunn and So held it Out at Armes End Only with that finger." Simon Willard concurred with this report; he had heard that "s'd gun was about or near seven foot barrill: and very hevie: I then tried to hold out s'd gun with both hands: but could not do it long enough to take sight." Four others had heard that Burroughs had carried a barrel of molasses with only two fingers for some distance without putting it down.[84]

Interestingly, only the male witnesses offered unusual strength as evidence that Burroughs had colluded with Satan and become a witch; his terrible strength, in sharp contrast to their own limited abilities, resonated with their notions of manliness and their expectations about how the devil might empower male witches. The women who testified against Burroughs claimed bodily afflictions similar to those they attributed to female witches. No extra strength was required to afflict women.

Since Puritans believed that Satan designed his attacks to fit his quarry, it made sense that women and men perceived Satan's tortures differently. Just as female victims were more likely to be physically tormented, the women witches themselves—the majority of the accused—also experienced greater bodily distress as Satan destroyed their bodies to capture their souls. Though men's bodies were hardly invulnerable, in women the devil sought easier marks.

Curiously, although a weak body and a vulnerable soul left one open to Satan, they might also encourage one's faith in God. Indeed, Cotton Mather and other ministers suggested that the frailty of women's bodies, compounded by the dangers of childbirth, gave women more reason to seek the Lord since death was more immediate.[85] Anne Bradstreet, bemoaning an illness that had plagued her for months, hoped that her soul would gain some advantage while her body was faltering. Accepting the belief that God inflicted bodily illness only for the good of the soul, she

84. *Salem Witchcraft Papers,* 1:160–78, quotations on 160–61.
85. Mather's suggestion perhaps helps to explain why more women than men became church members, especially later in the seventeenth century. See Cotton Mather, *Ornaments for the Daughters of Zion* (Boston, 1692); Benjamin Colman, *The Honour and Happiness of the Vertuous Woman* (Boston, 1716).

mused, "I hope my soul shall flourish while my body decays, and the weakness of this outward man shall be a means to strengthen my inner man." [86] Echoing Samuel Willard's biological reference to the feminine soul, Bradstreet called her soul the "inner man" and tried to dissociate its spiritual strength from her body's physical weaknesses.[87] She cultivated resignation: "And if He knows that weakness and a frail body is the best to make me a vessel fit for His use why should I not bear it, not only willingly but joyfully." Bradstreet went so far as to suggest that good health might divert her from the Lord. She wrote, "The Lord knows I dare not desire that health that sometimes I have had, lest my heart should be drawn from Him, and set upon the world." [88]

Perhaps women's weaker bodies brought them closer to God, as Bradstreet hoped. Women, then, had a particular potential for goodness, but their more fragile bodies also exposed them to Satan, perhaps encouraging a peculiar potential for evil—Eve's legacy. In the context of the witchcraft outbreaks, a time of extraordinary uncertainty and fear, New Englanders focused on the darker side of womanhood, emphasizing the vulnerability of women's bodies and souls to the devil, rather than their openness to regeneration. Women as witches were so threatening because their souls had asserted themselves to ally with Satan. Too impatient or too weak to wait passively for Christ's advance, witches strode out upon the devil's path. In the course of living their errand in the North American wilderness, Puritans thus constructed a gendered ideology and society that conceived of women, ironically, as closer both to God and to Satan.

86. Hensley, *Works of Anne Bradstreet*, 255. See also Hall, *Worlds of Wonder*, 198–210, for a discussion of the colonists' attitude toward illness and prayer. For example, Samuel Sewall recorded in his diary a note he posted on the church door concerning his son, Joseph, who, "being, after long sickness, in some good measure Restored, desires Thanks may be given to GOD: and begs Prayers, that he may profit by the Affliction." See *The Diary of Samuel Sewall, 1674–1729*, ed. M. Halsey Thomas, 2 vols. (New York, 1973), 2:695. Hall examines similar notes by Sewall in *Worlds of Wonder*, 232.

87. Bradstreet did not consistently refer to the body as male. In a poem titled "The Flesh and the Spirit," she posited the body and the soul as twin sisters, feuding with each other. The soul deplores that the body has made her into a virtual slave: "How oft thy slave, hast thou me made, / When I believed what thou hast said, / . . . My greatest honour it shall be / When I am victor over thee." See Hensley, *Works of Anne Bradstreet*, 216.

88. Ibid., 254.

4

❧

GENDER AND THE
MEANINGS OF CONFESSION

BY the end of the seventeenth century, more and more women were becoming brides of Christ, joining their churches as full members. Yet, ironically, the avalanche of accusations and confessions at Salem seems to suggest the opposite, that women were flocking to Satan. The outbreak at Salem is particularly vexing for historians in several ways: in addition to demonizing women, it reversed the seventeenth-century trend of acquittal for suspected witches; it witnessed women accusing other women more than had been typical in previous witch-hunting episodes; and it generated puzzling confessions from some of the accused women.[1] Bernard Rosenthal has shown that confession and strategic accusation of others were the two surest ways to avoid execution oneself.[2] Without denying the possibility of such calculation, I want to explore the causative influence of women's sense of their own depravity and their recognition of a similar basic corruption in other women. Simply put, women

---

1. On the peculiarities of Salem, see Bernard Rosenthal, *Salem Story: Reading the Witch Trials of 1692* (Cambridge, 1993), 1–7. Carol Karlsen argues that most of the witchcraft accusations throughout the seventeenth century were made by men, but in fact her evidence demonstrates that at Hartford and at Salem the primary accusations were made by young women against older women. See Carol F. Karlsen, *The Devil in the Shape of a Woman: Witchcraft in Colonial New England* (New York, 1987), 24–27, 222–23. In these cases, in contrast to others that Karlsen analyzes, property was a much less important issue, and the crisis precipitated not a solitary trial but a massacre.

2. Rosenthal, *Salem Story*, esp. 48–50.

were more likely than men to be convinced of their own complicity with
the devil, and given such convictions about themselves, they could more
easily imagine that other women were equally damned. Although some
clergy, magistrates, and laity voiced skepticism throughout the proceedings, the crisis escalated. For women as well as men, the relationship between womanhood and witchcraft was so firmly entrenched, as we shall
see, that women's accusations of other women and women's confessions
of their own collusion achieved at least a short-lived deadly credibility.

Women's and men's testimony against those accused was congruent
with female and male notions of sinfulness. Men typically presented instances of maleficium—cows made sick or butter turned rancid—to prove
a woman's witchcraft,[3] just as they renounced specific sins to testify to
conversion. Women were more likely to present spectral evidence. In all
the cases in which the accused were executed, there was invisible pinching and torturing of accusers during public examinations.[4] The pain they
displayed seemed a clear demonstration of a consensual pact between the
devil and the "witch." A witch's specter rendered explicit and immediate
what the mere fact of her womanhood made only implicit and potential—her inherent unworthiness and entanglement with the devil.

After the Hartford outbreak of 1662, one might have predicted that
witchcraft accusations were on the wane, vanishing with the rise in secu-
larism, which so many Puritan ministers decried. The intensity of the
Salem outbreak seems particularly absurd, given this trend. After the
Hartford crisis, in which approximately thirteen people were accused
and four executed, ministers and magistrates avoided the opportunity to
prosecute those suspected of witchcraft.[5] But at Salem their doubts may
have been eased (or at least temporarily suspended) because women
themselves, the brides of Christ, brought forth so many clearly convincing cases, complete with the specters to prove the devil's intrigues.

3. See Karlsen, *Devil in the Shape of a Woman*, 40; and Rosenthal, *Salem Story*,
56–60. Richard Weisman, *Witchcraft, Magic, and Religion in Seventeenth-Century Massachusetts* (Amherst, Mass., 1984), esp. 96–112, has interpreted the varying kinds of testimony brought against the accused as a split between elite and popular culture. What the
court sought to prove, he says, was the signing of the devil's pact, whereas the lay public was
content with proving instances of maleficium. The split, in my view, was gendered rather
than based on lay-clerical divisions.
4. Rosenthal, *Salem Story*, 44, 68.
5. On the official restraint before and especially after the Hartford outbreak, see Karlsen,
Devil in the Shape of a Woman, 27; and Weisman, *Witchcraft, Magic, and Religion*, 113–14.

Women's accusations against other women at Salem might be explained, in part, by the rage particular accusers felt toward those whom they accused, as Carol Karlsen suggests. Victims themselves of precarious economic and social circumstances, these young women perhaps feared for their future, worrying that they would end up alone, with no one to establish their dowries and find them husbands.[6] But I think it likely that envy and guilt mixed with rage to fuel their indictments. Many of the accusers had grown up in religious households, where they developed a strong notion of good and evil and, most important, the imminent possibility of their own damnation. Accusations of the pious, such as Rebecca Nurse, suggest not merely the rage of the disadvantaged but the envy of those who feared they would never be allowed to achieve such prominence and respectability. Finally, if the accusers had doubts about their own regeneration and perhaps about the reprobation and maleficence of the pious women they indicted, they may have felt the additional guilt inherent in giving false testimony before the court and God. In such cases, could renewed, more vigorous accusation provide a measure of self-justification?[7]

The community accepted the surprising shift in the pattern of witchcraft prosecution and believed the main group of accusers because the spectral evidence struck them as particularly compelling and because, as we have seen, women's vulnerability to Satan—even women who demonstrated their closeness to Christ—was even more plausible. By the end of the seventeenth century, women were joining the church in numbers equal or greater to those of male converts.[8] Men seem to have been think-

6. On the persistence of the myth that the original accusations sprang from fortune-telling sessions with Tituba, see Rosenthal, *Salem Story,* 10–14.

7. My thinking on these issues has been informed by discussions with John Murrin, and I am grateful for his insight and expertise.

8. Cotton Mather confirmed that women church members far outnumbered the men: "There are far more *Godly Women* in the World than there are *Godly Men.* . . . I have seen it without going a Mile from home, That in a Church of between *Three* and *Four* Hundred *Communicants,* there are but few more than *One* Hundred *Men;* all the Rest are *Women.*" See Cotton Mather, *Ornaments for the Daughters of Zion, or the Character and Happiness of a Virtuous Woman* (Cambridge, Mass., 1692), 44–45. See also Harry S. Stout and Catherine A. Brekus, "Declension, Gender, and the 'New Religious History,'" in *Belief and Behavior: Essays in the New Religious History,* ed. Philip R. Vandermeer and Robert P. Swierenga (New Brunswick, N.J., 1991), 15–37; and Gerald F. Moran, "'Sinners Are Turned into Saints in Numbers': Puritanism and Revivalism in Colonial Connecticut," ibid., 38–62. On the relation between declension and male piety, see Mary Maples Dunn, "Saints and Sis-

ing less about questions of salvation and damnation; women more. Yet as increasing numbers of women became church members and seriously contemplated the meaning of conversion and the possibility of their own salvation or damnation, their very faith could damn them. Some pious women found themselves accused of witchcraft by women whose own religious anxieties allowed them to conceive and present damning evidence. Some women denied the charges; others confessed; but all suffered the disadvantage of their womanhood in facing the dangerous and disturbing accusations. We turn now to confessing and denying women and how their responses to the charges fueled the court's willingness to continue and justified its proceedings.

Why would a woman confess to witchcraft? Why would she admit to signing the devil's book and participating in a devil's baptism? Very early in the Salem witchcraft episode of 1692, the court decided not to hang those who confessed, hoping that they could be persuaded to name others involved in this wicked affair. Surely the avenue of escape this decision provided helps to account for many of the approximately fifty confessions. I am not convinced, however, that self-preservation alone explains the admission of guilt at Salem, even though the accused faced the gallows. Furthermore, "Why did they confess?" might not be as pertinent a question to ask as "How did they confess?" Confessors' language suggests that the confessions and denials resonated with women's and men's more general confessions in Puritan churches.

Women and men, we have seen, thought about sin and guilt differently, whether they were applying for church membership or trying to convince the court that they were not witches. Women were more likely to interpret their own sins, no matter how ordinary, as tacit covenants with Satan, spiritual renunciation of God, evidence of their vile natures. Men tended to focus on particular sins such as carnality or Sabbath-breaking. Women were more convinced that they had embraced the devil; men were more confident that they would be able to reform their behavior and turn to God. And so if women believed more generally that they had covenanted with the devil, it did not take much for them to be convinced further that they had in fact accepted a more literal and physical invitation from Satan and become actual witches. During the Salem witchcraft

---

ters: Congregational and Quaker Women in the Early Colonial Period," *American Quarterly* 30 (Winter 1978), 582–601.

trials and other episodes, the distinction between implicit sins, which bound sinners to the devil and would take them to hell, and an explicit pact that turned sinners into witches became blurred, particularly for women.

When Alice Lake of Dorchester was about to be hanged, in 1651, she protested that she "owned nothing of the crime laid to her charge." Yet though she declared herself innocent of witchcraft, she nonetheless believed that she deserved to be exposed as a witch because, according to the minister John Hale, "she had when a single woman play'd the harlot, and being with Child used means to destroy the fruit of her body to conceal her sin and shame." Lake believed that her sexual transgression was enough to make her a witch. Although she had not signed an explicit compact with Satan, she concluded—and apparently Hale concurred— that she had covenanted with him through the commission of her sin.[9]

During the witchcraft episodes, not only when the accused confessed to signing the diabolical covenant with the devil but also when they vehemently denied any familiarity with Satan, like Alice Lake, they often conflated ordinary sins with witchcraft. Their transgressions could suggest, even to the sinners themselves, an insidious merger between regular sins and more active commitment to Satan in the form of witchcraft. At the heart of this ambiguity between sinning and witchcraft was the central idea of the covenant, which Puritans believed could bind them, individually and as a community, to God, but which, in a conflicting and darker manifestation, could chain believers to Satan.

Alice Lake's feminized denial was simultaneously a feminized confession. She disavowed witchcraft practice, yet acknowledged her sinfulness and was hanged; her response reintegrated her into the community, but it did not exonerate her on earth. Forty years later, during the Salem witch trials, however, confession *did* save lives, although the policy was never articulated explicitly. The biblical injunction, "Thou shalt not suffer a witch to live," prevailed in theory, but with reliable witnesses and evidence scarce, nothing was more valuable than an accused woman's confession. Admissions "proved" confessors' guilt, of course, but in practice the court sought confessions for other reasons as well. Convinced that

9. John Hale, *A Modest Enquiry in the Nature of Witchcraft* (Boston, 1702), 18. Hale commented that although Lake "did not effect it, yet she was a murderer in the sight of God for her endeavors, and showed great penitency for that sin." Quoted in David D. Hall, ed., *Witch-hunting in Seventeenth-Century New England* (Boston, 1991), 28.

the devil had confided in his victims, the court prolonged confessors' stays in jail so that they might name other conspirators. In some respects, then, for the court and community "witches" were more valuable alive than dead.

By September 1692 it had become clear that the court's policy of sparing confessors had encouraged (perhaps disingenuous) admissions of guilt. In an effort to stem this tide, the court decided that some confessors would stand trial, although none were hanged.[10] The Salem episode was thus different from previous ones, in which outright confessions were rare and fatal. Nonetheless, ambiguous responses like Alice Lake's exposed the accused woman as a sinner and a "witch." Confessors at Salem, though they survived the ordeal, inculpated themselves similarly.

The confessions and denials of those accused of witchcraft were intimately linked to Puritan women's and men's notions of sin, Satan, and self.[11] And they exhibited Puritan anxieties about secrecy. Presumably a

10. Rosenthal, *Salem Story*, 151–58.

11. The confessions of the accused witches at Salem and elsewhere earlier in the seventeenth century have remained a curiosity for historians of witchcraft. In John Demos's *Entertaining Satan: Witchcraft and the Culture of Early New England* (New York, 1982), confession is not explored at great length, primarily because it was an unusual feature of witchcraft episodes prior to the Salem outbreak. Chadwick Hansen, *Witchcraft at Salem* (New York, 1969), 92–95, asserts that the confessors were probably, like the afflicted girls, "hysterics subject to hallucinations" (94). Unable to find any other reason why they might have offered such elaborate details to the court—far more than were necessary for a confession—Hansen says that contemporaries found the confessions believable because they offered an explanation for the bizarre and frightening events in Salem. Paul Boyer and Stephen Nissenbaum, *Salem Possessed: The Social Origins of Witchcraft* (Cambridge, Mass., 1974), 214–16, emphasize the importance of public confession as a community ritual, through which the accused witch could be reintegrated into the community. Boyer and Nissenbaum contend that the ritual was therapeutic; the confessors admitted to deeds that remained merely "unacknowledged impulses" in both the accusers and the onlookers (215). This explanation helps to account for the court's focus on confession, but not for the confessors' admission of guilt, particularly among those who later recanted. In my view, confessing to witchcraft under certain circumstances was not essentially different from admitting to ordinary sin; in both cases, Puritans believed, the victim was possessed by Satan. What gave the "unacknowledged impulse" such power, then, was the knowledge that accusers and onlookers had sinned themselves and, by implication, made their own covenants with the devil. Weisman, *Witchcraft, Magic, and Religion*, 155–59, places the confessions within the framework of covenant theology, arguing that they served as a form of communal regeneration. He also makes the important point that the incidence of confession was low, despite emotional and some physical torture, until the court decided not to execute the

witch took the crucial and damning, covert, yet explicit step of signing the covenant in private. Civil and religious officials tried most assiduously to ascertain whether an accused witch had indeed signed a pact in blood with Satan not only to expose this secret sin and establish guilt but also to initiate the process of admission, repentance, and redemption. Once the witch inscribed the pact with the devil, Puritans believed, she could no longer keep Satan's possession a secret, so unambiguous and shocking was her sin.[12] Drawing a parallel between the inevitable disclosure of sin more generally and the notion of an evil female interiority, Obadiah Sedgwick declared that "secret sins will become publike sins if they be not cleansed. [T]he Child in the wombe hath not stronger throwes to get out of its private lodging, then sin secretly wrought to fly into open and manifest action."[13] Such was particularly the case for witchcraft. Elizabeth Knapp, the "possessed" servant of Samuel Willard, believed that signing the devil's pact would surely be exposed. During her ordeal, she expressed concern that "if shee were a witch, shee should bee discovered,

---

confessors. Rosenthal, *Salem Story,* 42–43, 151–52, concurs that confessors tried to save their own lives, although colluding with accusers was an even surer path to liberty. Richard Godbeer, *The Devil's Dominion: Religion and Magic in Early New England* (Cambridge, 1992), 204–11, emphasizes the emotional and physical torture to which the accused were subjected and suggests that the confessions stemmed from religious anxiety; confessors may have admitted that they entered the devil's service as a way of opting out of Christian fellowship. Some, he admits, may have been anxious about their salvation and so could have been convinced, temporarily, that they had actually succumbed to Satan. David D. Hall, *Worlds of Wonder, Days of Judgment: Popular Religious Belief in Early New England* (New York, 1989), 193; and Karlsen, *Devil in the Shape of a Woman,* 148, briefly suggest that in a culture that associated female discontent with witchcraft, it is not surprising that some women were finally persuaded (or, as Hall says, "fantasized") that they had become witches. This line of reasoning comes the closest to my argument; the women knew they were sinners, and so either way—implicity or explicitly—they belonged to Satan.

12. Samuel Willard wrote in his hypothetical dialogue between "S" and "B" that proof of a pact made in private required presumptive rather than convictive evidence. "Witchcraft is the esteemed Capital," he explained, "when the person is Guilty of being in Combination with the Devil; which must be proved by Presumptions; for who saw or heard them Covenanting?" See Samuel Willard, *Some Miscellany Observations on Our Present Debates Respecting Witchcrafts, in a Dialogue between S. & B.* (Philadelphia, 1692); reprinted in *Congregational Quarterly* 11 (1869), 403. On the difficulty of "proving" secret crimes, including treason ("compassing or imagining the death of a king") and witchcraft, see Katharine Eisaman Maus, "Proof and Consequences: Inwardness and Its Exposure in the English Renaissance," *Representations* 34 (Spring 1991), 29–52.

13. Obadiah Sedgwick, *The Anatomy of Secret Sins* (London, 1660), 11.

& brought to shamefull end; which was many times a trouble on her spirits." [14]

Knapp's personal worry about sin (especially secret transgression) and its exposure rehearsed larger community anxieties about corrupt dissemblers in their midst. In view of Puritan belief in upholding strict codes of behavior and cultivating assurance of salvation despite the virtual impossibility of meeting God's and the community's expectations, it seems inevitable that individuals would examine themselves privately and find themselves—their secret selves—wanting. Feelings of inadequacy and guilt, under the right circumstances, might be imaginatively compounded into confession of transgression not actually, or actively, committed.

Ministers fostering the spiritual regeneration of sinners stressed that salvation was possible (though never assured) only if the transgressors repented. Strict adherence to the framework of the covenant demanded confession and repentance as the only means for the guilty to be readmitted into God's graces, just as a conversion narrative, which acknowledged one's sinfulness and attested to one's regeneration, preceded initial church membership. Within the terms of the covenant, those guilty of witchcraft—as well as other more mundane sins—theoretically were able to confess, repent, and ultimately return to God's embrace.

Seventeenth-century church disciplinary proceedings and town records are filled with accounts of various misdeeds, ranging from stealing to fornication, and of sinners' requisite humbling. When Mary Hitchcocke came before the New Haven court in 1662, presumably for fornication (although the records are incomplete), she admitted "that her way had

14. Samuel Willard, *A Briefe Accounte of a Strange & Unusuall Providence of God Befallen to Elizabeth Knap[p] of Groton*, in *Groton in the Witchcraft Times*, ed. Samuel Green (Groton, Mass., 1883), 15. As Chapter 1 suggests, seventeenth-century conversion narratives uncover a pervasive interest in the idea of "secrecy." In a society in which neighbors watched each other so closely, perhaps secrecy took on special significance; only God on the Day of Judgment would reveal who had truly made a covenant with him and who with Satan. Ministers encouraged sinners to confess and repent their secret sins, suggesting that God would forgive and forget. In fact, some accused "witches" confessed and *were* rehabilitated by the community, but some believed that witches would not be so lucky when their secret pacts became known. Deodat Lawson preached during the Salem outbreak, "Therefore KNOW YE, that are guilty of such *Monstrous* Iniquity . . . to *enter* into Covenant with *Satan; He that made you will not save you, and he that formed you will shew you no favour.*" See Deodat Lawson, *Christ's Fidelity the Only Shield Against Satan's Malignity*, (Boston, 1704), 68.

bene very euill & sinful." Hoping to have her penalty reduced from corporal punishment to a fine, she acknowledged "that God had helped her to see it in some measure & shee desired the lord might helpe her to see it more." Elinor Glover sought a similar reduction, declaring "shee hoped that there was something of repentance begun in her which god would owne." [15]

Sometimes sincere remorse was not enough to mitigate the punishment. When Jacob Moline appeared before the court for fornication prior to his marriage, he was sentenced to a whipping, whereas his wife only paid a fine. Jacob was apparently a repeat offender, "not taken warneing thereby but proceeded now to higher acts of filthines." [16] Some sinners confessed reluctantly or not at all. When John Clearke came before the court for running away from his master, the court tried assiduously "to bring him to a sight of his euill & to an ingenious Confession of the same," but with little success. Finally it was decided to turn him over to the marshall, "soe he might be brought to a sight of his sin in a way of suffering, seeing it could not bee attained otherwise." [17]

If in civil cases sinners expressed contrition hoping for abated disciplinary measures and the court used physical punishment to encourage remorse, in ecclesiastical cases penitence was required for readmittance into church fellowship and attendance at the Lord's Supper. Some confessions were deemed satisfactory, such as that of William Franklin of the Boston congregation in 1653. After "acknowledgment in the publique face of the Congregation of his sinn whereby he had exersissed covetousness prid and frowardnes," the church reinstated him as a brother. Others were unacceptable. In 1640 John Underhill confessed to fornica-

15. Franklin Bowditch Dexter, ed., *Ancient Town Records: New Haven Town Records, 1662–1684* (New Haven, Conn., 1919), 2:8–9. When Isaac Moline and Hester Clark appeared before the court—he for "inveiglement of Mr. Davenporte's mayd servant," and she for "several gross miscarriages," including entertaining Moline and being "false in her speeches"—they both apologized after first denying various charges. Moline said "he was sorry for what he had done, & desired the Court to be as favourable to him as they could." Clark "also confessed that she had greatly sinned, & was sorry, & desired their prayers for her" (65–71).

16. Ibid., 11. Moline's name is also spelled Moloine throughout the records. Thanks to John Murrin, I know that this was Jacob Melyn, a Dutch exile from New Netherland in New Haven. The court eventually relented on his punishment when Melyn's family argued that in Dutch eyes a whipping could mean complete disgrace to a gentleman.

17. Ibid., 25.

tion and to reviling the governor and other magistrates and threatening to destroy the country. He admitted these transgressions, "but not in such measure of humiliation. . . . his Confessions being mingled with sundry Causelesse self Justifyings and some falshood," and he was excommunicated.[18]

Confessions had to be accompanied by sincere contrition. When Bethia Stanly appeared before the Beverly congregation in 1669 for fornication, she publicly acknowledged that "God had of late made her to see from his word ye greatness of her sin against God." According to the records, her confession appeared "somwhat hopefull yet not so full, nor convincing to ye world as was desired in regard of ye newness of it." Advised to take more time to repent, she returned four years later, in 1673, and was then reconciled to the church.[19] Similarly, after Anne Hett's excommunication from the Boston church in 1642 for "open blasphemous speeches of hatred against God, and for sundry scandalous attempts of drowning one of her Children, and likewise for her stubborne unrulinesse with her husband, as also for her Inordinate idle walking in her Calling, and further also for her willfull Contempt of Gods holy Ordinances," she was readmitted to the fellowship of the church one year later after "hir publike poenitentiall acknowledgement."[20]

In certain trials—especially those involving offensive speech—men were required to apologize publicly as part of their punishment. Jane Kamensky has analyzed the gender implications of these cases. Women's criminal punishment usually focused on symbolic silence (wearing a sign that announced their misdeeds, for example) rather than public verbal apology. Men, by contrast, were empowered by their public confessions, which ironically included a reiteration of the original offense, thus allow-

18. Richard D. Pierce, ed., *The Records of the First Church in Boston, 1630–1868*, Publications of the Colonial Society of Massachusetts, no. 39 (Boston, 1961), 53, 28.

19. Beverly First Church Records, *Essex Institute Historical Collections* 35 (July 1898), 188, 193.

20. Pierce, *Records of the First Church in Boston*, 37, 39. It was not unusual for cases to take months or years to resolve. After Joseph Williams of Salem had been publicly admonished by the church for theft, he never returned following his "space of repentance." When two church members sent for him, he did confess, although "his confession was more dry and more generall than was to be desired." Williams had friends to speak on his behalf, and the pastor had earlier heard him express "sundry poenitentiall expressions," and so he was restored "as a child of the Covenant in an unblamable state." See Richard D. Pierce, ed., *Records of the First Church in Salem, 1629–1736* (Salem, Mass., 1974), 121–22.

ing them to say again what they were now unsaying.[21] In church disciplinary proceedings and in other civil cases involving a broad range of misdeeds, women confessed and, as it were, publicly volunteered their apology. It was not part of their punishment per se but a necessary step for
their reintegration into the church or community. Neither Bethia Stanly
nor Anne Hett was particularly empowered by her show of appropriate
remorse, but without it their lives would have been considerably more
inauspicious.

The Salem witch trials epitomize the kind of confession required of accused women. Because of the supernatural nature of the devil's perceived
powers, witchcraft was a special case, difficult to prove without a confession. But confession, whether voluntary or coerced, had to follow certain
prescriptions, as we shall see. It was, in any case, the only way to avoid
damnation. The magistrates and the clergy explained to Martha Corey
during her examination, for example, "If you expect mercy of God, you
must look for it in Gods way by confession."[22] The laity also recognized
the significance of confession. Goody Bridges told the court that she had
urged Hannah Bromage to confess, "that being the way to eternal life."[23]

Let me state frankly that I do not believe the devil actually visited the
people of Salem and urged them to sign his book in blood, though many
of the accused, female and male, admitted to such an act. My purpose
here is to show the multiple meanings attached to such an admission.
Whether interpreted literally or metaphorically, signing the pact defined
one as a witch, the most egregious of sinners. The devil's pact took on

21. For a discussion of the ritualized performance of public apology among men convicted of unruly speech, see Jane Kamensky, "'Saying and Unsaying': The Fine Art of Eating One's Words in Early Massachusetts," unpublished paper presented at "Possible Pasts:
Critical Encounters in Early America" conference, University of Pennsylvania, Philadelphia, June 1994.

22. Paul Boyer and Stephen Nissenbaum, eds., *The Salem Witchcraft Papers: Verbatim
Transcripts of the Legal Documents of the Salem Witchcraft Outbreak of 1692*, 3 vols.
(New York, 1977), 1:250.

23. Ibid., 1:143. On the importance of confession in criminal court cases, see Gail Sussman Marcus, "'Due Execution of the Generall Rules of Righteousnesse': Criminal Proce-
dure in New Haven Town and Colony, 1638–1658," in *Saints and Revolutionaries: Essays
on Early American History,* ed. David D. Hall, John M. Murrin, and Thad W. Tate (New
York, 1984), 99–137. On the relation between confession and reform, see John M. Murrin,
"Magistrates, Sinners, and a Precarious Libery: Trial by Jury in Seventeenth-Century New
England," ibid., 152–206, esp. 188–97. On the ritual of confession and repentance, see
Hall, *Worlds of Wonder,* 169–86, and passim.

such great significance in seventeenth-century New England—in both elite and popular belief—because of its reference to the covenant with God, one of the most prominent features of Puritan religious thought.[24] The significance of the devil's pact, like that of the covenant with God, rested on its voluntary nature. Those who admitted signing crossed the forbidden line between sinner and witch. Puritans knew that all sin was a covenant with Satan, but willfully putting it down on paper was a shockingly explicit evil. A typical indictment charged that the accused "Wickedly Mallisitiously & Felloniously A Covenant with the Devill did make & Signed [pap'r] to the Devill & by him was [ ] Baptized by the Devill By which Wicked Diabollicall Covenant with the Devill make by the Said [accused] shee become a detestable Witch."[25] The specific act of signing denoted the renunciation of Christian baptism and the creation of the identical bond with Satan.[26] Usually some form of persuasion was brought to bear by the devil, one of his shapes, or one of his accomplices, a witch. The coercion could take the form of torture or simply beguilement by the devil's attractive offers and temptations.

24. For an analysis of the relation between Calvinism and witchcraft which stresses the importance of the devil's compact, see John L. Teall, "Witchcraft and Calvinism in Elizabethan England: Divine Power and Human Agency," *Journal of the History of Ideas* 23 (1962), 21–36. See also Clive Holmes, "Popular Culture? Witches, Magistrates, and Divines in Early Modern England," in *Understanding Popular Culture: Europe from the Middle Ages to the Nineteenth Century,* ed. Stephen Kaplan (New York, 1984). On the relation between the Puritan deity and the witch, see Ann Kibbey, "Mutations of the Supernatural: Witchcraft, Remarkable Providences, and the Power of Puritan Men," *American Quarterly* 34 (1982), 125–48.

25. See, for example, *Salem Witchcraft Papers,* 1:134, 325, 63. Some of the indictments mentioned the details of the covenant; others cited the "Detestable Arts called Witchcrafts and sorceries" practiced by the accused. See ibid., 3:807. In cases in which the indictments charged the accused with acts of witchcraft without specifically mentioning the devil's covenant, the pact proved equally significant in the course of the trial. See, for example, 3:701, 2:434, 2:519–29.

26. The renunciation of Christ in favor of the devil appeared in European accounts of Satan's pact as well. For example, the confession of Isabel Becquet, from the Royal Court of Guernsey, acknowledged that the devil "then made her express detestation of the Eternal in these words: I renounce God the Father, God the Son, and God the Holy Ghost; and then caused her to worship and invoke himself in these terms: Our Great Master, help us! with a special compact to be faithful to him." See M. J. H. Heucher, *Magic Plants; being a Translation of a Curious Tract entitled De Vegetalibus Magicis,* ed. Edmund Goldsmid ([no city], Scotland, 1886), 36. Heucher's tract was not dated, but the editor presumed it was written during the seventeenth century. The appendix, from which I have quoted, included other confessions from the Royal Court of Guernsey, dated 1617. See also Jeffrey Burton Russell, *Witchcraft in the Middle Ages* (Ithaca, N.Y., 1972), 208.

In the case of Mary Bridges Jr., the devil appeared in the shape of a black bird and offered her money and fine clothes. She admitted that she had been baptized by the devil, and that "he would have her serve him & would have her to touch a paper: which she did with her fingers & it made a red mark." Mary Lacey Jr. confessed that the devil urged her to recruit more witches, threatening, "if we will not make other persons sett there hand to the Book he will tear us in peaces." When the court asked her if she had his book in her possession, she explained, "no the Divel Keeps it & he goes along with us. & we perswade persons, & their he setts downe ther names in Blood." [27] Mary Walcott testified that it was Sarah Buckley and not the devil who persuaded her to sign. Buckley "brought me a book and would have me write my name in it or elce give my consent that she might write it for me. I told her that I would not touch her book nor write in it, nor give consent to her tho she killd me then she choaked me." Similarly, Ann Putnam Jr. testified that when the accused witch John Willard brought the book for her to sign, "he did sett upon me most dreadfully and beat me and pinched and almost choaked me to death; threatening to kill me if I would not writ in his book: for he tould me he had whiped my little sister sarah to death and he would whip me to death if I would not writ in his book." [28]

Confessors usually mentioned that they signed the book in red, signifying blood, although sometimes they used either their finger or a pen and black ink to make a mark upon the page. The accused, Mary Barker, told the court that "sometime last sumer she made a red mark in the devils book with the fore finger of her Left hand." [29] William Barker, too, "did syne the devils book with blood brought to him in a thing lyke an Inkhorn that he dip't his fingers there in and made a blott in the book which was a confirmation of the Covenant with the devil." [30] Samuel Willard's servant, Elizabeth Knapp, confessed in 1671 that when she consented to sign the devil's book he brought her a knife with which he cut her finger. He caught her blood in his hand and then, she said, "took

27. *Salem Witchcraft Papers,* 1:135, 2:522.
28. Ibid., 1:149, 3:851.
29. Ibid., 1:59. Sarah Wardwell, for example, testified that she signed a piece of paper by putting her finger to it and making a black mark. Mary Warren also mentioned signing by a black mark. See 3:791, 799.
30. Ibid., 1:65.

The Salem trial records include accounts of witches flying on poles, as in this woodcut depicting the activities of Lancashire witches in 1612, from Matthew Hopkins, *The Discoverie of Witches,* 1647. The accused confessed to riding to witch meetings and participating in the Lord's Supper and devil's baptism, while theologians debated the devil's power to transport people through the air (from Cotton Mather, *On Witchcraft* [Mt. Vernon, N.Y.: Peter Pauper Press, Inc., 1950]. Reprinted with permission).

a little sharpened sticke, & dipt in the blood, & put it into her hand, & guided it, & shee wrote her name with his help."[31]

The devil's book itself was as mysterious as the ritual of signing. Since it was presumed that the covenant was sealed in private, accounts of what the book looked like were based on hearsay and varied from witness to witness. In 1671 when Knapp claimed she was possessed by Satan, she said that he "presented her a book written with blood of covenants made by others," presumably to assure her that many of her friends had already signed.[32] In testimony against Abigail Williams, Joseph Hutchinson claimed that he had often heard her talk about the

31. Willard, *Briefe Account,* 14.
32. Ibid., 8.

book: she "said that there was two Books one was a short thike book & the other was a Long booke. . . . She said the bookes ware as rede as blode. . . . She said thar was many lines riten & at the end of Evary line thar was a seall." Mercy Lewis swore that her old employer, George Burroughs, brought her what seemed to be a brand new book and urged her to write in it, assuring her that this was merely a book that had always been in his study. Skeptical because she could not recall ever seeing such a book and brave enough to resist his tortures, Lewis told him that she would not sign even "if he throde me down on 100 pitchforks."[33] Whether the devil's pact was written in a book or simply on a piece of paper, whether the accused witches signed in red blood or black ink, whether they saw many or few names, it is clear that the court anxiously awaited the details of the making of a covenant.

In a culture that so celebrated "the Book," it is not surprising that the court anticipated—and even conditioned—responses of this nature. It was equally eager to hear the details of the devil's baptism, a Satanic sacrament that mocked and reversed one's original baptism and promise to keep the Lord's covenant. Samuel Wardwell declared that "he was baptised by the black man at Shaw shin river alone and was dipt all over and beleeves he renounced his former baptisme."[34] Sarah and Thomas Carrier both admitted that their mother had baptized them at the river; Thomas recalled that she "pulled of his Cloths & put him into the River & that his Mother then told him he was hers for Ever."[35] Cotton Mather was greatly alarmed at this abomination whereby "people to be, (as is some confess'd) Baptized by a Fiend using this form upon them, *Thou art mine, and I have a full power over thee!* afterwards communicating in an Hellish *Bread* and *Wine,* by that Fiend administred unto them."[36]

33. *Salem Witchcraft Papers,* 3:853, 1:169.

34. Ibid., 3:784. On the relation between the devil's baptism and Baptists, see Rosenthal, *Salem Story,* 130–34.

35. *Salem Witchcraft Papers,* 1:203.

36. Cotton Mather, *The Wonders of the Invisible World* (Boston, 1693), in *The Witchcraft Delusion in New England,* ed. Samuel Drake, 3 vols. (Roxbury, Mass., 1866), 1:111. Just as some of the accused disclaimed signing the pact, some of them would admit that they had attended a baptismal feast but denied taking part. Deliverance Hobbs, for example, named several of the accused along with the minister George Burroughs and the devil in a large white hat, all of whom took part in the sacrament. According to the court record, "She herself affirms did not nor would not Eat nor drink, but All the Rest did who were there present, therefore they Threatened to Torment her" (*Salem Witchcraft Papers,* 2:423).

The confessions, denials, and accusations by the afflicted and others who testified need to be read carefully. Together this oral and written evidence can "tell us" not only about the "narrative" of the trials but, as significant, about women, men, and the power of Puritan covenant theology. The process of cultural negotiation—between women and men; between the clergy and the magistrates; and between sources of authority and the laity—can be seen quite clearly in the trial transcripts. Admittedly, the court records of Salem and other towns have their limitations; often it is difficult to tell if they are verbatim transcripts or accounts reconstructed after the event. Sentences appear in fragments or are lost altogether, and first-person accounts often shift to the third person, casting doubt on the proximity of the voice to that of the defendant. Some of these problems are mitigated by the sheer volume of the transcripts. Despite their deficiencies, the trial records portray a cultural and religious world that was deeply gendered.

Although women and men both understood the meanings of confession, they confessed to the charges of witchcraft or denied them in distinctly different ways. And the testimony of their neighbors—either for or against those accused—betrays a gender division as well. A confessing woman was the model of Puritan womanhood, even though she was admitting to the worst of sins, for she confirmed her society's belief in both God and the devil. She validated the court's procedures, as we shall see, and corroborated Puritan thought concerning sin, guilt, and the devil's wily ways. Apology was critical. It was not enough to describe the devil's book and baptism. A good Puritan woman/witch needed to repent of her obvious sins. The cultural performance of confession created a paradigm of perfect redemption, and during the Salem trials the confessing woman was rewarded with her life.[37]

In confessing, these women succumbed to the unbearable pressures of their own and their community's expectations of proper female behavior.

37. On the relation between apology and public execution, see Lawrence W. Towner, "True Confessions and Last Dying Warnings in Colonial New England," in *Sibley's Heir: A Volume in Memory of Clifford Kenyon Shipton*, Publications of the Colonial Society of Massachusetts, *Collections* no. 59 (Boston, 1982), 523–39; Ronald A. Bosco, "Lectures at the Pillory: The Early American Execution Sermon," *American Quarterly* 30 (Summer 1979), 156–76; J. A. Sharpe, "'Last Dying Speeches': Religion, Ideology, and Public Execution in Seventeenth-Century England," *Past and Present* 107 (May 1985), 144–67; and Karen Halttunen, "Early American Murder Narratives: The Birth of Horror," in *The Power*

What they confessed to and the manner in which they confessed can tell modern readers about the constraints and boundaries of Puritan womanhood. Denials are equally telling; women who insisted on their innocence of the crime of witchcraft often unwittingly implicated themselves because they admitted to being sinners. Ironically, those who would not confess to witchcraft and allow themselves to be forgiven, yet who did admit to sin, as any good Puritan should, were executed. They were unable to convince the court and their peers that their souls had not entered into a covenant with the devil; they could not wholeheartedly deny a pact with Satan when an implicit bond with him through common sin was undeniable. The sense of the depraved female self which emerges from women's conversion narratives merged with the community's (and each accused woman's own) expectations about the rebellious female witch.

Susannah Post's admissions, delivered at her examination in August 1692, contained the elements of a respectable confession. She acknowledged that she "had bin in the Devils snare three years: the first time I saw him he was like a Catt: he told her he was a prince: & I was to serve him I promised him to doe it the next shape was a yellow bird: it s'd I must serve him: & he s'd I should live well: the next time he appeared like a black man that time he brought a book & she touched it with a stick that was Dipt in an ink horne & it made a red mark." [38] Here description of the events was ordinary enough, paralleling and elaborating ministers' representation of the devil's powers in the context of the meetinghouse. No doubt the very ordinariness of her tales contributed to her audience's belief.

What is particularly "womanly" about Post's confession is not the detailed description of the devil's appearance or the specific information about the meeting she claimed to have attended but her admission that she had made a mistake. During her confession "She s'd she was now willing to renownce the Devil & all his works: & she went: when bid & begged forgivnes of the afflicted & could come to them and not hurt

---

of Culture: Critical Essays in American History, ed. Richard Wightman Fox and T. J. Jackson Lears (Chicago, 1993), 67–101. See also Emil Oberholzer Jr., Delinquent Saints: Disciplinary Action in the Early Congregational Churches of Massachusetts (New York, 1955); and N. E. H. Hull, Female Felons: Women and Serious Crime in Colonial Massachusetts (Urbana, Ill., 1987).

38. Salem Witchcraft Papers, 2:647.

them." [39] Similarly, Abigail Hobbs told the court that she had made a covenant with the devil for which she now sought repentance. "I will speak the truth," Hobbs said. "I have seen sights and been scared. I have been very wicked. I hope I shall be better, if God will help me. . . . I hope God will forgive me." [40] Despite these confessions—or, I believe, because of them—the court spared Susannah Post and Abigail Hobbs. Their regret and willingness to turn from the path of evil to the path of righteousness, expected of all decent Puritan women, transformed their confessions from tales of depravity and sin to narratives of redemption.

Those confessions that were filtered through the court and written down by a court official present a certain problem of evidence for the modern reader. It is impossible to know "what really happened." Perhaps the accused did confess that the devil diverted them from praying to God, as Mary Osgood apparently did in her confession of September 8, 1692. But the possibility exists that the justice who penned her confession, John Higginson, imposed his own interpretation. We will never know if Osgood actually uttered the words inscribed in the record, if she said them because she had learned what to say to save her own life, or if the court supplied the acceptable script for her. But if establishing the "truth" of Osgood's narrative remains impossible, its cultural significance

39. Ibid. On the individual and social implications of repentance, see Hall, *Worlds of Wonder,* 166–212; on the witchcraft confessions, see esp. 192–96. For a discussion of women and repentance in eighteenth-century Connecticut, see Cornelia Hughes Dayton, "Taking the Trade: Abortion and Gender Relations in an Eighteenth-Century New England Village," *William and Mary Quarterly,* 3rd ser., 48:1 (January 1991), 19–50. See also Lynda E. Boose, "Scolding Brides and Bridling Scolds: Taming the Woman's Unruly Member," *Shakespeare Quarterly* 42:2 (Summer 1991), 179–214. Jane Kamensky says that women's criminal punishment usually focused on symbolic silence (wearing a sign that announced their misdeeds, for example) rather than public verbal apology. See Kamensky, "Saying and Unsaying," 7. By contrast, during the Salem episode, verbal apology coupled with regret constituted a successful confession.

40. *Salem Witchcraft Papers,* 2:405. One petition, presented on behalf of Dorcas Hoar, shows the importance attached to repentance. Apparently Hoar confessed, although her confession has not survived. Four men wrote to the court requesting delay of her execution (ultimately she was reprieved). They agreed that she was guilty of "the heynous crime of witchcraft . . . & how & when shee was taken in the snare of the Devill," but they asked for more time in order that she might ask for forgiveness: "And being in grat distress of Conscience [Hoar] earnestly craves a little longer time of life to realize & perfect her repentance for the salvation of her soule" (see 2:403).

for the community that endorsed it is undeniable. Whether heartfelt or tactical, Osgood's cultural performance helped produce or reproduce particular gender categories and arrangements, helped construct or reconstruct female subjectivity in Puritan New England.[41]

Osgood's confession contained a number of ideas about the devil and witchcraft that would have made it satisfactory to both the court and her peers. It told how the cat appeared "when she was in a melancholy state and condition" and diverted her from praying to God. "Instead thereof she prayed to the devil; about which time she made a covenant with the devil," and she consented to worship him. She renounced her former baptism, was transported through the air, and was able to name others who similarly rode a pole to a witch meeting. On the issue of afflicting others in order to coerce them into joining the devil's minions, Osgood's confession concedes she gave "consent the devil should do it in her shape, and that the devil could not do it without her consent." [42]

Consent was crucial, and mention of it in the confession validated not only Puritan theology but the court's procedures as well.[43] The clergy, we recall, had expressed ambivalence about spectral evidence, ultimately advising the court that the devil had power to assume an innocent, nonconsenting person's shape. If the court had heeded the ministers' advice, it could no longer have accepted spectral evidence, inasmuch as there would be no way of telling whether a particular person had given the devil permission to use her (or his) shape. Yet the court persisted, and countless witnesses testified that they had been afflicted by particular accused witches' specters.

Osgood's confession, then, validated the court's proceedings. The court specifically asked her, "Do you know the devil can take the shape of an innocent person and afflict?" And she answered, "I believe he cannot." Her testimony carried authority. The court inquired, "Who taught you this way of witchcraft?" and Osgood implicated someone with more

41. For a provocative analysis of similarly problematic sources, see Natalie Zemon Davis, *Fiction in the Archives: Pardon Tales and Their Tellers in Sixteenth-Century France* (Stanford, Calif., 1987).

42. *Salem Witchcraft Papers*, 2:615.

43. According to Bernard Rosenthal, "the witch-hunt became as much an affirmation of the process as a search for witches." See Rosenthal, *Salem Story*, 49.

knowledge of the spiritual world than even the ministers—Satan himself. Osgood's expertise[44] on this matter confirmed prevailing popular opinion during the trials, despite the ministers' caution; she stated quite clearly during her examination, "The Lord would not suffer it so to be, that the devil should afflict in an innocent person's shape."[45] Ironically, while admitting her own complicity in the devil's plots, she succeeded in authenticating the court's and the laity's notions of the devil's limited powers and saved her own life.

Osgood verified yet another element of Puritan belief concerning Satan's intrusion, thus making her confession particularly valuable as a morality tale. After describing at some length the various rewards the devil offered her in exchange for her complicity, she acknowledged that he had not delivered on a single promise. Not only did she have to reconcile herself to this disappointment, but in fact, the conditions of her life took a turn for the worse as a result of her ill-fated pact. According to the court recorder, "He promised her abundance of satisfaction and quietness in her future state, but never performed any thing; and that she has lived more miserably and more discontented since, than ever before."[46] Puritans knew full well that the devil was prone to offer material or spiritual rewards but to deliver only despair.

Ann Foster's confession in July included similar elements. Foster admitted that the devil had appeared to her six years before and that she had promised to serve him two years, "upon w'ch the Devill promised her prosperity & many things but never performed it." According to the transcripts, "She saith that she formerly frequented the publique metting to worship god. but the divill had such power over her that she could not profit there & that was her undoeing."[47] Here again, Foster's particular drama would have sounded familiar to the court and its listening audience. Puritans knew the devil's tactics. Obviously the devil would have

44. Ironically, Osgood's expertise, as recognized or invented by the court, was based on her alleged experience, the very reality or unreality of which was itself the object of the court's deliberations.

45. *Salem Witchcraft Papers*, 2:616.

46. Ibid. Mary Lacey Jr. also conceded that the devil did not keep his word: "He bid me to be afraid of nothing. & he would not bring me out. but he has proved a lyer from the begining." Despite her admission, the court still offered, "you may yet be deliverd if god give you repentance." See 2:520.

47. Ibid., 2:343.

offered enticements, failed to uphold promises, and kept her from prayer; Foster's perhaps formulaic recitation of such details rendered her performance convincing and her tale culturally useful.

It might be tempting to see these confessing women as clever manipulators of the court. Were they cognizant of their power to mock authority with their tales of the devil's misdeeds and their own collusion, followed by clever apologies comprising all the elements apparently required by the court? They knew what the court wanted to hear, especially by September 1692 when it was clear that confessors were spared. To embrace this line of analysis completely, however, would be to misread the evidence. Women (and men) came to know their parts because confession and belief in the devil were integral components of their religious world. Successful confessions confirmed cultural expectations in a number of ways. Women formed a pact with the devil; women apologized; and the court was justified in basing convictions on spectral evidence.

It was the women who *denied* any collusion with Satan or those who initially confessed but later recanted who, by their refusal to admit complicity with the devil, displayed a measure of independence in the face of authority.[48] Women who denied guilt may have believed that they had the weight of God's witness on their side. At her execution Sarah Good defiantly insisted she was no witch and warned her minister, "You are a

48. Rarely did women consistently deny other kinds of charges in church or civil proceedings. Like Goodwife Lines in New Haven in 1655, they might deny for a time but then come around to a confession. Lines "strongly denied [stealing] at first, as she did the other things, but after confessed them." Later she "stiffly denied sundrie times" stealing a tray; "yet after confessed she stole it." On the issue of abusing her husband and calling him a devil, "she confessed the thing is true, onely she remembers not that she repeated the word deuill so often." See *Ancient Town Records*, 1:246–47. In the Wenham congregation, when Sarah Fiske was accused of maligning her husband, Phineas, and behaving inappropriately during a Sabbath service, she denied the charges, instead blaming Phineas for "false witness bearing," not taking her side in the dispute, failing to pray for her, and acting cruelly toward her. The church concurred with Phineas's denials, found him innocent, and urged Sarah to admit her sins and apologize. Finally, months later, after reluctantly admitting publicly some "evil in these particulars whereas she should have kept secret and as the duty of a wife and as . . . her carriage at that time," the church allowed her to give her conversion relation. See Robert G. Pope, ed., *The Notebook of The Reverend John Fiske, 1664–1675* (Salem, Mass., 1974), 25–29, 32, 34, 40–47. Sarah Fiske's case is discussed in Charles Lloyd Cohen, *God's Caress: The Psychology of Puritan Religious Experience* (New York, 1986), 154–55.

lyer; I am no more a Witch than you are a Wizard, and if you take away my Life, God will give you Blood to drink." [49]

Denying women testified that their innocence would be vindicated, if not in this world, then in the next, on Judgment Day. Ann Pudeator was convicted and executed; she insisted she knew nothing of the afflicted women who testified against her, "nothing in the least measure about it nor nothing else concerning the crime of witchcraft for w'ch I am condemned to die as will be known to men and angells att the great day of Judgment." Abigail Faulkner Sr. declared, "Thankes be to the Lord I know my selfe altogether Innocent & Ignorant of the crime of witchcraft w'ch is layd to my charge: as will appeare at the great day of Judgment." [50]

Such protestations unfortunately fell on deaf ears. Vehement denial and absolute refusal to confess, in effect, repudiated Puritan theology, contradicted the court's proceedings, and invalidated notions of proper female decorum.[51] Faulkner, for example, negated the court's stance on spectral evidence. When the afflicted went into fits, she announced, "it is the devill dos it in my shape," implying that he did it without her permission.[52] Though the court had accepted the "expert" testimony of

49. Robert Calef, *More Wonders of the Invisible World: or The Wonders of the Invisible World Display'd in Five Parts* (1700), reprinted in *Narratives of the Witchcraft Cases, 1648–1706,* ed. George Lincoln Burr (1914; New York, 1968), 358. On the various literary and historical representations of Sarah Good, see Rosenthal, *Salem Story,* 87–90.

50. *Salem Witchcraft Papers,* 3:709, 1:334.

51. Steadfast denial was considered far beyond the bounds of acceptable female behavior. The First Church of Boston excommunicated Ann Hibbon (or Hibbens) in 1640, not only for her dispute with some joiners whose rates she considered exorbitant but for her "obstinate Judgeing and Condemning of them" for lying, and perhaps most egregiously of all, for refusing to make "any humble and penitentiall acknowledgement thereof." The records state that Hibbens condemned the church's admonition and "still continued Impenitent and obstinate in these things, not hearkning to her husband at home; nor to the brethren and sisters in private, noe nor yet to the whole Church in Publique." See Pierce, *Records of the First Church in Boston,* 32–33. Hibbens did apologize, in part, not for the accusations she made but for speaking to others about it rather than taking it immediately through the proper disciplinary channels. See "Church Trial of Mistress Ann Hibbens," in *Root of Bitterness: Documents of the Social History of American Women,* ed. Nancy F. Cott (New York, 1972), 47–58. On Hibbens's unusual case, see Jane Kamensky, *Governing the Tongue: The Politics of Speaking in Early New England* (New York, forthcoming 1998). Not surprisingly, in 1656, after the death of her husband, Anne Hibbens was accused of witchcraft. See Karlsen, *Devil in the Shape of a Woman,* 150–52.

52. *Salem Witchcraft Papers,* 1:327, 2:551.

Mary Osgood, which confirmed its own view, it dismissed Faulkner's claim, or at least considered it disingenuous, because Faulkner failed to admit guilt. Ironically, by denying the witchcraft accusation, Faulkner disputed the reality of witchcraft itself and by implication undermined her own expertise.

Susannah Martin, another of those executed, had the audacity to laugh during her examination at what she called "such folly." She would not admit even that the afflicted were bewitched, much less that she (or her shape) bore any responsibility. When pressed, "How comes your appearance just now to hurt these," she used her biblical knowledge to challenge the legitimacy of spectral evidence: "He that appeared in sams shape a glorifyed saint can appear in any ones shape," referring to the biblical Witch of Endor who conjured before Saul the shape of the undeniably holy Samuel. Martin's denials and hermeneutics were not accepted.[53]

Female deniers had an especially difficult time proving their innocence because they had to prove not only that they had never signed the devil's pact but also that they had never even implicitly covenanted with the devil through ordinary sin. Few women, however, lacked guilt and remorse for prior sins and shortcomings, and the community persistently linked former transgressions with particular accusations of witchcraft. Petitioners on behalf of the accused, similarly, depicted those they fought to acquit as unblemished. It was necessary to show that the souls of the accused had not bonded with the devil in any way.[54]

Neighbors who deposed against defendants coupled their evidence with testimony besmirching the accused's religious profession. Knowing that one could not be faithful to Christ and in covenant with Satan at the same time, those testifying sought to demonstrate a tenuous relationship with God. During Elizabeth How's examination, Joseph Safford told the court he had overheard Major Appleton's wife say, "I was mistaken . . . for I thought goode how [that is, Goodwife How] had bene a precious

---

53. Ibid., 2:551. In fact, the devil does not appear at all in the biblical passage (1 Samuel 28); Susannah Martin's diabolical interpretation suggests the strength of the Puritans' association of witchcraft with the devil.

54. Men, as we shall see, were seldom placed in such a bind, and even when they were indicted, male subjectivity functioned in ways that allowed men more easily to own their sins while disowning their essential depravity.

saint of god but now I see she is a witch for she hath bewitched mee and my child and we shall never be well." Safford further claimed that not long after his wife tried to defend How publicly at the church meeting, his own son began to act strange, and then his wife "was taken after a Raving frenzy manar expresin in a Ragin manar that goode how . . . was Justefyed befor god and continued in this fram for the space of thre or four hours aftar that my wife fell into a kind of a tranc for the spac of two or thre minits." [55]

Safford presented his case prototypically. Those speaking against the accused did not make random charges of maleficence; the discourse was religious, and the accused became suspect for not being good Christians. During the course of Rebecca Nurse's examination, Ann Putnam Sr. declared, "Because I would not yeald to hir hellish temtations she threatened to tare my soule out of my body: blasphemously denying the blessed God and the power of the Lord Jesus Christ to save my soule and denying severall places of scripture which I tould hir of." [56] Various kinds of charges were brought against Nurse; the most serious marked her as a pawn of the devil. Certainly an innocent person would not blaspheme Jesus Christ or deny the Scriptures. Only a witch—one who had made an explicit covenant with Satan—would demonstrate that degree of impiety, and those with established "implicit" covenants were more likely to take the next step with the devil.

As part of the religious discourse of their accusations, accusers situated themselves in a godly framework. Ann Putnam Sr. reminded the court of her saintliness when she said, "as soon as I was caryed out of the meeting house dores it pleased Allmighty God for his free grace and mircy sake to deliver me out of the paws of thos Roaring lionn: and the jaws of those tareing bears that ever sence that time they have not had power so to afflect me." [57] She effectively ensured the validity of her claims by presenting herself as deserving of God's mercy while attributing nothing less than apostasy to Rebecca Nurse.

<hr>

55. *Salem Witchcraft Papers*, 2:452. For a perceptive analysis of the relation between women's speech and witchcraft accusations, see Jane Kamensky, "Words, Witches, and Woman Trouble: Witchcraft, Disorderly Speech, and Gender Boundaries in Puritan New England," *Essex Institute Historical Collections* 128 (October 1992), 286–306.

56. *Salem Witchcraft Papers*, 2:604.

57. Ibid., 2:605.

In testifying against a person it was important to associate unseemly conduct, particularly that which challenged gender conventions or prescriptions of ideal womanhood, with witchcraft charges. In this way women's behavior was constrained. It is not only that women who defied cultural boundaries of polite decorum, for example, were singled out and accused of witchcraft, but that the very definitions of acceptability were created and contested during the trials themselves. John Westgate testified that he was at a tavern when the accused, Alice Parker, arrived and "scolded att and called her husband all to nought." Westgate took the husband's side in the marital dispute, suggesting to him that "itt was an unbeseeming thing for her to come after him to the taverne and raile after thatt rate." Alice Parker then called Westgate a rogue, and told him to mind his own business. The incident might have been forgotten, except that Westgate reconstructed it for the court, adding the crucial detail that "sometime afterwards" he heard a noise and a black hog ran toward him and threatened to devour him. During the ensuing scuffle he realized the hog "was Either the Divell or some Evill thing not a Reall hog, and did then Really Judge or determine in my mind that it was either Goody parker or by her meenes, and procuring fearing that she is a Witch."[58]

During the trial of another one of the women convicted and executed, Sarah Good, witnesses for the prosecution made the connection between offensive demeanor and witchcraft quite clear. William Good, Sarah's husband, had apparently said that he believed his wife either was a witch or would soon become one. John Hathorne asked William if he had ever witnessed any of the misdeeds or afflictions now attributed to his wife: "He answered no not in this nature but it was her bad carriage to him and indeed said I may say with tears that shee is an enimy to all good." William Good wedded the two serious offenses—disrespect of one's husband and covenanting with the devil. Sarah Good tried to deny the latter offense, informing the court that she never made any contract, nor did she hurt the afflicted children. In response to one of the accusations, she

58. Ibid., 2:632. On the misidentification of Alice Parker in the *Salem Witchcraft Papers,* see Rosenthal, *Salem Story,* 254n38. Similarly, Andrew Elliott deposed that Susannah Roots was "a bad woman" because when she lived with him and his wife Roots always absented herself from prayer and excused herself from meeting. Immediately after he told of Roots's impiety, Elliott segued into stories of hearing mysterious voices coming from Roots's room at night, thus implicating her in the devil's deeds.

also tried to explain, to no avail, that the reason she never attended church meeting was because she did not have appropriate clothes to wear. Yet in the course of her own examination the link her husband had made between good [or Goodwife Good] and evil was reiterated, "William good saith thatt shee is an enemy to all good shee saith shee is cleare of being a witch." [59]

The court, the accusers, and as will be demonstrated, the accused themselves understood that in order to prove one's guilt or innocence, evidence had to be presented which would speak to the accused person's status as a sinner or a saint. The members of the court may have seen themselves as unbiased interpreters of testimony, but they, too, participated in the drama that constructed—rather than simply uncovered—evil personas. During Sarah Good's review the court commented tellingly and without neutrality, "Her answers were in a very wicked, spitfull manner rejecting and retorting aganst the authority with base and abusive words and many lies shee was taken in." Mary Clarke also endured the court's biases and insinuations against her. After urging her to confess, "for the good of her soul," the court called in the local constable when she steadfastly refused. Asked to describe her "fame and reputation," the constable suggested her culpability with this reply: "they had [heard] she was or had been guilty of such things, but as to anything in particular he could not say." [60] The constable's deployment of mere rumor suggests the burden of proof that weighed against accused women.

In the midst of Sarah Osborne's examination the magistrates intervened more directly, leading the accused, and in the process fashioning the woman's/witch's subjectivity. Again and again the authorities tried to force Osborne to admit she had been in the devil's snare, and time after time she refused. Finally they asked, "Why did you yeild thus far to the devil as never to goe to meeting since?" Osborne would not admit that she had actually signed a covenant, but perhaps the magistrates could persuade her to concede the merit of this charge; although seemingly not egregious, the offense would still have placed her in the devil's camp and thus implicitly in league with him. Likewise, when the authorities could not bring Rebecca Nurse to confess, they seemed willing, at least as a tac-

59. *Salem Witchcraft Papers*, 2:357, 360.
60. Ibid., 2:357, 1:213.

tic, to accept an admission that she had felt the devil's lure. "Possibly you may apprehend you are no witch," they conceded, "but have you not been led aside by temptations that way?"[61] How could such a suggestion have been denied?

Testimony offered on behalf of the accused makes it clear that the witnesses and the accused knew that there was a difference between simply sinning and becoming a witch. They knew they could recognize someone who had stepped over the line, but they did not necessarily understand where that line would be drawn during the proceedings. And so, as part of their testimony, petitioners and witnesses for the accused participated in the same discourse as their foes, trying tirelessly to prove not only that the defendant was not a witch but that her life was so nearly flawless that no compact with the devil could be implied or even imagined, let alone established in court.

For a Puritan woman, good character meant carrying out one's Christian duty as daughter, wife, mother, and neighbor.[62] Nicholas Rice submitted a petition on his wife's behalf urging the court to release her from jail. In all the time they had been married, he asserted, "he never had any reason to accuse her for any Impietie or witchcraft, but the Contrary Shee lived w'th him as a good Faithfull dutifull wife and alwise had respect . . . to the ordinances of God while her Strength Remain'd." Rice thus confirmed that which the court and its audience already knew while attempting to mobilize this knowledge to save his wife: a witch could not possibly be a good, faithful, dutiful, and pious woman. Either one covenanted with the devil and thus clung to all one's sins, or one remained by the Lord, devoutly fulfilling earthly duties. As a good, pious woman, therefore, Goody Rice could not be a witch. James How Sr. attested that his daughter performed her obligations as both a daughter and a wife, "as becometh a Christion with Respact to my self as a father very dutyfully & a wififfe [wife] to my son very Carfull loveing obediant and kind," and he urged the court to reconsider its position on spectral evidence, "to se a differance between predigous and Consentes." James Allen testified that Mary Bradbury "lived according to the rules of the gospell, . . . [and] was a constant attender upon the ministry of the word; & all the ordi-

61. Ibid., 2:611, 585.
62. See Laurel Thatcher Ulrich, *Good Wives: Image and Reality in the Lives of Women in Northern New England, 1650–1750* (New York, 1982).

nances of the gospell; full of works of charity & mercy to the sick & poor. neither have I seen or heard any thing of her unbecoming the profession of the gospell." [63]

Witnesses for the accused, then, needed to convince the court that particular defendants were model Puritan women, and in so doing they participated in the reconstruction of their social world, its gender arrangements, and its definition of female identity—all of which had been fundamentally disrupted by the witchcraft crisis. Case after case had been presented in which women did not appear to conform to prescriptive norms of female deportment; assurances to the contrary—both among deniers and those who confessed—reaffirmed cultural commitment to these values. Thomas Hart, for example, persuaded the court that he never knew of any evil or sinful practice associated with his mother. In fact, he assured them that he would not have nourished or supported "any creature that he knew ingaged in the Druggery of Satan." Furthermore, his mother's credibility extended beyond the family. It was known to all the neighbors, Hart asserted, that his mother "lived asober [sic] and Godly life alwise ready to discharge the part of A good Christian." [64]

Testimony *against* the accused, similarly, linked unwomanly, sinful behavior with witchcraft. The magistrates inquired about all her sins, not merely witchcraft, when they asked Mary Easty, "How far have you complyed w'th Satan whereby he takes this advantage ag't you?" The loaded question suggested a continuum of transgression, from common sin to the signature of a pact, the slippery slope making it all the more difficult to determine who, in fact, had surrendered. Easty replied that she was certainly "clear of this sin," that is, signing the devil's pact. In fact, she stated in a petition that, as far as she knew, she was clear "of any other scandalouse evill, or miscaryage inconsistent with Christianity." [65] The magistrates were most interested in whether or not Easty had explicity bargained with Satan, but both she and the authorities appreciated the relation between sin and the devil. Through her casual sins, Mary Easty complied with the devil; how far the court believed she had actually yielded would determine her innocence or guilt in the witchcraft trials.

Some of the accused, like Mary Easty, completely disavowed any

63. *Salem Witchcraft Papers*, 3:720, 2:444, 1:121.
64. Ibid., 2:383–84.
65. Ibid., 1:288, 303.

"Trial of George Jacobs" printed by T. H. Matteson, 1855. Though fanciful, this romanticized nineteenth-century rendition of the 1692 witch trials accurately emphasizes the frenzy and chaos of the courtroom. The accused had difficulty denying their complicity with Satan when his activities, made visible by the afflicted accusers, presented themselves so clearly before their eyes (courtesy Peabody and Essex Museum, Salem, Mass.).

familiarity with Satan, through sin or witchcraft. Martha Corey responded to the examiners, "Why I am a Gosple-woman, and do you think I can have to do with witchcraft too[?]" Mary Bradbury insisted that she remained "the servant of Jesus Christ & Have given my self up to him as my only lord & saviour." She had tried to live her life "according to the rules of his holy word," and she stood "in utter contempt & defiance of the divell," finding "all his works as horid & detestible." Jane Lilly also denied complicity on any account: "The truth was she knew nothing of it nor was she Sencible if she was in the Devills snare." When presented with evidence that she afflicted some, she asserted "she never went: in body nor spirit nor had ever had any [inclynason] to witchcraft. . . . but she sa'd if she confessed anything of this she should Deny the truth & wrong her own soul." [66]

But other women mused about their souls, too, and admitted that the devil had been in their hearts—in other words, that they had sinned. Their admission of his presence, at least in the context of the witchcraft trials, was used to implicate them as witches. Hannah Bromage, for example, acknowledged "that she had been under some dead nes w'h respect to the ordnances for the matter of 6 weeks." Bromage admitted nothing more than one might recount in a conversion relation. She further conceded, however, that "a sudden sugge[s]tion come into her heed sayeing I can help thee with strenth." Bromage firmly claimed that she did not succumb to Satan's devices, and she forcefully responded to the voice in her head, "avoid satan." [67]

Though they echoed, in an unextraordinary way, the temptations the ministers often described in their sermons, Bromage's admissions were interpreted quite differently during the trials. The changed context of her testimony altered its meaning fundamentally. In contrast to confessions occurring in conversion narratives, in which prospective converts were

66. Ibid., 1:248, 116, 2:539. Not all the accused were able to convince others that they were loyal to God and not the devil. Edward Putnam and Ezekiel Cheever testified that Martha Corey claimed "shee had made a profession of christ and rejoyced to go and hear the word of god and the like." Putnam and Cheever warned her that "making an out ward profession" would not clear her name, "for it had often been so in the wourld that witches had crept into the churches." They tried to persuade her to confess, but Corey insisted that she had made a covenant with God; for their part, Putnam and Cheever claimed that she "made her profession a cloake to cover all" (1:261).

67. Ibid., 1:143.

allowed to follow admission of sin with repentance, in this volatile and mistrustful climate, Bromage's disclosure simply provoked further suspicion and investigation. The court immediately demanded to know in what shape the devil appeared. Perhaps to distance herself from any involvement with Satan's physical appearance, she replied that "she believed the devil was in her heart."[68] Bromage was later acquitted for lack of evidence, but her testimony about the devil in her life suggests that there was indeed a very fine line between ordinary sinning and witchcraft, and that women tried to assess the states of their souls sincerely, even if doing so could expose them to the charge of witchcraft. Hannah Bromage's rather innocuous admissions, particularly the formulaic one that the devil was in her heart, signified that she had been a sinner; but even sinners, like witches, had given their souls to Satan and had become his servants.

Rebecca Eames's confession expressly blended more typical tales of Satanic encounters with admission of a prior sin of adultery. She explained to the court that immediately after making a black mark with her finger, sealing the covenant, "she was then in such horror of Conscienc that she tooke a Rope to hang herselfe and a Razer to cutt her throate by Reason of her great sin in Committing adultery & by that the Divell Gained her he promiseing she should not be brought out or ever discovered."[69] Her confession displayed terrified confusion—was she horrified by the evil pact or by confrontation with her previous sin of adultery? Or did she believe she had effectively covenanted with the devil by virtue of her earlier sexual violation?

If in their narratives of conversion women constructed an image of themselves, not merely of their sins, as entirely retrograde, in this more dangerous context, too, we see women embrace a sense of themselves as essentially depraved, as sinners bound to the devil. Although Rebecca Nurse, for example, denied any explicit pact with Satan, she could not say she was without sin, and in fact, she blamed some unknown lapse for her predicament: "Well as to this thing I am Innocent as the child unborne but . . . what sine hath god found out in me unrepented of that he should Lay such an Afliction upon me in my old Age."[70] Women such as

68. Ibid.
69. Ibid., 1:128.
70. Ibid., 2:594.

Nurse, Eames, and Bromage could not help but search within themselves and sometimes confess unwittingly, convinced that they actually were in the devil's snare, that something they had thought or done had festered in their souls and would eventually be exposed.

Simon and Mary Chapman attested that their friend, the accused Elizabeth How, "was a woman of a fliktion and morning for sin in hur selves An othars." In fact, they claimed, How used to bless God when afflictions came her way because it made her examine her own heart. Of the accusations of witchcraft, Simon and Mary Chapman heard How say, "Thoh i am a gret sinar yit i am cler of that." Elizabeth How knew that she sinned; no true saint could claim otherwise. She also knew that her heart should lie with God and not with Satan. She used her sins, as her ministers taught, as occasions to strengthen her devotion to the Lord. She and her supporters refused to admit that she had made an explicit pact with Satan; they believed that, in spite of her previous sins, she was "a woman throu in that gret work of conviktion and convertion." [71] In other words, she was a woman possessed by God and not by the devil.

Admitting to one kind of sin while denying the other was rarely successful; the court was more likely to interpret any admissions of sin in the worst possible light. Alice Parker said "she wished God would open the Earth and Swallow her up presently, if one word of this [witchcraft accusation] was true and make her an Example to Others." She did not deny the seriousness of the charge, nor did she question the validity of the proceedings. She simply did not believe that the accusation was true in her case. She did consent that she was a sinner, however, and perhaps that admission contributed to the court's guilty verdict. She avowed, "If she was as free from other sins as from Witchcraft she would not ask the Lord mercy." But as if to confirm her admission that she was not free of other sins, at that very moment Mary Warren had a "dreadful fit" in full public view; her tongue hung out of her mouth until it turned black, according to the record. Asked why she tormented Warren this way, Parker responded helplessly, "If I do, the Lord forgive me." [72]

Some women simply broke down under the enormous pressure to confess and repent. Faced with the constant, bizarre afflictions of the accusers, accused women began to believe that they were in some way re-

71. Ibid., 2:441.
72. Ibid., 2:624.

sponsible. In the midst of the proceedings, several of the citizens of Andover submitted a petition to the Salem court protesting the accusation of five of their fellow townspeople. Citing the accused's "sober godly and exemplary conversation," the fifty-three men and women spoke of their surprise that these five would have been indicted. Furthermore, the petitioners referred to the unbearable pressure the accused endured from their friends and families to admit their guilt; this stress "did unreasonably urge them to confess themselves guilty." At first, the five women refused to accept blame. Their petitioners suggested, however, that in the process of maintaining their innocence, these women may have implicated themselves unknowingly and erroneously: "But these good women did very much assert their innocency, yet some of them said they were not without fear least Satan had some way ensnared them." The accused could honestly testify that they had never signed an explicit pact with the devil, but aware of the devil's guile and power and their own helplessness, demonstrated indeed by their very incarceration, they had to fear that in some way Satan might have lured them into his trap. Even though these five women "knew nothing by themselves of that nature [witchcraft]," they were "at length persuaded publickly to own what they were charged with." [73]

Recantations by women who had initially confessed can provide additional clues about women's guilt and reprobation and about women's place more generally. Margaret Jacobs wrote to her father from the Salem jail that she had confessed by reason of "the Magistrates Threatnings, and my own Vile and Wretched Heart." Harassment seems to have played a role; her own guilt arising from past sin—a heart absent from God and thus committed to Satan—reinforced her decision. Like Jacobs, Rebecca Eames cited pressure, along with her own general sinfulness, as causes for her confession. In a later statement, she characterized her confession as completely false and stated that she had been "hurried out of my Senses by the Afflicted persons . . . saying they knew me to be an old witch and If I would not confesse it I should very Spedily be hanged . . . w'ch was the Occasion *with my owne wicked heart* of my saying what I did say." [74]

Recanters recognized that they now had to repent for the serious sin of lying. Margaret Jacobs related that her false confession wounded her soul

73. Ibid., 2:618–19.
74. Ibid., 2:490, 1:284, emphasis added.

and that she retracted it because the Lord "would not let me go on in my Sins." After she had falsely confessed she had spent a horrible night "in such horror of conscience that I could not sleep for fear the devil should carry me away for telling such horrid lies." Recognizing the imminence of her death, she chose to die "with a quiet conscience." And happily, she reported, since coming to this decision she had "enjoyed more felicity in spirit, a thousand times, than I did before in my enlargement." [75] Women who took back their statements established themselves publicly as liars; clearly they were in the devil's camp with or without explicitly signing the book. The public drama of retraction further emmeshed them in the discourse of depravity, repentance, and forgiveness; as women, their lies confirmed their self-image, as well as public perception of them, as sinners, as essentially unworthy, and thus they endorsed their subordination not only to God but to (male) authority.

If recanters mentioned the pressure on them to confess, it was left to others to suggest that perhaps the original admissions had been unfairly coerced. The fifty-three petitioners for the five Andover women proposed that "confessing was the only way to obtain favour," and that this "might be too powerful a temptation for timorous women to withstand." Increase Mather's report on his conversation with Mary Osgood confirmed the ease with which one might yield to the temptation to give the court what it wanted to hear. When the court asked her when she first covenanted with Satan, Osgood said she did not know. When pressed to come up with a time, according to Mather, "she considered that about twelve years before (when she had her last child) she had a fit of sickness, and was melancholy; and so thought that that time might be as proper a time to mention as any." Concerning the devil's shape, Mather contended that the court had insisted to her that he had appeared and then required her to tell his shape. As it happened, she had seen a cat the day she was apprehended and, according to Mather, "not as though she any whit suspected the said cat to be the Devil, in the day of it, but because some creature she must mention, and this came into her mind at that time." [76]

75. Ibid., 2:491. Jacobs was not executed, despite her recantation. Rosenthal, *Salem Story*, 230n49, suggests that by the end of the trials, the authorities were not executing anyone as young as thirty-eight.
76. Ibid., 2:619, 617. On Mather's role in securing recantations of the Andover confessions, see Stephen Foster, *The Long Argument: English Puritanism and the Shaping of New England Culture, 1570–1700* (Chapel Hill, N.C., 1991), 262.

Using his left (sinister) hand, a man signs the devil's book, committing himself body and soul to Satan. When accused women confessed to signing the book, they exposed not only their perceived sinful natures but sometimes a much greater sense of guilt, which developed as the boundaries separating common sins and the egregious sin of covenanting with the devil became blurred. Men's admissions of guilt were more typically qualified and ambivalent, as they distanced themselves from charges of direct collusion with Satan (from Cotton Mather, *On Witchcraft* [Mt. Vernon, N.Y.: Peter Pauper Press, Inc., 1950]. Reprinted with permission).

Mather was not alone in recognizing that the court wanted to hear and believe certain things, particularly from women. Sarah Churchill's confession was motivated by three circumstances, she later told her friend Sarah Ingersoll. She had been threatened and told "thay would put her in to the dongin," and she had persisted in her story for so long that it seemed impossible for her to back out of it. The third reason was most insightful: Churchill believed "that If she told mr Noys but ons [once] she had sat hur hand to the Book he would be leve her but If she told the truth and saied she had not seat her hand to the Book a hundred times he would not beleve hur." [77]

Churchill's apperception was more true for women than for men. Not only was it far more unusual for a man to be accused of witchcraft than a woman, but when men were accused, or when they confessed, their

77. *Salem Witchcraft Papers,* 1:212.

gender mattered as well. Unfortunately the surviving records of male examinations are scant. Instead of detailed records of conversations between
the court and accused men, we are more often left only with indictments,
warrants, or complaints, making it difficult to reconstruct events and
their nuances. The lack of such evidence, in and of itself, might suggest
that cases against men were pursued less vigorously than those against
women, perhaps because most people believed that witches were women.
Nonetheless, men's confessions and denials were different in their substance and in their reception. Men, by and large, did not confuse their
own ordinary sinning with witchcraft. They did not enter into the particular feminine drama of Puritan redemption and forgiveness during the
witchcraft crisis. When accused (generally because they were related to
an accused woman), either they boldly confessed, weaving elaborate tales
of the devil's doings, or they offered tentative and tactical admissions, or
most frequently, they denied the accusation and did so audaciously. Apparently, men did not feel the need to defer to the court's procedures as
did women. They were impertinent, though they sometimes paid for
their insolence with their lives.

In the few documented cases in which a lively exchange occurred, notions of proper male behavior were created or reinforced in the proceedings of the court. As in the trials of women, Puritan New England's social
order and gender arrangements were defined, rehearsed, and endorsed.
John Willard, for example, was brought before the court on charges of
witchcraft, but another offense, that he violently beat his wife, assumed a
significant role in the proceedings. Just as women's "feminine" behavior—
or the lack of it—became inextricably linked with suspicions of witchcraft, so too did Willard's abusive proclivities. Peter Prescot was concerned not with any act of maleficence for which Willard may have been
responsible but that Willard himself "with his own mouth told him of his
beating of his wife." Aaron Wey admitted, somewhat hesitatingly, "If I
must speak, I will, I can say you have been very cruell to poor creatures."
And finally, his choice of words hinting at the supernatural, Benjamin
Wilkins offered evidence of Willard's "unnatural usage to his wife."[78]

78. Ibid., 3:824. For a complete discussion of Willard's case, as well as those of the
other three men who hanged on August 19, 1692, see Bernard Rosenthal, *Salem Story*,
107–50. Rosenthal says that a profound cultural shift after the July hangings made it possible for men to be executed for witchcraft.

In the case of George Burroughs, former Salem Village minister, testimony against him frequently mentioned his inappropriate behavior
toward his wife. John and Rebecca Putnam both observed that when
the defendant lived at their house he was "a very sharp man to his wife,
notwithstanding to our observation shee was a very good and dutiful
wife to him." Mary Webber said that when she was Burrough's neighbor
six or seven years back, she heard his wife "tell much of her husband un-
kindness to her and that she dare not wright to her father to acquaint
[him] how it was with her." Webber described how the minister's wife
"had beene much affrighted," but it is not clear from the transcript if she
was afraid of Burroughs's violence or of the noise in the chimney which
turned out to be "something like a white calfe." [79] Witnesses merged the
two offenses—spousal abuse and witchcraft—thus gendering the witch's
(and the devil's) crime. Women were likely to be taken as witches if it
also could be proven that they displayed some sort of offensive carriage
as wives, mothers, or daughters. Men were more likely to be considered
witches if they had abandoned their duties as husbands and fathers.

Ann Putnam Jr.'s testimony against Burroughs linked abusive behavior
with yet another serious offense found in men's trials: murder. Putnam
claimed that she saw the ghosts of Burroughs's two former wives, clothed
in winding sheets. These two women told her "he had been a cruell man
to them. and that their blood did crie for vengance against him." They
told her that Burroughs had murdered both of them: "One tould me that
she was his first wife and he stabed hir under the left Arme and put a
peace of sealing wax on the wound." The other victim said he "kiled hir

79 *Salem Witchcraft Papers*, 1:153, 176, 163. Hannah Harris also mentioned that Burroughs "often scolded wife," and she attributed his wife's serious illness to this abuse. See
1:163. Bernard Rosenthal has shown how George Burroughs's trial revolved around religious dispute. It seems that Burroughs, former Salem Village minister, was more a Baptist
than a Puritan. He eschewed the Lord's Supper and refused to baptize his own children. Indeed, in the summary presentation of evidence, Burroughs was asked when he had last participated in the Lord's Supper. He admitted that "it was so long since he could not tell" and
that when he did attend Sabbath meetings in Boston and Charlestown he avoided it; in the
next sentence he denied that his house was haunted, and then conceded that none but his eldest child had been baptized. Massachusetts Bay prohibited execution of Baptists in 1692,
but if Burroughs were proven a witch, he could be hanged. After Burroughs's examination
a new script emerged, as accusers increasingly spoke of baptism by "the black man" and renounced their former baptisms—as both the devil and the Baptists required. See Rosenthal,
Salem Story, 129–38.

in the vessell as she was coming to se hir friends," and both women told Putnam she should tell the magistrates of these crimes.[80]

Quite likely, Burroughs was singled out because he had run afoul of Puritan orthodoxy. Yet during his trial, and the trials of other men as well, accusers, witnesses, and the court conjoined ideas about masculinity and male witchcraft. As we have seen, the devil deployed his powers unequally. He attacked the bodies of women but mainly the property of men, and he granted men unusual strength. In the accusations, too, notions of maleness pervaded the discourse.

John Proctor was one of five men to be executed for witchcraft; yet his attitude toward the court nonetheless reveals the efficacy men possessed. Proctor's petition to the court, declaring his innocence, was entirely different in character and tone from any petitions offered by women. Comparing the procedures to "Popish Cruelties," Proctor challenged the court by mentioning the barbarous torture used on three other men, Andrew and Richard Carrier and his own son, William Proctor. He wrote of the Carriers that they "would not confess any thing till they tyed them Neck and Heels till the Blood was ready to come out of their Noses, and 'tis credibly believed and reported this was the occasion of making them confess that they never did." [81] William refused to confess, Proctor explained, even though he endured such agonies. Proctor did not question the reality of the devil's substantial powers; in fact, he attributed the suspicion against him to "the Delusion of the Devil." But he was able, nonetheless, to transcend the world of magic, challenge the court, and demand either a change of venue or new judges; at the very least he requested that the ministers to whom he addressed his petition attend the trials. The record does not indicate the court's response to his requests.

Other men also questioned the court or the accusers and addressed their shortcomings—something that women did ever so carefully, if at all. When Mary Easty dared to suggest to the court that it might isolate the afflicted people and examine them carefully to avoid fraud, she did so

---

80. *Salem Witchcraft Papers*, 1:166. Likewise, during John Willard's examination the court reminded him that the accused spoke of murder charges against him as well as witchcraft. Hearing Willard deny that he hurt the afflicted, the court said, "Well they charge you not only with this but with dreadfull murthers, & I doubt not if you be guilty, God will not suffer evidences to be wanting." See ibid., 3:823.

81. Ibid., 2:689.

tactfully, and "humbly begg[ed]" the magistrates to accept her petition, "from a poor dying Innocent person." John Jackson Sr., by contrast, asked about his appearance at a witch meeting, replied, with no apologies, that "these persons was not in their Right mind." George Jacobs Sr., one of those executed, mocked the very notion of witchcraft when he provoked the court, "You tax me for a wizard, you may as well tax me for a buzard I have done no harm." And later during his examination, Jacobs seems to have thrown up his hands in despair, pronouncing, "Well: burn me, or hang me, I will stand in the truth of Christ, I know nothing of it." [82]

In their denials, men were better able than women to distinguish their prior sins from the immediate accusation of a devil's pact. They did not conflate their sinful pasts with their alleged diabolical presents. William Hobbs admitted that he had not been to church for some time, but did not interpret this deficiency more broadly, as anything more than a minor breach. He told the court only that he had been ill; as to the charges of witchcraft, he said, "You may judge your pleasure, my soul is clear." In stark contrast to so many accused women, though he had just admitted to one sin, Hobbs could still insist that his soul was clear. For Hobbs, apparently, his infraction did not connote even an implicit covenant with the devil. The court pushed him to admit his guilt on both counts; missing prayer service simply invited the devil. They told him, "If you put away Gods ordinances, no wonder that the Devil prevails with you." That the devil worked that way, Hobbs granted, but he willfully insisted nonetheless, "I do not know anything of that nature." [83]

Henry Salter similarly admitted that he had told lies in the past as well as "been in drink" but to the charges that he used a key, the Bible, a sieve, and a scissors for his witchcraft, he replied, "I never knew of any such thing." The court pressed neither Salter nor Hobbs as it did the

---

82. Ibid., 1:304, 2:467, 475, 476. When Martha Corey tried to point out to the court that the clothing worn by her supposed specter did not match the clothing Corey herself actually wore, what could have been exposure of her accusers and the magistrates was interpreted as the cunning machinations of a witch. See 1:260–62. Susannah Martin's appeal to the court citing the biblical episode of Saul and the Witch of Endor as precedent for the invalidity of spectral evidence was similarly ineffectual. As we have seen, the magistrates would not budge from their insistence that consent was required before the devil would take one's shape. See 2:551.

83. Ibid., 2:425, 427.

women, even though both acknowledged some sin. And neither man seems to have associated his own guilt with a more serious pact with the devil.[84]

Women's circumstances altered the nature of the cases brought against them. A woman risked being damned regardless of her response. If she embraced a sense of herself as a terrible sinner because she missed church meeting or lied or drank or committed some other common sin, then, convinced of her implicit covenant with the devil, she could easily implicate herself as a witch, though she denied that charge. If she instead steadfastly maintained her innocence, separating her prior sins from the extraordinary offense of witchcraft, the court could nonetheless convict her, convinced by her obstinacy in refusing to confess and repent. Neither Hobbs nor Salter was hanged; a woman who dared to deny sinfulness more likely would have been.

Men also confessed in their own way, when they did so at all. Two of the ten male confessions came from thirteen-year-old boys. Stephen Johnson's perfunctory confession sounds more like the typical female one. The boy described the various guises in which the devil appeared to him and the details of his baptism and told the court how he afflicted others. At the end, the document reads, "he Says he is Sorry for w't he has done Renounces the Divel & all his Works & then Could Take the afflicted by the Hand w'th out hurting of them." [85] Patriarchy—rule by fathers—subordinates children as well as women; in that context, Stephen Johnson's confession was complete, and he was not killed.

Some confessions were extracted by torture. The court records indicate that Richard and Andrew Carrier were "Carried out to another Cambbre and there feet & hands bound." Shortly thereafter Richard was brought back in again and the court asked, "Rich'd though you have been Verry Obstinate Yett tel us how long agoe it is Since you ware taken in this Snare," whereupon Richard said everything he knew—or thought the court wanted to hear—to avoid more pain. His elaborate tale included particulars about the devil's book, the baptism, how he arrived at the devil's meetings, and the exact manner in which he afflicted others ("I doe it by Roling up a handcherchif & Soe Imagining to be a representa-

84. Ibid., 3:723.
85. Ibid., 2:510. Another thirteen-year-old boy, John Sawdy, also appears to have confessed, although there is no surviving document. See 3:725.

tion of a person"). He told the court that the devil had his permission to afflict others.[86]

Richard Carrier's story was believable because he followed so many of the unspoken guidelines for confession, but it was also gendered. It contained no apology, and the admissions did not follow the female model. At one point Carrier wavered, indicating an ambivalence about what he admitted to doing. In an attempt to relieve himself from some of the responsibility for his actions, he announced, "the Divel Doth it Some times the Divell Sturred Me Up to hurt the Ministers Wife."[87] Richard Carrier felt compelled to acknowledge the afflictions happening before his eyes in the courtroom, and he wanted the torture to stop, but he did not want to own completely his own involvement. Woven into his story was an alibi: the devil made him do it. Even with this intricate narrative, Carrier never saw himself as the evil sinner, bonded to Satan by his own transgressive self or even for his particular transgressions.

Two other men displayed a similar divergence in their confessions. John Jackson Jr. confessed that the devil asked him to serve him, but significantly, he declared that he never took the ultimate, voluntary step of signing the devil's book. He did admit that the devil appeared to him in the shape of a black man, in the form of cats, and in the persona of his Aunt How, but he "would not own that ever: the Devill babtized him nor: that ever he had signed: to the Devils book." Joseph Ring, of Salisbury, was never accused of witchcraft, but his testimony against others came remarkably close to a confession. He told of how he had endured many strange happenings at the hands of the accused witches Susannah Martin and Thomas Hardy. Ring was "almost frited out of his witts" by the noises and shapes these two presented to him, not to mention the meetings and feasts that he was forced to attend. During his ordeal, a man used to come to him, he recounted, and promised him anything he

---

86. Ibid., 2:527–29. We do not know if men were tortured more frequently than women. The mere threat of torture may have been enough to persuade some women, convinced of their sinful natures anyway, to confess. For a discussion of emotional and physical torture, see Godbeer, *Devil's Dominion*, 206–10.

87. *Salem Witchcraft Papers*, 2:529. Nor did Samuel Wardwell's confession conform to the female model. He later recanted his confession but was hanged anyway. For a discussion of the court's change in procedure regarding spectral evidence in Wardwell's trial, see Rosenthal, *Salem Story*, 154–56. Wardwell thought he would die whether he confessed or retracted, and later chroniclers have lauded his choice to tell the truth. See 3:784.

wanted, "all delectable things psons and places Imaginabl." But Ring steadfastly refused the offers. "On[e] time the book was brought," Ring recalled, "and a pen offerd him & to his apprehension ther was blod in the Ink horn but *he never toucht the pen*." [88] Like John Jackson Jr., Ring firmly denied signing. Admission of that deed would have closed their cases; a confessed pact with Satan would have proven that the devil, rather than Christ, had taken possession of them. Yet, by admitting much less than Ring about involvement with the devil, a woman would have exposed herself to prosecution that Ring managed to escape.

Andrew Carrier, Richard's younger brother, also conceded the devil's intrusion, but his confession seems almost amusing in its ambivalence. With a hesitating stutter he admitted that the devil had offered him a house and land in Andover. Unable to resist that tempting offer, Andrew was ready to sign the book. He saw that the ink was red, but he could not make out the rest of the names on the list; he saw the devil's seal, but he could not discern the stamp because it was nighttime; he went to the meeting and saw others there, but he had forgotten their names; he drank the wine, but did not eat the bread; and he witnessed the Lord's Supper, but did not hear the exact words used at the administration of the sacrament.[89]

Despite Andrew Carrier's irresolution and Richard Carrier's lack of apology and acknowledged distance from the devil, their confessions saved the brothers from the gallows. Neither were pressured to admit past sins, nor did they in any way associate their character with their purported deeds. Because the court, the accusers, the witnesses, and even the accused themselves all believed that women were more likely to be witches than men, women had much more difficulty establishing their innocence. In their denials, women were required to demonstrate that their souls rested with God rather than with Satan. Even in their confessions, women's cultural performance conformed to the Puritan model of depravity, redemption, and forgiveness, not only because the court and the community seemed to require this discourse but because the accused women themselves embraced this construction of female subjectivity. Women did not confess tentatively like Andrew Carrier; such vacillation

88. *Salem Witchcraft Papers,* 2:469, 565–66, emphasis added.
89. Ibid., 2:530.

was apparently a man's privilege. The court demanded that women's confessions include testimony to their essential sinfulness, as well as admission of past misdeeds and alliances with the devil, whether great or small, explicit or implicit.

Even a retracted confession—perhaps especially a retracted confession—constituted an archetype of Puritan womanhood. When Margaret Jacobs admitted that she had lied, she begged the court to "take pity and compassion on my young and tender years," and she promised to pray forever, "as she is bound in duty, for your honours happiness in this life and eternal felicity in the world to come." Margaret Jacobs needed to prove she was not bound in the devil's snare (she said she was not guilty of witchcraft, "nor any other sin that deserved death from man"), and at the same time she was obliged to proclaim her status as a good—that is, essentially sinful and dependent—Puritan woman.[90]

Thus during the witch trials gender arrangements that subordinated women and prescribed their behavior were culturally reaffirmed as women attested to their own sinfulness, either in their confessions or in their denials. Women constructed a sense of themselves, a female subjectivity, that was endorsed by the cultural process. If they publicly affirmed their depraved nature, their lives were spared. Those who failed to conform, those who denied and therefore hanged, cast themselves not only as witches but as rebels against the entire order—male authority and God himself—because they would not admit that their past sinfulness had ensnared them in the devil's clutches. Puritans did not admit that women were more sinful than men and hence more likely than men to become witches. But in the process of negotiating their beliefs and ideals in practical ways, both women and men embedded womanhood in the discourse of depravity.

90. Ibid., 2:492.

5

SATAN DISPOSSESSED

OF the Salem witchcraft trials Perry Miller wrote, "The intellectual
history of New England up to 1720 can be written as though no such
thing ever happened. It had no effect on the ecclesiastical or political situation, it does not figure in the institutional or ideological development." [1]
In this chapter I argue that Miller was wrong. The concept of evil changed
as a result of the witchcraft trials. Puritan ideas about Satan and thus Puritan theology shifted subtly. People no longer thought of the devil as a
physical entity; his powers were relegated to the realm of the merely spiritual. Still the tempter, Satan sought to destroy souls in order to bring them
to hell. But post-Salem sermons and early and mid-eighteenth-century
conversion narratives suggest that ministers and laity conceived of a less
proximate Satan, one who tempted sinners and physically presided over
hell, rather than one who preyed on people and possessed souls in the immediate, living world. Sinners still perceived the devil as a threat to their
salvation, but both women and men were more easily assured that he
could be conquered spiritually.

As Satan receded into the background, Puritans took more responsibility for their own sins and their own souls. Not surprisingly, given the
gender distinctions of the seventeenth-century conversion narratives, the
post-Salem accounts of women and men also differ markedly. All pushed

1. Perry Miller, *The New England Mind: From Colony to Province* (Boston, 1961), 191.

the devil aside, but women's sense of their natures remained more pessimistic right through to the Great Awakening and beyond. As we shall see, men tended to blame their sins for corrupting their souls; women more often blamed their corrupt souls—their essence—for producing sinful behavior. During the Great Awakening, when the devil reappeared, albeit in a more metaphorical guise, women continued to struggle against his temptations, balancing a sense of depravity like that felt by seventeenth-century women with a newer awareness of their freedom to choose Christ actively.

Of course, factors other than the witch trials helped diminish Satan's powers in the early eighteenth century. Historians have described fundamental changes, both material and cultural, including intellectual transformations associated with the advent of an "Age of Reason." Such social, economic, and intellectual trends are beyond the scope of this book and have been well analyzed elsewhere.[2] New, "enlightened," "rational" ways of thinking and greater engagement with a more complex, commercial, cosmopolitan world may indeed have helped to push Satan further from people's thoughts.[3] Here, however, I am more interested in local,

2. Jeffrey Burton Russell has argued that John Milton's traditional portrayal of Satan was the last and that the image of the lord of evil was altered by the dual effects of rationalism and romanticism: "The most vulnerable part of theology, the Devil thus helped weaken the old structure further, and the new philosophies and ideologies of the eighteenth century provided the tools with which to pull it down." See Jeffrey Burton Russell, *Mephistopheles: The Devil in the Modern World* (Ithaca, N.Y., 1986), 128 and see esp. 77–128. See also Herbert Leventhal, *In the Shadow of the Enlightenment: Occultism and Renaissance Science in Eighteenth-Century America* (New York, 1976); Jon Butler, *Awash in a Sea of Faith: Christianizing the American People* (Cambridge, Mass., 1990); David D. Hall, *Worlds of Wonder, Days of Judgment: Popular Religious Belief in Early New England* (New York, 1989), 106–10. On the other hand, it is not completely clear that the advent of new rational, catholic, and cosmopolitan attitudes toward the world, especially associated with a creeping commercialization in eighteenth-century New England, were as widespread or influential as historians have imagined. See, for example, Christine Leigh Heyrman, *Commerce and Culture: The Maritime Communities of Colonial Massachusetts, 1690–1750* (New York, 1984). Especially in Essex County, the site of the 1692 witchcraft crisis, the coagulation of orthodoxy, even in seaport towns such as Gloucester and Marblehead, seems more an obstacle than an aid in explaining the declining fear of Satan as an immediate, physical threat.

3. Declining fear of Satan is sometimes seen as an index of a more general decline in religious belief. Yet secularization is by no means a necessary byproduct of economic growth and complexity, as Christine Heyrman demonstrates for the maritime Essex County communities of Gloucester and Marblehead, where social stability, religious orthodoxy, local-

contingent events, specifically, the excesses of the Salem trials, the unnec-
essary deaths, accusations, and reprisals that made people wary of seeing
Satan's intrusion so readily in everyday affairs.[4] Though theology appeared unchanged in ministers' sermons, in the post-Salem world ministers suggested that the devil's direct interference was quite uncommon and
that his temptations more typically took the form of spiritual assaults
than of physical abuse.[5]

---

ism, and insularity developed in tandem with commercial expansion. Heyrman's conclu-
sions might thus encourage us to seek shifts in New Englanders' attitudes toward the devil
elsewhere, in the more concrete and proximate crisis of 1692. For other works that emphasize social continuity over change in eighteenth-century New England, in addition to
Heyrman, *Commerce and Culture,* see especially James Henretta, "Farms and Families:
Mentalité in Pre-industrial America," *William and Mary Quarterly,* 3rd ser., 35 (1978),
3–32; Christopher Jedrey, *The World of John Cleaveland: Family and Community in
Eighteenth-Century New England* (New York, 1979); and Michael Zuckerman, *Peaceable
Kingdoms: New England Towns in the Eighteenth Century* (New York, 1970).

4. Changes in Puritan New England, especially in the social and legal sphere, have been
well documented and analyzed in Cornelia Hughes Dayton, *Women before the Bar: Gender, Law, and Society in Connecticut, 1639–1789* (Chapel Hill, N.C., 1995). Dayton traces
the shift from a single sexual standard for women and men to a dramatic reassertion of Europe's double standard; during the height of Puritans' insistence on moral godly behavior
for both sexes in the seventeenth century, women entered the court system regularly. Frequently whipped, fined, or humiliated, women had their voices heard. In the early eighteenth
century, says Dayton, anglicization, commercialization, and the emergence of a middle class
ultimately changed the work of the court and created barriers to women's use of the court
system. A contributing cause, I maintain, was the immoderation of the witch trials. Men
may well have thought that women had had their moment in public, as accusers, deniers,
and confessors, only to precipitate the worst travesty of justice in the region's history. As
New England society underwent "refinement," moral transgressions, which earlier had
linked women with the devil, were no longer regulated by the community in court. Women
were effectively and publicly silenced. See Richard Bushman, *The Refinement of America:
Persons, Houses, Cities* (New York, 1992).

5. As we shall see, immediately after the trials (1693–1720s) the devil's presence was
significantly downplayed by the laity in their conversion narratives and in ministerial sermons. During periods of revival (after the 1727 earthquake, for example, and during the
Great Awakening), the powers of both God and the devil were resurrected. Lay narratives
and clerical sources characterized Satan, however, as a tempter and not as the possessor of
souls. On the problem of declension as an interpretive category, see, for example, Harry S.
Stout and Catherine A. Brekus, "Declension, Gender, and the 'New Religious History,'" in
Belief and Behavior: Essays in the New Religious History, ed. Philip R. Vandermeer and
Robert P. Swierenga (New Brunswick, N.J., 1991), 15–37; Gerald F. Moran, "'Sinners Are
Turned into Saints in Numbers': Puritanism and Revivalism in Colonial Connecticut,"
ibid., 38–62; David D. Hall, "On Common Ground: The Coherence of American Puritan
Studies," *William and Mary Quarterly,* 3rd ser., 44 (April 1987), 193–229.

Concerning Satan's appearance, ministers found themselves stranded between Scylla and Charybdis; they wanted their audiences to think of Satan as a spiritual rather than a physical presence, and yet they could not deny that spirits sometimes presented themselves concretely to the public. To do otherwise might suggest that the victims and accusers at Salem had all been deluded or fantastic liars. Samuel Willard relied on biblical wisdom to explain Satan's powers in this respect. In a series of sermons preached in 1701, he continued to maintain that the devil could assume a bodily shape, thus vindicating the suffering at Satan's hand professed at Salem. Yet, significantly, Willard qualified his interpretation. The devil tempted people, he argued, incorporeally; the devil's nature as an angel was simply not suited to appear visibly before his victims. Although he had the ability, according to Willard, he "rarely useth it." "Men and Angels are of two distinct kinds," Willard explained, "and were not made for *sensible Communion* ordinarily one with the other." Although Willard never mentioned the Salem episode directly, he asserted that "such apparitions therefore are beside the order of ordinary Providences."[6]

If the devil's appearance was so unusual, then ministers had to confront his outrageous activities at Salem while honoring the people who had been executed. Many felt tremendous guilt that the episode had reached such extraordinary proportions. In 1696, after the death of his daughter, Samuel Sewall, one of the Salem judges, had heard Latin passages from Matthew, which translated, "If ye had known what this meaneth, I will have mercy and not sacrifice, ye would not have condemned the guiltless." He recorded in his diary that this verse "did awfully bring to mind the Salem Tragedy."[7] Three years later Sewall posted a petition on a fast day begging forgiveness from his fellows as well as from God for Salem. According to the notice, Sewall was, "upon many accounts, more concerned than any that he knows of, Desires to take the Blame and Shame of it, Asking pardon of men, and especially

6. Samuel Willard, *The Christians Exercise by Satans Temptations: or, An Essay to discover the methods which this Adversary, useth to Tempt the Children of GOD; and to direct them how to escape the mischief thereof* (Boston, 1701), 88.

7. Samuel Sewall's Diary, 1674–1700, *Collections of the Massachusetts Historical Society*, 5th ser., 5, excerpts reprinted in *What Happened in Salem: Documents Pertaining to the Seventeenth-Century Witchcraft Trials*, ed. David Levin (New York, 1960), 89.

desiring prayers that God . . . would pardon that sin and all other his sins." [8] Just after the fast, Cotton Mather recorded in his diary that he had been "afflicted last night with discouraging thoughts as if unavoidable marks of Divine Displeasure must overtake my family for not appearing with vigor enough to stop the proceedings of the judges." [9]

Michael Wigglesworth shared the concern and the guilt of Sewall and Mather. Convinced that "innocent blood hath been shed & that many have had their hands defiled therewith," Wigglesworth wrote in 1704 to Increase Mather, urging swift restitution to the families whose lives had been destroyed by the witchcraft accusations. Wigglesworth did not suggest that the devil of whom the accusers spoke did not exist; but he did intimate that perhaps it was not actually the devil but either his acts of trickery or his imitators—evil men and women who emulated the devil—that had plagued the Bible Commonwealth. Placing blame on the "Devil's impostures," rather than the devil himself, Wigglesworth created a distinction that had not previously existed. He was convinced that "it was done ignorantly," and he sought assurance that the devil would not reappear, while expiating all involved from complicity in Salem's immoderations. Despite the likelihood that the devil's deceptions, not the devil himself, had instigated the episode and despite its unhappy conclusion, officials had nonetheless acted honestly, Wigglesworth implied, and he hoped for forgiveness. He offered the biblical example of Paul, who had "shed the blood of gods saints, and yet obtained mercy, because he did it in ignorance." He was convinced that God would show his subjects mercy if, like Paul, they bewailed their sins, shamed themselves, and made a "Publick and Solemn acknowledgment of it, and humiliation of it." [10]

Five years later some of the victims of the trials or their grown children appealed to the General Court seeking a reversal of attainder and compensation for their financial losses incurred as a result of the trials. It was not until 1711 that the General Court passed a bill reversing the convic-

8. Excerpted in *What Happened in Salem*, 90.

9. Quoted in Richard Weisman, *Witchcraft, Magic, and Religion in Seventeenth-Century Massachusetts* (Amherst, Mass., 1984), 175. Weisman offers a detailed account of the confessions by clergy and judges following the Salem trials, 160–83.

10. Michael Wigglesworth to Increase Mather, May 22, 1704, photocopied collection of manuscripts at the Massachusetts Historical Society, Boston.

tions of twenty-two people. The language of the bill seemed carefully for-
mulated to avoid the issue of Satan's intrusion. The question of spectral
evidence—whether or not the devil could assume the shape of an innocent person—was purposely left unanswered. The bill stated that in 1692
"several Towns within this Province were Infested with a horrible Witchcraft or possession of devils." The wording of the bill left Salem's visita-
tion from the invisible world ambiguous. Whether there had indeed been
actual witchcraft—people willfully giving their bodies and souls over to
the devil—or whether they had all been the unwitting victims of the
devil's possession was left untouched. The bill simply reminded its audience that her majesty, the late Queen Mary, had requested in 1693 that in
the future, "all proceedings against persons accused for Witchcraft, or
being possessed by the Devil," be confronted with "the greatest Modera-
tion and all due Circumspection."[11]

In any case, no one publicly mentioned fraud as a possible explanation
for the episode, as opposed to the conventional interpretation that it represented an intrusion from the spirit world. By contrast, in 1720 when
three young girls in Littleton, Massachusetts, claimed that a neighbor's
specter was afflicting them, the town's minister speculated that the cha-
rade was likely "the contrivance of the children of men." Firmly avowing
belief in the devil, while venturing a more mundane explanation for the
affliction—an explanation corroborated by the eldest girl's admission—
Ebenezer Turrell remarked, "Where one relation is exactly according to
truth, there are two, at least, that are wholly the fruit of wild imagination, or intolerably mixt with deceit and falsehood." Turell's fascinating
account of the incident, written eight years later, should be read as nothing less than a morality tale, intended to teach parents to raise their children to uphold God's word, rather than to succumb to the deceptions
and lies of the devil. According to Turrell, the devil appeared in Littleton
not as the leader of a band of witches but as the tempter who successfully
lured these girls into an outlandish hoax. For Turrell, then, Satan's accomplices were not the accused but the weak, deluded, and ungodly
accusers.[12]

11. Both quotations in David Levin, *What Happened in Salem*, 139.
12. Ebenezer Turell, "Detection of Witchcraft," *Collections of the Massachusetts Historical Society*, 2nd ser., 10 (1823), 6–7. This kind of storytelling, invoking the tragedy at

Ideas had changed in the twenty-eight years since the Salem trials. Belief in Satan had not waned, but his ubiquitous intrusion was no longer
credible. The clergy played a part in altering the Puritan worldview. The
shift in the theology of the devil was by no means dramatic. Ministers
continued to teach that Satan was a force to be reckoned with, but their
tone also implied their hope that congregants would not see Satan lurk-
ing behind every tree waiting to lure sinners into his service as witches.
Samuel Willard, for example, did not deny that the devil was responsible
for people's temptations, but he carefully explained that it was the temptation and not the devil that entrapped the sinner. The temptation,
Willard warned, "may attack him in the Morning when he awakes, and
follow him to his lying down again at Night, & give him disturbance in
his business all the day long, and break his rest." Sometimes the sinner
would successfully withstand temptation; at other times "it ensnares
him, and leads him away after it; it imposeth upon him, and deceives
him, and he yields without making any resistance." Willard's guarded interpretation admitted that Satan possessed the unregenerate. Indeed, he
quoted biblical passages that warned, for example, "They are led captive
at his will, 2 Tim.2.26." [13] The Bible, of course, could not be disputed;
nevertheless, Willard's exegesis of these portions focused directly on the
temptations, rather than on the devil, who lay indirectly behind them.

Willard continued to warn his congregants of Satan's relentless pursuit,
his dogged persistence to distract sinners from God. The difference in the
post-Salem years was that ministers no longer concentrated on Satan's
possession of souls. The devil tempted and persuaded, but ultimately
ministers avoided talking about sinners as those who had abandoned
their souls to the devil's control. Willard explained that though "perfect

---

Salem but still insisting on the reality of devils and other spirits, can be seen in eighteenth-
century published pamphlets, often taking the form of allegorical morality (and sometimes
political) lessons. For example, see *A Most Unaccountable Relation of one Miss Sarah
Green, A Widow* . . . [etc.] (n.p., 1762), dated pamphlet, American Antiquarian Society
(hereafter AAS), Worcester, Mass.; *The Wonder of Wonders! or, The Wonderful Appearance of an Angel, Devil, and Ghost, to a Gentleman in the Town of Boston* . . . [etc.]
(Boston, 1774), dated pamphlet, AAS; *The Prodigal Daughter: or A Strange and Wonderful
Relation* . . . [etc.] (Boston, c. 1742–54), dated pamphlet, AAS.

13. Willard, *Christians Exercise*, 27. Willard (9) also quoted John 8:44: "They will do
his lusts," and Eph. 2:2: "He works in them with power."

This wicked Wretch, quite void of Grace & Shame,
She seem'd to be well pleased at the same;
Said, I'm resolv'd your Counsel for to take,
And be reveng'd for what they've done of late.
　Where do you live, pray tell me where to come
That I may tell you when the Job is done,
He said, my Name is Satan, and I dwell
In the dark Regions of the burning Hell.
　At first she seem'd to be something surpriz'd,
But

The Prodigal Daughter: or a strange and wonderful relation (Boston, between 1742 and 1754). By the mid-eighteenth century the devil could appear guileful but nonthreatening as a handsome and charming young man, as in the illustration to this morality tale concerning a "proud and disobedient" daughter and her parents. The devil visited the "wicked Wretch, quite void of Grace & Shame," urging her to poison her parents because they would not indulge her many extravagances (courtesy American Antiquarian Society, Worcester, Mass.).

happiness consists in a full freedom from all evil, and an entire fruition of all good," this would never be achieved "so long as we are every moment in hazard of being assailed with the Temptations of our most virulent adversary, and are too often drawn away *by them* to wound our Conscience, and disturb our peace." The devil constantly assaulted one's soul with temptations, but the sinner's undoing was in yielding to the allurements. It was the temptation and not Satan that drew sinners away and wounded their consciences. Avoiding inference of the devil's physical intrusion, Willard shifted his focus away from Satan and counseled that the only way "to get rid of these temptations . . . [was] to seek earnestly for help & strength from him, to help us to encounter and vanquish them." [14]

Ministers approached the question of responsibility for sin more directly in the post-Salem years. If the message to the public had been somewhat ambiguous in the seventeenth century—blaming both Satan and one's own inward concupiscence—in the years after the witch trials ministers insisted that one's own self, and not Satan, was to be held completely accountable for sin. Willard, for example, emphasized that those who had sinned had "made choise of it." The indwelling sin in humankind had so distorted understanding and judgment that sin became the reflection of a "spontaneous and deliberate Election and Embracement of these delusions." Innate depravity, not the devil, created the delusions, which sinners then willfully embraced. As if, perhaps, to allay any misguided attempts to blame Satan's interference in sin, Willard maintained, "and yet this is all *voluntary;* there is no outward force laid upon them to cause them thus to do, but is a fruit of the native Corruption which is in them." [15]

14. Ibid., 112–24, 137 (emphasis added), 140. In the seventeenth century Willard had been persuaded that the devil not only tempted people but could molest them physically and speak through their bodies. When his servant Elizabeth Knapp became possessed by Satan in 1671, Willard wondered "whither shee have covenanted with the Devill or noe," but he did not doubt her possession. He pitied her condition and urged that others show similar compassion. As a victim of Satan's possession, "shee is a monument of divine severitye, & the Lord grant that all that see or hear, may feare & tremble." See Samuel Willard, *A Briefe Account of a Strange & Unusuall Providence of God befallen to Elizabeth Knap[p] of Groton* (1671) in *Groton in the Witchcraft Times,* ed. Samuel Green (Groton, Mass., 1883), 21.

15. Samuel Willard, *Reformation the Great Duty of an afflicted People. Setting forth the Sin and Danger there is in Neglecting of it, under the Continued and Repeated Judgments of God* (Boston, 1694), 28, 29.

In a later series of sermons, Willard acknowledged that Satan might introduce temptation, but he warned against blaming him for every allurement. "It was our Duty," he counseled, "both not to have been ignorant of his devices, and to have withstood him steadfastly." He made this point several times in these sermons, insisting, "The Devil shall bear his own blame, and God will punish him for all the malicious practices which he useth against his people: but you must bear your own blame, which is due to you for yielding to the Temptation." Willard criticized his flock for placing too much blame on the devil: "There is a great noise and cry that some make, the Devil, the Devil, he hath tempted me, he was too sly and hard for me, and a great deal of anger seems to be vented upon him." Willard was not denying the devil's role in sin; in fact, he acknowledged that one of the devil's tricks was to "keep us from a due sense of and sorrow for our own folly which we have acted in it, and thereby hinder our true and soaking Repentance." The biblical example that he used to illustrate his point, however, removed the devil from the focus of sin. When David sinned by numbering the people after God had warned him not to, Willard explained, he "doth not so much as mention Satan, tho' he had provoked him to it, but takes all to himself. David said unto God, I have sinned greatly, because I have done this thing." [16] Willard's tone and the biblical example he provided suggested that he wanted his listeners to accept the guilt for their sins personally and to leave Satan out of it.

Sinners—and female sinners, in particular—in their conversion narratives placed far more blame on themselves than did those sixty years earlier, before Satan's blatant intrusion at Salem. Whereas earlier converts tended to cite both sin and Satan for their errant ways, women in the eighteenth century blamed primarily themselves. Esther Bissell believed in 1700 that she was the "wickedest wretch that ever breathed" because she was utterly unable to submit to God's will: "[I] could freely own that it was my own fault, and from the wickedness of my own heart that I was not converted." If God ever did bestow free grace upon her it would be "mere mercy," she claimed, because "I had nothing to commend me to God, and deserved nothing but death and damnation." Abigail Strong re-

16. Willard, *Christians Exercise,* 57, 149, 57–58. See 2 Sam. 24. In fact, the devil did not appear at all in this passage; God had incited David to count the people and then punished him for it.

lated that she "had such a sight of my own vileness," and that she "was utterly unworthy of the least mercy from God, and that if God had after all my pains and prayers, denied mercy to me and left me to perish in my sins, it would have been no more than I deserved, and this I can still freely own." [17]

Women assumed that their despicable and rebellious souls would damn them. Whereas in the seventeenth century women had tended to ignore their actual sins, focusing almost exclusively on their base souls, in the immediate post-Salem years, women repented for their actual sins, like men, but clearly gave their souls primary responsibility. When Ann Fitch gave her relation in February 1701, she portrayed herself as an active sinner, citing her unwillingness to engage in secret prayer, her temptations to forgo private counsel, her slothfulness, her ignorance of God, and her inability to heed her father's advice on his deathbed. So convinced was she of the power of her own sinfulness, that she believed she had caused her father's death "because God was angry with me for my sins." Fitch's sins were no worse—indeed, they were more innocuous—than those of many men; yet still she believed she "had a very wicked heart," and she moaned, "I thought it was a dreadful thing that I had such a nature in me as that I hated God, and then I also saw that I had greatly provoked God by trusting in my own righteousness." [18] First and foremost came her wicked nature; the sins she committed merely reflected and corroborated her vileness.

Although men also blamed themselves more than Satan, they put more emphasis on their sins, assuming that these had ruined their souls. Sins were the root of the problem and men's corruption was more contingent and less inevitable; their souls became culpable only after the commission of actual sins. Joshua Loomis's conversion narrative exemplifies this tendency. Loomis mentioned his drinking, his temptations to neglect public worship of God (which he took to be the devil's temptation), and his fears that he had committed the unpardonable "sin against the Holy

17. Kenneth P. Minkema, "The East Windsor Relations, 1700–1725," *Connecticut Historical Society Bulletin* 51 (Winter 1986), 7–63, Esther Bissell, July 24, 1700, Abigail Strong, September 14, 1725. This collection consists of fourteen narratives from the First Church of East Windsor, Connecticut, from 1700 to 1725, recorded by pastor Timothy Edwards, father of Jonathan Edwards. Ten of them are from 1700–1702, two from 1722, and two from 1725.

18. Ibid., Ann Fitch, February 26, 1701.

Ghost." Loomis admitted that because of all these sins he was in a miserable condition. He lamented, "And then I saw more than ever before what a great sinner I had been *by reason of* my actual sins, and that I had a very wicked heart, so that I thought I was the wickedest, vilest creature in the world." Like the female sinners, Loomis recognized his sins and his reprobation. But he believed his sins to be at the heart of his problems. Regarding a particularly egregious sin, which he dared not mention, he admitted that his soul had become tarnished: "Because I have herein and that over and over committed a sin that in itself is great and gross wickedness, it being of a scandalous nature and a very shameful and odious sin in the esteem of all sober people, *so that in and by it I have made my self vile.*"[19]

Loomis's emphasis on sins at the expense of the soul and his representation of his vileness as earned rather than inherent can perhaps explain why the devil appeared more frequently in the early eighteenth-century male narratives than in the female accounts. Admittedly, in the published East Windsor relations, Satan appears only four times—twice in Loomis's account, again when a male sinner recalled a biblical passage concerning the devil in hell, and once as a tempter in an anonymous narrative, which I take to be that of a man because of the nature of the professed transgressions. Satan's presence was decidedly different in these few instances from that of the seventeenth-century narratives. Here he was only rarely mentioned, as the tempter or as a reminder of hell, and even these few examples focused on the sinner's own failings. When Satan did emerge, infrequently, men mentioned him because they were atoning for specific sins that were conventionally associated with the devil's temptations. Women, on the other hand, though they sometimes specified various sins, expressed and hoped to expiate the wretchedness and rebelliousness of their very souls. And since Satan was no longer seen as the possessor of souls, he lost his prominent place in women's narratives.

In general, male as well as female converts distanced themselves from the devil. The anonymous (male) sinner first berated himself for sinning against God, keeping vain company, excessive drinking, "foolishly and sinfully spending my precious time, disgracing my self and relations and wringing and rending my precious soul." Only at the end of his narrative

19. Ibid., Joshua Loomis, February 27, 1701, emphasis added.

did he reprove himself for his "other late disorderly sinful actions and carriages which are well known by my neighbors." These transgressions alone had been caused "by the influence and instigation of the Devil and my own proud, froward, rebellious spirit and desperately wicked heart." Unfortunately we do not know what kind of wretched activity, perhaps more heinous than his itemized sins, compelled this sinner to shift some of the guilt to the devil.[20]

In the post-Salem years, male and female sinners placed more blame on themselves for submitting to temptation than they did on Satan's lures. More important, they emphasized their unworthiness in the sight of God. The notion that Satan controlled sinners had faded away; early eighteenth-century converts feared God's wrath rather than Satan's possession. The anonymous sinner admitted that his sins had been a "very provoking thing to God," and he begged forgiveness for "openly dishonor[ing] God." Hannah Bancroft was convinced that "God was very angry with me for them [her sins] and that I was in great danger of eternal damnation and that I was so great a sinner that I was the worst in the place." Joshua Willis Jr. testified that "the thoughts and fears of falling into the hands of an angry God stirred me up to take more pains for an interest in Christ." And Abigail Rockwell lamented, "I saw my self guilty before God, and that He was very angry with me, and that if I died in the condition that I was then in I should perish for ever, and was much afraid that I should die in my sins."[21] Eighteenth-century converts feared God more than the devil; they expected God to punish them for their sins, and they anticipated that God would cast them aside on Judgment Day and banish them to hell.

Of course, seventeenth-century conversion narratives contained elements of the same anxiety; sinners knew that God would determine their fates. But in the years before Salem repentent sinners feared Satan's possession of their souls in this life, and they presumed that as his slaves they would be sent to hell. John Furnell, for example, a carpenter and miller who gave his relation in 1645, admitted that "God had suffered Satan to assault me with many temptations." As a consequence of submitting to sin, Furnell believed that he was held captive. "It is true," he said, "Satan

20. Ibid., anonymous narrative, n.d.
21. Ibid., anonymous narrative, n.d., Hannah Bancroft, November 1700, Joshua Willis Jr., December 24, 1700, Abigail Rockwell, March 18, 1702.

had many wiles to keep his prisoners in awe and bondage." Roger
Haynes, the son of the governor of Connecticut, disclosed that he had
had "many slavish fears of the devil and going to bed lest before morning
I should fall to eternal sorrow." [22] Satan terrified these sinners; their sins
had made them slaves to the devil. In the post-Salem world Satan appeared in sinners' thoughts occasionally as the tempter, but these later
converts did not concern themselves with Satan's subjection. Rather than
fear the devil's enslavement, they worried about God's wrath.

Like their predecessors, eighteenth-century converts were troubled
when they felt that their hearts had grown distant from God. They spoke
about sin in the same terms; sin drew one from the Lord. If the earlier
sinners replaced that void with Satan, the post-Salem sinners avoided
that characterization of sin. Eighteenth-century sinners repeatedly described their hearts as full, not with the devil exactly but with the malig-
nant residue of their own evil behavior. Esther Bissell, for example,
owned that her heart "had been full of pride [and] enmity against God,
blasphemy and unbelief, atheism, and in a word empty of all good, and
full of all evil." Hannah Bancroft testified "in general that I was empty of
all good and very full of sin and wickedness." Joshua Willis Jr. claimed
that his "heart was very full of pride, unbelief, deceit, self-righteousness,
and enmity against God and all good." [23]

Forced to confront their own responsibility for their predicament,
early eighteenth-century sinners carried the burden of their sins in their
souls, instead of conceiving of sins more generally as the shackles of Satan.
They understood their transgressions or their emptiness as weights that
lay heavy on their consciences; either their souls (if they were women) or
their sins (if they were men) would justifiably anger God and send them
to join the devil in hell.[24] Joshua Loomis, for example, reflected "in particular about my actual sins," and realized that he was "full of all sin and

22. *Thomas Shepard's Confessions,* ed. George Selement and Bruce C. Wooley, Publications of the Colonial Society of Massachusetts, *Collections,* no. 58 (Boston, 1981), 206, 168.

23. "East Windsor Relations," Esther Bissell, July 24, 1700, Hannah Bancroft, November, 1700. Joshua Willis Jr., December 24, 1700.

24. As if to add to this image of sin as a millstone around one's neck, eighteenth-century
sinners usually listed particular sins they had committed, including drunkenness, gambling,
slothfulness, and keeping bad company. Whereas earlier converts focused on their distance
from God in a more general sense, these converts mentioned those transgressions for which
they carried the most grief. See ibid., passim.

empty of all good, and that I could do nothing to help my self." He did not mention the devil at all in his contemplations about the state of his soul; Satan appeared only when Loomis speculated about his future. At the moment he realized the enormity of his sins and the hopelessness of his situation, Loomis imagined that he was about to die and knew he could not escape God's wrath. He lamented, "I thought it was just with God to cut me down, and cast me into hell, and that I stood just upon the very brink of it, and therein wanting nothing but God's word and the devil would throw me in." Several times in his relation Daniel Skinner mentioned that "my sins lay as a heavy burden upon me." Briefly assuaged by the biblical message, "Come unto me all ye that labor and are heavy laden and I will give you rest," Skinner soon plummeted again into the depths of despair. "Then after this," he remembered, "I was in the dark, and them words come to me, depart from me ye cursed into ever lasting fire prepared for the devil and his angels." [25]

The deathbed narrative of Mary Clark Bonner, recorded by a member of her family after her demise in 1697, vividly portrays an active Satan, but his role is limited to frightening Bonner and tempting her to believe that her positive thoughts about her salvation are delusory. At first Bonner was filled with comfort, and when she thought of God she exulted, "He is Come he is Come he is Come and has Spocken powerfully to my Soul telling me my Sins are forgiuen!" Later, doubts returned, and she was convinced that her former joy had been a deception. Her neighbor, Mrs. Champney, spoke gently to her and "bid her not give way to the temptation of Satan." Just as the devil's threat seemed to abate, Bonner cried, "The Deuil Came upon me Like a Lyon[,] almost a frighted me out of my wits." But she was able to force Satan out of her imagination aided by the comforting words of her minister, William Brattle. Ultimately, Mary Clark Bonner resolutely concluded that what she had experienced were no more than temptations. Assured that she was going to Christ, she died with "one hand Lifted up and her Eyes to heauen." [26]

25. Ibid., Joshua Loomis, February 27, 1701, Daniel Skinner, n.d. See also Samuel Belcher's relation in Kenneth P. Minkema, "A Great Awakening Conversion: The Relation of Samuel Belcher," *William and Mary Quarterly*, 3rd ser., 44 (1987), 121–26. Belcher stated, "I found that I was Dead in trespasses and Sins, and I thought what a Dreadfull thing it was to fall into the hands of an angry God" (125). Belcher's language echoes Jonathan Edwards's famous sermon *Sinners in the Hands of an Angry God*.

26. Robert Trent, "'The Deuil Came Upon me like a Lyon': A 1697 Cambridge Deathbed Narrative," *Connecticut Historical Society Bulletin* 48 (Summer 1983), 115–19.

By the early eighteenth century, then, the sinner's relationship to Satan had changed. Sinners feared that if they succumbed to Satan's devices they would anger God, rather than lose their souls to the devil. Satan still plagued people with various temptations, but significantly, neither female nor male sinners insisted that the devil possessed their souls because they had sinned or that they had sinned because the devil possessed them. As the century progressed Satan appeared most commonly as the tempter. His powers were distinctly diminished; his victims could successfully reject his advances, free of the immediate fear that he might capture their souls.

In the conversion narratives of the 1720s, Satan appeared slightly more frequently, in both men's and women's accounts, than he did in the immediate post-Salem years, although references remained unusual and limited. Significantly, women's and men's narratives became less distinctive. Both sexes now specified sins for which they repented, and both sexes now considered themselves vile, rebellious creatures toward whom God would be justly angry. The devil tempted sinners in one-third of these accounts (five of fourteen), and he appeared similarly in male and female narratives.[27]

As in the years immediately following the Salem trials, the sinners invoked the devil only when they described particular sins that plagued them. By the 1720s, women lamented their particular sins as much as men, thus creating a place in their narratives for the devil as tempter. Frances Bancroft, for example, in 1722 admitted that she had "been sorely exercised with the temptations and besettings of Satan in evil thoughts cast in very forcibly upon me." In 1727, Mehitable Osgood said that because of "Satans temptations and a deceitfull heart" she neglected looking to God and closing with Christ, and she "shamefully neglected" her duty. Both of these women acknowledged their innate depravity. Bancroft thought she "was so vile a creature, and so polluted

---

27. In *Disorderly Women: Sexual Politics and Evangelicalism in Revolutionary New England* (Ithaca, N.Y., 1994), Susan Juster describes the androgyny of these pre-Awakening narratives. She maintains, however, that neither male nor female sinners focused on individual sins and that both tended to confess their innate depravity. Thanks to the generosity of Kenneth Minkema, I have been able to use the previously unpublished Lynnfield "Earthquake" Relations of 1727. All ten of the narratives (eight of which were given by women) mentioned specific sins as well as the sinners' corrupt nature. See Kenneth Minkema, "The Lynn End 'Earthquake' Narratives of 1727," *New England Quarterly* 69 (September 1996).

with sin that [I] could not but wonder that God should bare any regard to [me]." Osgood similarly speculated that she was "such a poor vile Creature that God would utterly reject me as dross & reprobate silver."[28] But Satan could ease his way into their imaginations not as a possessor of their innately depraved souls but rather as an annoying seducer to sin.

It could be argued that the androgyny of the 1720s narratives reflects a convergence of "feminine" and "masculine" notions of sin and the soul. Women never abandoned feelings of worthlessness and vileness, although they were more likely to mention particular sins and to recognize what men seem to have believed earlier—that, as Abigail Hodgman put it in 1727, "sin was a soul ruining thing." It not only reflected the pitiful condition of women's souls; it actively destroyed them. Men, on the other hand, adopted a more "feminine" approach toward sin. Although they continued in the 1720s to lament specific sins, such as "going into company," neglecting the Lord's Supper, forsaking prayers, or thinking about the vanities of the world, they also stressed, as Jonathan Pearson related, "my Miserable and undone Condition by nature." Pearson went so far as to suggest, like women of a previous generation, that his sins merely reflected that nature. He admitted, "Mine Iniquityes did testifye against me"—meaning that the commission of these sins betrayed the vileness of his soul, which could no longer go unnoticed. Indeed, his sins appeared to him "in a crimson Colour."[29]

Whether sins ruined the soul or the already depraved soul committed the sins, converts in the pre-Awakening years kept the devil at arm's length. But during the Great Awakening, Satan reappeared with a vigor unseen since before the Salem trials. Although he seemed undaunted, assiduous in his temptations and lures, Great Awakening sinners—women and men—proved successful in thwarting his advances.

Hannah Heaton, a Connecticut farm woman, pictured Satan in her mid-eighteenth-century autobiography either as tempting her to abandon belief in God or as bound powerless in hell. The devil would send such "darting" thoughts to her mind: "How do you know says satan that there is a iesus [Jesus] or a heauen." When she felt despair he whispered

28. "East Windor Relations," Frances Bancroft, June 8, 1722; Minkema, "Lynn End Narratives," 486.

29. Minkema, "Lynn End Narratives," 484, 489.

to her, "Hang your self." Satan tried to convince her that she need not bother with prayer anymore, that she had prayed enough already, and that her father, who had died recently, was lying—body and soul—in the grave, implying that his soul had not risen to heaven. Following her father's death, Satan plagued Heaton for several days; she wrote that he inquired of her, "How do you know that the byble is the word of God [says Satan] then i said thus haue i not felt the power of gods word in my heart many a time but ah says the temptor should you not feel the power of a wonderful history that told of great and terrible things done in forrain countries." [30]

Hannah Heaton mentioned Satan only as the tempter. She did not conceive of her soul in bondage to the devil. The devil harassed but did not overtake her. Ultimately, she was able to put the devil in his place. God assured her, "Let satan say what he will he is a lier o satan you will not onely be bound but cast into the bottomles pit and a seal sat upon you." [31] Satan's place, Heaton suggested, was not in Connecticut. Though he appeared in her thoughts and plagued her with temptations, when she put her mind to it, Heaton could unequivocally send the devil away.

Heaton's dreams were also filled with images of Satan in hell. Many of those she recorded warned of the "great trial." On one occasion she dreamt of a cave "full of burning flames like a gloing oven," and Satan, in the "shape of a great snake all on a flame with his sting out," running toward a "wicked prophane" man. This dream prophesied for her what the wicked would endure in hell, and she prayed for their conversion. [32] Satan appeared as the tempter and as the warden of souls in hell, but not as the possessor of souls in this life.

Susan Juster has argued that in Great Awakening narratives women expressed greater vulnerability to Satan's temptations, suggesting a return to the unspoken association in the seventeenth century between women and the devil. Hannah Heaton and Susanna Anthony, Great Awakening converts, offered vivid accounts of Satan's devices, which would surely have left them vulnerable to accusations of witchcraft had

30. Barbara E. Lacey, "The World of Hannah Heaton: The Autobiography of an Eighteenth-Century Connecticut Farm Woman," *William and Mary Quarterly*, 3rd ser., 45 (1988), 280–304, quotation on 284, 285.
31. Ibid.
32. Ibid., 286.

With bitter Pains, my Child I did you bear,
I taught you how the Lord of Life to fear,
Whole Days and Nights I did in sorrow spend,
To bring you up now to my Discontent.

Quite void of Grace you in your Sins do run,
You slight my Counsel after all I've done,
Instead of Obedience which you ought to pay,
Your Parents Lives you're seeking to betray.

The Prodigal Daughter: or a strange and wonderful relation (Boston, between 1742 and 1754). Illustrating the young daughter's solicitations by the devil, the artist here portrayed Satan traditionally. In the eighteenth century, women still struggled with the devil's temptations; yet even the most persistent battles remained spiritual and they could be overcome (courtesy American Antiquarian Society, Worcester, Mass.).

they been uttered fifty years earlier. Heaton admitted that she "felt the devil twitch my cloaths," and Anthony conceded "that satan seemed to have had full power of me." Depicting the agony of her soul as she battled temptations, she described how she believed she had "twisted every bone out of its place: and have often since wondered that I never disjointed a bone when, through the violence of my distress, I wrung my hands, twisted every joint, and strained every nerve; biting my flesh; gnashing my teeth; throwing myself on the floor." [33]

Women such as Heaton and Anthony may have included physical allusions to their spiritual battles with the devil, but their interpretations of Satan's powers remained metaphorical rather than literal. Although they portrayed the devil's immediate presence so vividly, they managed to keep him at bay. Anthony made sure to tell her readers: "Blessed be God, satan was never permitted to present any thing to my bodily eyes, or ears; nor did I ever think I heard any voice, or saw any vision, either from heaven or hell." She insisted that these battles took place only in her mind and that her "fancy, or imagination, was never carried away." [34]

Susanna Anthony's Satan never failed to put temptations in her path, but she conceived of these as spiritual roadblocks to be ultimately surmounted. She articulated her spiritual journey as "the inward exercises of my mind, in respect to the state of my soul," rather than as a literal battle between God and the devil for her soul. Anthony believed that when she needed reminding and "further humbling," God sent Satan, but only metaphorically. Recalling one particular moment in which she began to feel secure, Anthony admitted, "And God was pleased again to let satan loose, *as it were,* upon me; until I became a very terror to myself." In response to this temptation to kill herself, as with many others

33. Lacey, "World of Hannah Heaton," 285; *The Life and Character of Miss Susanna Anthony,* ed. Samuel Hopkins (London, 1803), 23–24. Juster argues convincingly that women more than men embraced the direct relationships between their souls and God and the devil. See Juster, *Disorderly Women,* 60–62. Although an extensive reading of the mid-century conversion narratives is beyond the scope of this book, I would say that women converts, like the men, were able to overcome Satan's devices, no matter how direct, and find relief from God in ways inconceivable to sinners in an earlier era. Richard Gildrie has also noticed that when Great Awakening converts experienced physical symptoms such as those of Susanna Anthony, their tortures were no longer interpreted as diabolical intrusion but as part of the positive work of conversion or as signs of mental anguish. See Richard Gildrie, *The Profane, the Civil, and the Godly: The Reformation of Manners in Orthodox New England, 1679–1749* (University Park, Penn., 1994), 234–35.

34. *Life and Character of Anthony,* 23.

peppered throughout her narrative, Christ appeared to Anthony, and her soul "was taken up in admiring the glorious Redeemer." "Her temptations," not Satan himself, fled, and hope prevailed above her fears.[35]

Nathan Cole, a carpenter and farmer of Kensington, Connecticut, handled the devil's intrusions similarly. Cole had recorded his "spiritual travels" in 1765, detailing his anguished introspection of the preceding twenty-five years. After his conversion, inspired by George Whitefield's preaching at Middletown, Connecticut, in 1740, Cole was beset with many temptations from the devil. Satan cast doubt on the genuineness of Cole's conversion and tempted him to test it by suicide: "Well Satan comes upon me and says there is one way to know quick; destroy your self says he and you will soon know; for if you be converted you will certainly be saved; and if not you never will be converted, there fore destroy your self and you will know at once."[36] The devil tormented Cole for three months with these thoughts. Cole "went groaning about and begging for help of God; and bidding Satan depart and be gone saying to him I won't, I won't, avoid Satan, be gone, but he still followed me very Close." Then the devil introduced a new temptation, suggesting to Cole that if he truly were converted then he would not be troubled by suicidal thoughts, for no saints in the Bible had suffered them. Finally Cole found his deliverance from the devil's persistent assaults. He sought an "experienced Christian" and unburdened his anguish; his friend reassured him that Satan had tempted Christ to destroy his body, "and if he might tempt him, much more may he tempt his followers." Cole recorded, "A ray of divine light broke into my Soul that moment; and the Devil lear'd away ashamed." Thus, with help from friends and God's mercy, Cole successfully resisted the devil again and again. The devil doggedly pursued him, but Cole, either through prayer or the counsel of other Christians, managed to conquer the temptation, no matter how insistent, and emerged victorious, spiritually strengthened.[37]

35. Ibid., 31, 33, emphasis added.

36. The revival in Northampton, Mass., came to an abrupt halt after Jonathan Edwards's uncle Joseph Hawley committed suicide, in despair over the state of his soul. Edwards blamed Hawley's tragic act on the withdrawal of God and the rage of Satan, although he also admitted that family members were prone to melancholy and that Hawley's mother had died of it as well. See Patricia J. Tracy, *Jonathan Edwards, Pastor: Religion and Society in Eighteenth-Century Northampton* (New York, 1980), 116–18.

37. Michael Crawford, "Spiritual Travels of Nathan Cole," *William and Mary Quarterly*, 3rd ser., 33 (1976), 101, 103. For an analysis of Cole's diary, see also Daniel B. Shea Jr.,

Cole's embroilments with Satan, and those of Hannah Heaton and Susanna Anthony as well, were of a different nature from those of the seventeenth century. There was little of the fear that is so palpable in the conversion narratives of sinners in the 1640s. Neither Cole, Heaton, nor Anthony ever expressed concern that the devil would possess their souls.[38] These converts feared death and the possibility of hell, but they had a greater sense of efficacy, even the women. Men and women both acknowledged their vileness, but the pessimism was countered by their agency in opting to ignore temptations and choose Christ.

The seventeenth-century demonization of active female choice, dependent as it was on the image of a feminine soul battling a masculine Satan, had disappeared. Seventeenth-century women could be damned either way: if their souls waited passively for Christ, they could be faulted as dissatisfied women, to be appeased only by the devil, but if women chose God overtly, their assertiveness would have been seen as a sure sign of their damnation. Satan's demotion from master of souls to master of hell freed women converts to make a positive choice. Regarding her conversion, Susanna Anthony could record in her diary in 1743, "Then, O my soul, sit down again, and make another deliberate choice . . . let it be great, noble, and free." Anthony was emphatically not submissively waiting for Christ; hers was a deliberate decision, as she repeatedly emphasized. "With all the faculties and powers of my soul," she declared, "I freely, resolutely, cheerfully, and unreservedly, entered into this covenant. . . . I am the Lord's, body, soul, and spirit." Despite Anthony's pessimistic claim that she remained a "vile, ungrateful wretch," she knew she would close with Christ.[39]

Spiritual Autobiography in Early America (Princeton, 1968), 208–21. Cole also recorded the spiritual crisis of his wife; Satan tried to convince her that she had not really been converted because she still battled temptations, and Cole's "heart sunk down for fear Satan should get the victory and drive her into total despair; or clear out of her witts." Fortunately, after Cole endured a "3 or 4 hours dispute with satan, for as he put these things into her mind so she spake them to me," he was able to fight the Devil with "the sword of the Spirit which is the word of God; and I told her it was no sin to be tempted, but it was sin to yield to the temptation" (ibid., 104–5).

38. Anthony mentioned possession of her soul only once, and even this mention was qualified, "I seemed as one really possessed of the devil" (*Life and Character of Anthony*, 23).

39. Ibid., 49, 61, 122. Barbara Lacey has interpreted Hannah Heaton's diary similarly: "Deity and devil were vividly alive in her mind, and she was free to choose between them." See Lacey, "World of Hannah Heaton," 285.

In the 1744 funeral sermon preached for his daughter, Deborah Prince, the Reverend Thomas Prince of Boston spoke of her spiritual trials. She bemoaned what "a vile creature" she was, as she "complained of her Stupidity, Hardness of Heart, blindness of Mind, Impenitence and Unbelief; censuring and condemning herself of all Good." But on her deathbed her words voiced desperate confidence. "O I love the LORD JESUS with all my Heart! I see such an Amiableness, such an AMIABLENESS in Him; I prize Him above a thousand Words!" Not only was she ready to resign herself to Christ, but she spent her last words encouraging others, including her friends in the Female Society and her father, to "live nearer to God," and "to be more careful after CHRIST and grace," so that they, too, might experience her joy.[40]

Optimism found its way into Nathan Cole's narrative as well. Cole frequently thought about hell before his conversion experience, but he never believed that God's vengeful decision to send him to hell would be justified. He "was loaded with the guilt of Sin" and "carried Such a weight of Sin in my breast or mind, that it seemed to me as if I should sink into the ground every step." He pitied himself for this condition. "Poor-Me-Miserable-me," he wrote. And during this time of despair, convinced that he would see hell, Cole admitted that "hundreds of times [I] put fingers into my pipe when I have been smoking to feel how fire felt; And to see how my Body could bear to lye in Hell fire for ever and ever." Despite his obvious anxiety and despair, when Cole considered that God had chosen some to be among the elect and others to be cast into hell, he could not abide the possibility that he should be among the latter. He said, "I thought God was not Just in so doing. . . . My heart then rose against God exceedingly, for his making me for hell."[41]

Like Susanna Anthony, though before his conversion he was terrified by the prospect of hell and harbored "black despairing fears of death," he remained assured, after his conversion, that he would be able to over-

40. Thomas Prince, *The Sovereign God Acknowledged and Blessed, both in Giving and Taking away. A Sermon Occasioned by the Decease of Mrs. Deborah Prince on Friday, July 20, 1744. In the 21st Year of her Age. Delivered at the South Church in Boston, July 29* . . . (Boston, 1744), reprinted in *Women and Religion in America*, ed. Rosemary Radford Ruether and Rosemary Skinner Keller, vol. 2: *The Colonial and Revolutionary Periods: A Documentary History* (New York, 1983), 344–45.

41. Crawford, "Spiritual Travels of Nathan Cole," 94.

come evil temptations, conquer sin, and enter heaven. He was surprised that he should be the victim not of Satan but of temptations, which he listed as covetousness, selfishness, malice, and envy. "I was not willing they should live in my breast," he declared, "but that I would immediately make war with them and cast them out with all my might." His tone was positive; he insisted, "I will not lose my happiness of my mind for these evil tempters for I never can feel happy with them in me, I will conquer or die in the cause." Cole confided to another Christian friend that he could successfully rid himself of these tempters and take control "by turning my mind into the ways of Gods Commands, and so walk as well I can."[42] Cole's spiritual autobiography was written after his conversion, after he had lived as a Christian for twenty-five years; but even the most pious seventeenth-century convert would not have been so confident that he or she was among the elect. Indeed, total assurance would have been seen as a sure sign of damnation.[43]

Satan no longer possessed the souls of sinners in this world; eighteenth-century sinners battled their own selves (apparently easier opponents), not the devil himself. In the post-Salem era, Satan was more likely to be found in hell, where he awaited the sinner's arrival. Even Cotton Mather, perhaps one of the most vigorous and obsessive supporters of the devil's powers, talked about the devil in different terms in the early eighteenth century. Mather's devil of 1717, for example, did not directly possess the souls of the sinners he seduced. Instead, Mather described the souls who entered hell as those who had "gone away with the Satanic Image depraving of them, and prevailing in them."[44] Mather made a fine distinction: these souls went to hell with the image of Satan imprinted on them; earlier souls cleaved to the devil himself as he spirited them away.

42. Ibid., 116, 112, 113.

43. Thomas Shepard wrote that "the greatest part of a Christian's grace lies in mourning for the want of it." See Thomas Shepard, *God's Plot: The Paradoxes of Puritan Piety Being the Autobiography & Journal of Thomas Shepard*, ed. Michael McGiffert (Amherst, Mass., 1972), 198. McGiffert has explored the cycle of anxiety and assurance, what he called the Sisyphean sequence, in the introduction to Shepard's autobiography. Edmund S. Morgan explains, "The Puritans' strength lay not in confidence but in lack of it." See Edmund S. Morgan, *The Puritan Family: Religion and Domestic Relations in Seventeenth-Century New England* (New York, 1944), 5.

44. Cotton Mather, *Hades Look'd into: The Power of our Great Saviour Over the Invisible World, and the Gates of Death Which lead into that World* (Boston, 1717), 19.

More important, Mather focused on the devil's conveyance of his reprobate charges to hell rather than on his everyday, earthly activities. In a 1713 sermon Mather explained that "when people do Evil, they obey the Devil, who is the Evil One. By their Obedience to the Devil, People Resign themselves up to the Possession of that Evil One." But the devil's possession served no other purpose than to bring those sinners to hell. "It is with surprize, that we hear the Language of those Monsters, who wish *the Devil to take them,*" Mather counseled. "Ah, Fool-hardy Sinner; As often as thou Sinnest, thou dost monstrously Resign thy self to the Wicked One, and *bid him to take thee.*" Mather discussed the devil's possession in terms of the sinner's ultimate fate. He did not say that a sinner's heart was filled with Satan or that the sinner did the devil's bidding. Satan possessed sinners in order to take them to hell. Emphasizing where they would end up, Mather warned ominously, "Sinner, dost thou know what thou dost?"[45]

In a world in which the devil no longer inspired such fear, ministers substituted hell's gruesome horrors to persuade sinners to repent.[46] Seventeenth-century clerics had also employed graphic images of hell to persuade congregants to turn to God, but their portrayals included a vivid depiction of Satan in this life. By contrast, in the post-Salem world, ministers hoped fear of hell alone would motivate sinners to convert. In 1713, for example, Solomon Stoddard published a sermon titled *The Efficacy of the fear of Hell, to restrain Men from Sin.* Stoddard argued that a cautious fear of hell allowed people to "avoid those paths that lead to Hell." He lamented that too many people were "not sensible of the dreadfulness or danger of Damnation" and thus sinned freely. Neither the actions of one's parents or rulers, nor shame, nor the possibility of mercy and deliverance would be quite enough, in Stoddard's view, to dissuade sinners. "But if they were afraid of hell," he insisted, "they would be afraid of sin."[47]

45. Cotton Mather, *Advice from the Watch Tower: In a Testimony against Evil Customes. A Brief Essay to Declare the Danger and Mischief of all Evil Customes, in General* (Boston, 1713), 12, 13, emphasis added.

46. Perry Miller, *Jonathan Edwards* (N.Y., 1949), 155. Miller maintained that at the turn of the century ministers began "to employ the fear of hell as a whip and a goad," but he did not place this development within the context of Satan's recession, a trend associated with the Enlightenment.

47. Solomon Stoddard, *The Efficacy of the Fear of Hell, to Restrain Men from Sin* (Boston, 1713), 4, 5. Stoddard suggested that the fear of hell would work particularly well

Stoddard held nothing back in describing the miseries of hell. He started comparatively gently with the assurance that the damned "will be in Distress, they rest not Day nor Night; their Misery will be overbearing to them." He continued, "They will wish they had not been, they will wish they could cease to be." Pleasures that sinners formerly enjoyed in this world would no longer have any meaning for them; companions with whom they shared their misery would be no comfort to them. Because of all their rebellion and the "contempt that they have cast upon God," said Stoddard, these sinners "will be standing Monuments of the Vengeance of Heaven." [48]

Surely Stoddard intended to frighten his audience with his vivid and horrifying portrayal of hell. Using biblical examples (Matthew 8:12, Judges 13, Jeremiah 38:6), he likened hell to a dark dungeon, where "the Children of the Kingdom shall be cast into outer darkness," and explained, "When Persons are in a Dungeon, they are confined, and have no Liberty." He quoted from Revelations 21:8, "They shall have their part in the Lake that burneth with Fire and Brimstone, which is the second Death." Hell would approximate the fiery Sodom: "The People were in a miserable Condition, when streams of Fire and Brimstone fell from Heaven upon their Houses, and upon their Ground, and upon their Bodies, Men, Women, Children, all like light Torches, their Bodies blazed." And then to press his point Stoddard described the land of Tophet, where human sacrifice had been offered to a pagan deity: "There they burnt them as Sacrifices to the Devil, and made a noise with Trumpets and other Instruments, that they might drown the noise of the Cryies of the poor Children, they could not bear their Roarings." Simply stated, Solomon insisted, "Hell is worse than all these." He reminded his audience, "These Miseries will never have an End. . . . This makes every part of their Misery Infinite, their Pain will be Infinite, the Terrour Infinite." [49]

Cotton Mather described hell similarly, as "the Prison of the Damned," where "miserable Prisoners have an uneasy Confinement upon them."

---

on young sinners: "If they had a sense of Hell-fire they would not dare to do what now they are bold to do; they would have no Heart to prosecute their carnal Designs; they would be deaf to Temptations; no Arguments would prevail with them, they would as soon be perswaded to handle an Iron burning hot, as to practise their former ways" (21–22).

48. Ibid., 23.

49. Ibid., 25, 26–27. See also Matt. 5:29; Isa. 30:3.

He explained that "in the Invisible World there are Quarters in which the ungodly Souls of Men, whose Day of Grace is over with them, are Imprisoned. . . . These are seiz'd by Dragons, and are drag'd into a Place of Dragons." The confinement would be made all the more unbearable for sinners because they would be forced to reside with legions of devils, "who rose up in Rebellion against God, and so became full of Aversion for all the Things that are Holy, and Just & Good." Mather's point in this particular sermon was that both the visible and the invisible world were ultimately under the government of God; in articulating this message, however, Mather focused on the damned and the devils in "those dark Cells; those doleful, wo[e]ful, tremendous Caverns . . . where things worse than Rattle-Snakes coyl about them, hideous Fiends are their Companions, and their Tormentors."[50]

Jonathan Edwards, pastor at Northampton, Massachusetts, has provided perhaps the best-known portrait of hell. "So that thus it is, that natural men are held in the hand of God over the pit of hell," he told his congregation. "They have deserved the fiery pit, and are already sentenced to it; and God is dreadfully provoked, his anger is as great towards them as to those that are actually suffering the executions of the fierceness of his wrath in hell. . . . [T]he devil is waiting for them, hell is gaping for them, the flames gather and flash about them, and would fain lay hold on them and swallow them up."[51] Even if, as some argue, Edwards used the image of hell as a metaphor, surely he simultaneously conveyed a powerful sense of its material terrors to his listeners.[52] The Reverend Stephen Williams of neighboring Longmeadow admitted in his

50. Mather, *Hades Look'd Into,* 4, 15, 19, 16, 23. Joseph Green in 1696 fastened on the anguish of hell's perpetuity and the misery of the devils' company. At Judgment Day, he explained, "O how will they [sinners] be cast down to think that they are lost forever, and that they must lye in hell soul & body in extremity of pain unto all eternity; and then they shall meet with Devils, which will torment & spit their malice in their faces and will laugh them to scorn bec. they hearkened to them and suffered them to tempt them and lead them to eternal darkness." See Joseph Green, "Commonplace Book of Joseph Green," Publications of the Colonial Society of Massachusetts, no. 34 (Boston, 1943), 209.

51. Jonathan Edwards, *Sinners in the Hands of an Angry God* in *Selected Writings of Jonathan Edwards,* ed. Harold P. Simonson (New York, 1970), 103.

52. See ibid., 18. Some scholars contend that Edwards, although remembered for his "hellfire" sermons, actually conceived of hell as a state of mind rather than a literal fiery inferno. See Alan Heimert and Andrew Delbanco, eds., *The Puritans in America: A Narrative Anthology* (Cambridge, Mass., 1985), 410–11.

diary that when Edwards delivered an impassioned sermon in Enfield, Connecticut, "the shrieks and cries were piercing and amazing." [53]

Yet eighteenth-century Puritanism did not rely as heavily as one might imagine on the fear of hell, despite the sermonic emphasis on the miseries of the inferno. As we have seen, the laity seemed more optimistic and assured about their salvation than had seventeenth-century sinners. Converts like Nathan Cole, Hannah Heaton, Deborah Prince, and Susanna Anthony may have been plagued by the tempter, but ultimately they were successful in turning their hearts to God, and they hoped, with some conviction, that they were among God's elect. Struggling Puritans sought the help of sermons from the previous century as well as contemporary spiritual writings, suggesting perhaps that the post-Salem shift in theology and worldview was a matter of degree. Yet, whereas older works, such as Thomas Hooker's popular *Poor Doubting Christian Drawn to Christ* (originally published in 1629), remained vital, indeed became classics, other sermons and tracts settled into obscurity because they spoke less compellingly to mid-eighteenth-century men and women.[54]

During a particularly difficult time, Nathan Cole found Hooker's *Poor Doubting Christian* an invaluable aid against a building sense of despair. Hooker's sermon outlined the "main hindrances" that kept people from Christ. Most seventeenth-century sermons concerned with sin and salvation featured Satan prominently, as did several demonological treatises.[55]

---

53. Quoted in Patricia J. Tracy, *Jonathan Edwards, Pastor: Religion and Society in Eighteenth-Century Northampton* (New York, 1979), 133. Tracy suggests that Edwards preached *Sinners in the Hands of an Angry God* in several towns he visited on his way to New Haven in the summer of 1741.

54. Thomas Hooker, *The Poor Doubting Christian Drawn to Christ. Wherein the Main Hindrances, Which Keep Men from Coming to Christ, are Discovered* (1629; Boston, 1743). For the publishing history of Hooker's book, see Sargent Bush Jr., "The Growth of Thomas Hooker's *The Poor Doubting Christian,*" *Early American Literature* 8 (Spring 1973), 3–20. Bush considers Hooker's book, which went through fifteen editions in the seventeenth century, and was reprinted into the nineteenth century, one of the Puritans' most enduring pieces of sermonic literature. The work was atypical of Hooker, for it contained an unusual message of optimism and positive thinking, and it minimized the Puritan belief in predestination and the uncertainties of one's future. For an analysis of Hooker's writings, see Sargent Bush Jr., *The Writings of Thomas Hooker: Spiritual Adventure in Two Worlds* (Madison, Wis., 1980).

55. See, for example, Thomas Brooks, *Precious Remedies against Satan's Devices* (London, 1652); Richard Gilpin, *Daemonologia Sacra; or A Treatise of Satan's Temptations* (1677; London, 1867).

Hooker's sermon focused instead on human failings, most notably pride and haughtiness; Satan emerged infrequently, only to encourage human infirmities. Hooker questioned the devil's powers even to do that much: "This is the Policy of the Devil, who (if he can) will make a man to see Sin thro' his own spectacles." Hooker undermined the devil's ability and suggested that his wily ways were far from universally successful. The main hindrance, according to Hooker, was either that sinners never realized the enormity and severity of their sins and, so, erroneously believed that they had no need of Christ or that they saw so much wickedness that they feared Christ would consign them "to that ever-burning Lake of Fire and Brimstone." Hooker offered hope for sinners who fell into either category. He reassured his audience that even those who believed "the Word" was ineffectual were, by their pessimism, made more aware of their hardness and deadness and thus might remain hopeful that they could overcome their sins and Satan. Hooker suggested that the moment when one hit the depths of despair was the best time to seek the Lord. "It is the last Refuge that the Devil hath," Hooker said of this spiritual despondency, "and if he miss of this, his Force is gone for ever." [56]

Hooker's *Poor Doubting Christian* contained an unusually optimistic message; perhaps it was this positive emphasis that inspired its repeated publication. Other seventeenth-century sermons, indeed, other sermons Hooker delivered, had suggested that it was nearly impossible to extract a sinner from the devil's clutches. In 1637 Hooker had told his congregation, "We can pitty poore drunkards, and sorrow for them, but we are as able to make worlds, and to pull hell in pieces; as to pull a poore Soule from the paw of the divell." [57] But sinners one hundred years later had no need for such pessimism. The devil would plague them, and he would continue to beset women more severely than men, but he could nonetheless be conquered in the end.

In the seventeenth century, to sin meant to absent oneself from the Lord and consequently to bond one's soul to the devil. In the post-Salem years, sin did not place one's soul in the devil's clutches. Sin was increasingly divorced from Satan. Nathan Cole, for example, did not believe that the privation of God meant attachment to Satan; in his mind it

56. Hooker, *Poor Doubting Christian*, 6, 7, 22.
57. Thomas Hooker, *The Soule's Humiliation* (London, 1637), 37.

meant only a godless hell: "Once I had a God but now I have lost him; and it is the loss of God that makes hell." [58] Men and women who sinned would surely end up in hell, where the devil waited, but by the mid-eighteenth century, the language of possession and bondage had changed. The devil might tempt and perhaps lure one to sin, but it was the temptations themselves on which sinners dwelled, rather than on a notion of Satan's inescapable possession. No longer enslaved, sinners—female and male—could have more hope for their salvation. They conceived of a devil in hell, a God in heaven, and the ability to choose between the two. Even women—who perhaps still perceived the devil's threats more palpably than men—were able to select Christ. At least in this regard, women were no longer damned.

58. Crawford, "Spiritual Travels of Nathan Cole," 99.

EPILOGUE

GENDER, FAITH, AND
"YOUNG GOODMAN BROWN"

I<small>N</small> 1774 Isaiah Thomas printed Ezra Gleason's *Massachusetts Calendar; or an Almanack*. Its cover, picturing a "Wicked Statesman [the American governor of Massachusetts, Thomas Hutchinson], or a Traitor to his Country, at the Hour of D<small>EATH</small>," employed traditional religious imagery and represented the transformed meaning of the devil by the late eighteenth century. The deposed Hutchinson meets his demise at the hands of the grim reaper, while a monstrous devil behind him displays a list of the traitor's crimes. Though Satan continued to engender fear and loathing and remained a symbol of evil, his direct or immediate threat to New England seems devalued in the illustration.[1]

Other political cartoons of the American Revolution which offered caricatures of the devil similarly employed him allegorically, as a representation of evil, or even lampooned Satan and those, like Lord Bute or George III, who were associated with him. One cartoon, for example, depicted two devils, complete with wings and pitchforks, pushing the seventeen Rescinders in the Massachusetts Assembly into hell's furnace. The title read, "A Warm Place—Hell," and a caption declared, "There puny Villians damn'd for Petty Sin." Another cartoon, titled, "The Parl'nt dissolv'd, or the Devil turn'd Fortune Teller," pictured Lord North and an unidentified minister sitting with a horned devil—half man, half

1. Ezra Gleason, *The Massachusetts Calendar; or an Almanack for the Year of our Lord Christ 1774; Being the second after Bessextile or Leap Year* (Boston, 1774).

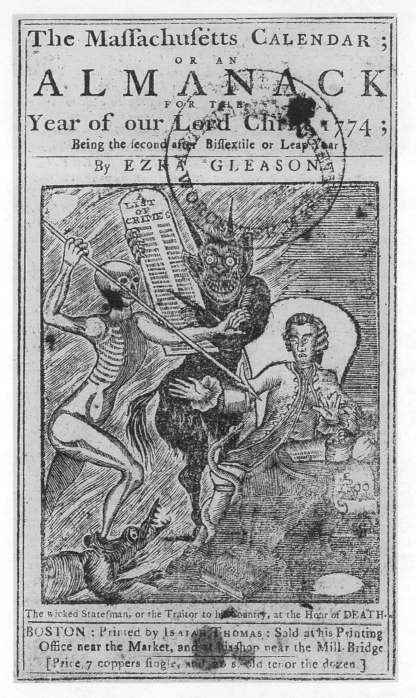

Ezra Gleason, *The Massachusetts Calendar: or an Almanack*: In 1774, the cover of Gleason's almanac pictured "Wicked Statesman [the American governor of Massachusetts, Thomas Hutchinson], or a Traitor to his Country, at the Hour of DEATH," illustrating the transformed meaning of the devil by the late eighteenth century. While the deposed Hutchinson meets his demise at the hands of the grim reaper, a monstrous devil behind him displays a list of the traitor's crimes (courtesy American Antiquarian Society, Worcester, Mass.).

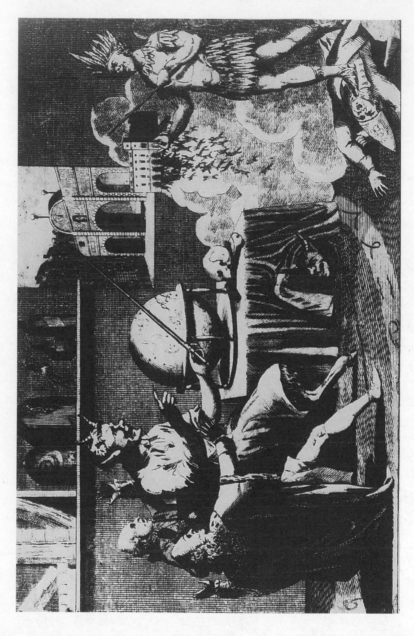

"The Parl'nt. dissolv'd, or, The Devil turn'd Fortune Teller" (c. 1774): Political cartoons of the American Revolution offered caricatures of the devil, employing him allegorically, as a representation of evil, or even lampooning Satan and those, such as Lord Bute or George III, whom they associated with him (Library of Congress).

beast—as he conjured up an image of America, standing on top of a fallen British soldier and shaking all the tiny inhabitants of Parliament onto the floor.[2]

Such representations would have been considered sacrilegious in an earlier time, when Satan was not merely semiotic but physically, horrifically present. And by the nineteenth century, when Nathaniel Hawthorne wrote his vivid portrayals of the Puritans, most notably "Young Goodman Brown" (1835) and *The Scarlet Letter* (1851), his audience clearly conceived of sin and Satan in ways quite different from those of seventeenth-century New Englanders. Following "Young Goodman Brown" on his terrifying errand into the demonic woods helps us see these changes more clearly.

Despite recent salutary revision, the modern understanding of the Puritans has been largely shaped, for better or worse, by the nineteenth-century Victorian imagination. Hawthorne's evocative tale "Young Goodman Brown" tells us as much about the nineteenth century as it does about the seventeenth. The mere fact that Hawthorne could speak of the devil in so unholy a context, in a popular short story, betrays a dramatically altered conception of sin. Yet Hawthorne, who sought to understand and convey a critical sense of the Puritans' worldview, perceptively recognized their fear of Satan's possession of souls. His representation in this story nicely captures the anxiety and turmoil that beset Puritan men and women and their communities.

The literary scholars who have analyzed "Young Goodman Brown," with few exceptions, have paid more attention to Hawthorne's style and

2. Michael Wynn Jones, *The Cartoon History of the American Revolution* (New York, 1975), 32, 57. Belief in witches, as in the devil, declined, so that by 1787 Isaac Bickerstaff could include in his almanac the following light verse, which constructed witches simply as nighttime figments of people's imaginations: "PALE Fear does Things so like a Witch, / 'Tis hard t'unriddle which is which, / that makes Men in the Dark see Visions, / And hug themselves with Apparitions; / And when their Eyes discover least, / Discern the subtlest Object best." See February page in Isaac Bickerstaff, *An Almanack, For the Year of our Lord Christ 1787 . . .* (Hartford, [1786]). Surprisingly, in 1787 in Philadelphia, just a few blocks from where members of the Constitutional Convention debated the excesses of democracy, a woman was pelted to death "under the imputation of being a *witch* . . . by an ignorant and inhuman mob." At the proceedings against her tormenters, the justice declared witchcraft an "idle and absurd superstition." If the woman had been young and alluring, rather than old and infirm, he sarcastically suggested, perhaps her wiles would indeed have been "calculated to charm and bewitch us." See Edmund S. Morgan, "The Witch and We, the People," *American Heritage* 34 (August–September 1983), 10, 11.

Lo! Mother Shipton and her Cat,
Quite full of Conjuration,
And if more Conjurers could be found
'Twere better for the Nation.

"Lo! Mother Shipton and her Cat": By the early nineteenth century a witch and her familiar made their appearance in Philadelphia's 1814 Peter Pry's Puppet Show. The representation and accompanying text present the witch comically, rather than with revulsion (courtesy American Antiquarian Society, Worcester, Mass.).

intentions than to the tale's historical verisimilitude.[3] My purpose is somewhat different. Appreciating Hawthorne's historical as well as literary talents, we can see the story as a window into the seventeenth-century Puritan mind.[4] Many of the themes I have explored here appear in this work. Indeed, "Young Goodman Brown" can provide a convenient summation of the Puritans' gendered "theology of Satan."

The tale opens as a young, recently married Goodman Brown prepares to leave his wife, appropriately named Faith, and embark on an unknown journey. His wife begs him to stay and spend the night with her, but Brown insists that he must attend to a pressing matter between dusk and sunrise. As he makes his way through the dark, foreboding forest, he is heartened by his firm resolve to confront Satan this one last time, to overcome his temptations, and to lay aside his evil ways, and he vows to renew his faith in God come morning. Goodman Brown's first steps into the woods symbolize the ambivalence of a faithful Puritan. He knows full well his evil intentions, knows himself for the sinner he is, but he has convinced himself nonetheless that he is a saint and will ultimately go to heaven.

3. Some critics have read the tale for its psychological insight into the distortions of the human mind, completely ignoring Hawthorne's explicit sense of time and place. See Frederick C. Crews, *The Sins of the Fathers: Hawthorne's Psychological Themes* (New York, 1966), esp. 99–106. Others have been preoccupied with the seeming impossibility of spectral evidence and have interpreted the story symbolically rather than literally. As twentieth-century critics, they have been convinced that Young Goodman Brown arrives at a hasty conclusion concerning the depravity of man because the devil does not enter into the shapes of people in order to win souls. See D. M. McKeithan, "Hawthorne's 'Young Goodman Brown': An Interpretation," *Modern Language Notes* 67 (February 1952), 93–96; Paul W. Miller, "Hawthorne's 'Young Goodman Brown': Cynicism or Meliorism?" *Nineteenth-Century Fiction* 14 (December 1959), 255–64; Thomas F. Walsh Jr., "The Bedeviling of Young Goodman Brown," *Modern Language Quarterly* 19 (December 1958), 331–36.

4. Michael J. Colacurcio's "Visible Sanctity and Specter Evidence: The Moral World of Hawthorne's 'Young Goodman Brown,'" *Essex Institute Historical Collections* 110 (1974), 259–99, most closely parallels my own views on Hawthorne's story. Colacurcio acknowledges that, although the author may have been making a statement about human nature and the uncertainties of life, he firmly grounded the story in the history of Puritan New England. The story cannot be adequately understood without a knowledge of that world. See also B. Bernard Cohen, "Deodat Lawson's *Christ's Fidelity* and Hawthorne's 'Young Goodman Brown,'" *Essex Institute Historical Collections* 104 (1968), 349–70; David Levin, "Shadows of Doubt: Specter Evidence in Hawthorne's 'Young Goodman Brown,'" *American Literature* 34 (1962), 344–52; and Jerome Loving, "Pretty in Pink: 'Young Goodman Brown' and New-World Dreams," in *Critical Essays on Hawthorne's Short Stories,* ed. Albert J. von Frank (Boston, 1991), 219–31.

The traveler is fearful, expecting to see perhaps a "devilish Indian," perhaps even the devil himself. Soon he confronts "the figure of a man, in grave and decent attire."[5] Hawthorne does not introduce the reader to the companion, although he mentions that Brown is not surprised to see him there. It is evident that the person, or "figure," who carries a staff resembling a black snake, is none other than Satan, albeit in the shape of a somberly clad middle-aged man. Now alarmingly aware and forced to confront the implications of his trip, Brown tries in vain to reverse his original plans. "Friend," he pleads, "having kept covenant by meeting thee here, it is my purpose now to return whence I came. I have scruples touching the matter thou wot'st of" (278). He pleads that he comes from a long line of good Christians, not one of whom would ever have dared to walk with Satan. But the devil disagrees. He points out that, in fact, he had known Brown's father as well as his grandfather and had walked the same journey with them.

Thus begins the young man's night. He finds himself torn between his commitment to God and the devil's seductions. Doubt about his own faith is compounded by the devil's assurances that many of the town's most prominent citizens will be joining them at the meeting in the woods, including Goody Cloyse, the old woman who taught Brown his catechism in school and remained his spiritual adviser. As their paths cross in the forest, Cloyse greets Brown's sinister companion with obvious recognition and reveals in a matter-of-fact way the shocking news that this devil appears in the very figure of Goodman Brown's grandfather. Hawthorne thus employs the notion, common in the seventeenth century, of the specter: the devil has taken the shape of one of his witches, Brown's grandfather, an ostensibly pious man who had nonetheless been a sinner and had apparently given his soul to the devil.

For a moment Goodman Brown decides to end his journey, and he yearns to spend "that very night, which was to have been spent so

5. Nathaniel Hawthorne, "Young Goodman Brown," in *Nathaniel Hawthorne: Tales and Sketches* ed. Roy Harvey Pearce (New York, 1982), 277. The story was originally published in *New-England Magazine* in 1835. All quotations are from the 1982 edition, cited hereafter in the text. On the relation between fear of the Indians and fear of the demonic, see Dennis Edward Owen, "Satan's Fiery Darts: Explorations in the Experience and concept of the Demonic in Seventeenth-Century New England" (Ph.D. diss., Princeton University, 1974), 100–213; William S. Simmons, "Cultural Bias in the New England Puritans' Perception of Indians," *William and Mary Quarterly*, 3rd ser., 38 (1981), 56–72.

wickedly, but so purely and sweetly now, in the arms of Faith!" (281). His oscillation between righteousness and temptation, between dreams of heavenly glory and nightmares about the devil's horrible communion, parallel the anxieties suffered by many seventeenth-century New Englanders. Momentarily convinced that he has the resolve to turn from the devil, Brown shouts, "With heaven above and Faith below, I will yet stand firm against the devil!" (282). So sinners of that earlier time had tried to rebuke Satan and reject his temptations. As we have seen, conversion narratives and diaries disclosed strenuous efforts to avoid Satan, the hope that invocation of God would drive the devil away. During the witchcraft episodes as well, many of the victims testified that they had seen the devil in various guises, but they shouted at him to vanish, hoping to mobilize their faith in God by invoking him.

Brown's hopes are dashed almost immediately, for he realizes that the voices he hears in the forest are coming from people he knows well, both the presumed saints and the notorious sinners of his own village. And then through the din he hears a woman's voice, asking in a sorrowful tone for some favor, as the crowd at the meeting urges her to continue. With "grief, rage, and terror," Brown shouts out, "Faith!" (283). His discovery of Faith's pink ribbon confirms his worst fear, that his wife has been seduced by Satan. Dejected and full of despair, Brown understands at that moment, "There is no good on earth; and sin is but a name. Come devil," he beckoned, "for to thee is this world given" (283).

Faith's soul, unprotected in her fragile body, has been more vulnerable to Satan than a man's would be, just as Goodman's Brown's "better half," his Faith, had been left defenseless at home. Faith had begged her husband to stay: "A lone woman is troubled with such dreams and such thoughts, that she's afeard of herself, sometimes. Pray, tarry with me this night, dear husband, of all nights in the year!" (276). Women knew themselves to be loathsome sinners, already committed to the devil. Faith, too, seems to need protection from herself, from her own knowledge that she has surely taken steps into the devil's world. Hawthorne links the notion of women's self-abnegation with the common interpretation that women would fall into the devil's trap more easily than men.

Faith's seduction by the devil, though never explicit, assumes the pattern we have seen. Hawthorne suggests that she had asked the devil for a favor; one of his favorite ploys, according to the clergy, was to offer his victims some kind of reward—earthly delights, perhaps, or escape from mundane burdens. His most cunning trick was to tempt sinners with assurances of salvation, with easier means to heaven which circumvented the divine pact, based instead on a diabolical covenant. Was Faith successfully entrapped by the devil, or was the whole episode another of the devil's tricks, meant to drive Brown to despair? Indeed, was the entire occurrence a mere nightmare, rather than a reality for young Goodman Brown? Ambiguity reigns in the tale, as it does in Brown's mind, but Faith's presence in those dark woods, whether real or fantastic, has a dramatic effect on the terrified and defeated young man.

The very thought that Faith has joined the devil's minions drives Goodman Brown still further into the forest, "giving vent to an inspiration of horrid blasphemy." Hawthorne writes, "Thus sped the demoniac on his course," suggesting that Brown had indeed been possessed; he runs as if the devil had entered his body, even without his consent (284). As he approaches the meeting he confronts an alarming sight—the specter of a prominent New England minister—and hears a voice call out, "Bring forth the converts!" As Brown steps forward he sees not only the form of his own dead father beckoning him but also Goody Cloyse, his catechism teacher (Cloyse had been accused at Salem), along with Martha Carrier, one of the women executed at Salem. The saints no less than the sinners have joined the devil.

The devil in the shape of the minister gathers his flock around him and urges them to examine themselves and each other. Of the supposed saints the figure explains, "Ye deemed them holier than yourselves, and shrank from your own sin, contrasting it with their lives of righteousness and prayerful aspirations heavenward. Yet here are they all in my worshipping assembly. This night it shall be granted you to know their secret deeds" (286). The somber specter describes the secret sins, of which even the most pious members of the community were guilty. He divulges tales of elders who secretly coveted their young maids, of young men who hastened their fathers' deaths so as to inherit their wealth, and of young women who buried their infants born out of wedlock. He urges his legion to admit and embrace their sin, which "inexhaustibly supplies more evil impulses than human power—than my power at its utmost—can make manifest in deeds" (287). The devil insists that "evil is the nature of mankind. Evil must be your only happiness" (287).

As the figure is about to dip his hand in what appears to be blood and baptize his new converts, Brown shouts out, "Faith! Faith! . . . look up to heaven, and resist the wicked one" (288). Here, Hawthorne's tale is dramatically interrupted, and Brown awakens from his nightmarish experience, unsure of what has actually occurred; like all Puritans, doubt about his own fate and the fate of others continues to plague the young man. He finds himself in the dark, quiet forest, all alone with his chilling memories. The next morning Brown cannot help but see his neighbors, the minister, and his wife, in a new light, or rather a darker shade. His suspicion of and contempt for hypocrites who continue to pray to God despite their apparently sinister allegiances, dictates his actions and thoughts. He even turns from Faith, both his wife and his reverence for God. Each sabbath, as he listens to the sermons, reminiscences of that night and consciousness of his own sin and that of the others overwhelm his being. "And when he had lived long," Hawthorne writes, "and was borne to his grave a hoary corpse, followed by Faith, an aged woman, and children and grandchildren, a goodly procession, besides neighbors not a few, they carved no hopeful verse upon his tombstone; for his dying hour was gloom" (289).

Hawthorne uses the images of the Salem witchcraft episode to tell his tale; women's particular vulnerability, the devil's appearance in various shapes, the witches' meeting, and the bloody sacrament can all be found in the Salem trial transcripts. But the Salem trials are mentioned only obliquely, through the inclusion of three accused women, Martha Carrier, Goody Cloyse, and Martha Cory (both Carrier and Cory were executed). Among his other concerns, Hawthorne probes the relation between sin and witchcraft. To sin meant to covenant with the devil. The people young Goodman Brown meets in the woods, the saints as well as the sinners, had all committed transgressions in their lifetime, and now, Brown believes, the devil has them in his possession. Did they actually sign a compact in blood, thereby making their covenant with Satan explicit? Hawthorne is purposely ambiguous. Young Goodman Brown would never know if his wife, Faith, had actually converted. And then Hawthorne asks, "Had Goodman Brown fallen asleep in the forest and only dreamed a wild dream of a witch meeting?" (288). For Goodman Brown, this is a deeply troubling question that he can never answer, and he can only imagine the worst. He lives the rest of his life suspicious of his friends, his neighbors, his minister, even his wife. His own covert sins and those of his fellows, real or imagined, have become remarkably clear to him in the forest that night. He realizes that he has covenanted with the devil, if only implicitly; he sees himself, his neighbors, even Faith, for the sinners—perhaps even the witches—that they are.

INDEX

Post-Salem Puritan theology (*cont.*)
  responsibility for sin, 5–6, 164, 170, 172–76
  Satan's physical presence, 167
  sin as burden, 177–78
Predestination, 1, 4, 16, 18, 19
Prescot, Peter, 156
Prince, Deborah, 186, 191
Prince, Thomas, 186
Proctor, John, 158
Proctor, William, 158
Prodigal Daughter, The: or a strange and wonderful relation, 171, 182
Property, 60, 117, 121n, 158
Pudeator, Ann, 142
Putnam, Ann, Jr., 73, 133, 157–58
Putnam, Ann, Sr., 69n, 144
Putnam, Edward, 150n
Putnam, John, 157
Putnam, Rebecca, 157

Recantations, 153–54, 163
Repentance, 22–23, 62, 137–38
"Return of Several Ministers Consulted, The," 75, 77–78, 87
Rice, Nicholas, 147
Ring, Joseph, 60, 161–62
Robinson, John, xiv
Rockwell, Abigail, 36, 37, 176
Roger, John, 117
Roots, Susannah, 145n
Roper, Lyndal, 67n, 95n, 113n
Rosenthal, Bernard, 8, 84n, 121, 127, 139n, 156n, 157n
Rule, Margaret, 91
Russell, Jeffrey Burton, 165n

Sacramental Meditations (Willard), 106
Safford, Joseph, 72n, 82n, 143–44
Salem Possessed (Boyer & Nissenbaum), 6
Salem witchcraft episode
  as cultural icon, 10
  descriptions of Satan, 70–75
  effects on Puritan theology, 166
  guilt about, 167–69, 169n–70n
  maleficence, 79, 82–83
  official responses, 8–9, 74–75, 77–79, 124
  peculiarities of, 121

  and Satan's threats to New England, 66–67
  sequence of events, 7–9
  and "Young Goodman Brown," 203
  See also Confessions; Spectral evidence; Witchcraft episodes
Salter, Henry, 159–60
Saltonstall, Nathaniel, 75, 77n
Sanctification, 2–3, 14, 62, 143–44
Satan as possessor of souls, 4, 58n
  vs. devil's pact, 57n, 73n, 84–85
  and original sin, 28
  and sin as absence of God, 45–47
  slavery analogy, 102–4
  See also Post-Salem Puritan theology
Satan, beliefs about, 55–92
  appearance, 70–71
  assurance offers, 62–63
  and body/soul definitions, 98–99, 110–12
  childhood lessons, 33–35, 61
  clergy/lay discourse, 3–5, 57, 72, 75–78, 83–89, 91–92
  and confessions, 139–41
  contemporary rhetorical use of, 10–11
  convictive vs. presumptive evidence, 78–79
  eighteenth-century beliefs, 5–6, 46n
  European roots, 60–62, 71
  folk beliefs, 79–83, 90, 91
  implicit presence, 63, 65
  importance in witchcraft episodes, 56–57
  and maleficium, 79, 82–83
  marital images, 65–66, 88–89, 106
  modern rhetorical use, 10–11
  multiplicity, 89–90
  omnipresence of, 4
  physical presence, 5, 67–69, 70, 71, 90, 111–12, 167
  political cartoons, 194–97
  and property, 60, 158
  sexual analogies, 106
  temptation methods, 58–60, 62–63
  threat to New England, xvi, 66–67
  torture, 111–12
  in *Wonders of the Invisible World,* 87–89

Weisman, Richard, 7n, 79, 86, 122n,
    126n–27n
Wellman, Elizabeth, 55
Well-Ordered Family (Wadsworth), xiii
Westgate, John, 145
Wey, Aaron, 156
Whitefield, George, 184
Whiting, Samuel, 24
Whitteridge (wife of Thomas), 54
Wigglesworth, Michael, xvi, 21, 47–48,
    107n
    on fear of God's wrath, 26–28
    guilt about Salem episode, 168
    on responsibility for sin, 49–50
Wilkins, Benjamin, 156
Wilkins, Bray, 118
Willard, John, 118, 133, 156, 158n
Willard, Samuel, xiv, 21, 66, 103
    and anxiety/assurance cycle, 17–19
    and essential depravity beliefs, 43–44
    on body/soul definitions, 96, 97, 98–99,
        105n, 106, 120
    on natural vs. converted states, 28–30
    on responsibility for sin, 48–49
    on spectral evidence, 76, 83–86, 87,
        127n
    on temptation methods, 58–59
    post-Salem theology, 167, 170, 172, 173
    witchcraft accusation of, 77n
Willard, Simon, 119
Williams, Abigail, 7, 134–35
Williams, Joseph, 130n
Williams, Stephen, 190–91
Willis, Joshua, Jr., 37, 176, 177
Willows, George, 47
Winship, Jane Wilkinson, 47
Winthrop, John, 100, 103n
Witchcraft beliefs
    and body/soul definitions, 107
    comical images, 197, 198
    convictive vs. presumptive evidence,
        78–79

European roots, 55–56
familiars, 112–15
and female dissatisfaction, 59, 107,
    127n
and female independence, 141–42
maleficium, 79, 82–83, 116, 122
vs. possession, 57n, 73n, 84–85
theological definitions, 79–80
See also Confessions; Devil's pact; Satan,
    beliefs about; Sin/witchcraft confla-
    tion; Spectral evidence; Witchcraft
    episodes
Witchcraft episodes
    alternative accounts, 6–7
    and body/soul definitions, 94
    European roots of, xv–xvi
    predominantly female victims, xvi–xvii,
        2, 95n, 110
    psychoanalytic perspective, 67n
    and responsibility for sin, 49n
    women's accusations, 121–23
    See also Clergy/lay discourse; Confes-
        sions; Salem witchcraft episode; Satan,
        beliefs about; Witchcraft beliefs
Witch of Endor, 76, 143, 159n
Women
    dissatisfaction, 58n, 59, 107, 127n
    empowering roles, xi–xiv
    internalization of ministerial messages,
        1–2, 12–13, 36, 37–39, 43–44, 47
    See also Body/soul definitions; Confes-
        sions; Female essential depravity be-
        liefs; Gender differences
Wonders of the Invisible World (Mather),
    87–89, 90

Young, Alice, 57n
"Young Goodman Brown" (Hawthorne),
    197, 199–204

*Elizabeth Reis teaches history and women's studies
at the University of Oregon.*